Advance Praise for *What Entrepreneurs Need to Know About Government*

"Many practitioners in the field of entrepreneurship look upon government as the enemy. It is feared, misunderstood, scorned and viewed as something to hide from and avoid. This book provides a powerful resource for the entrepreneurs and their support structure to use to comprehend the role of government—for both good and trouble! The government can be a source of assistance if you know what is available. The entrepreneur should also be fully aware of the government's role as the "policeman" of business, so that they can prevent trouble. This book will be a key ingredient in helping the entrepreneur to understand the role of government, optimize their relationships with government, and transform it from a feared antagonist into a market force that can be managed, and even turned into a potential resource."

Dr. W.F. (Fred) Kiesner
Conrad Hilton Chair of Entrepreneurship
Loyola Marymount University, Los Angeles

"Truitt's book provides a clear and comprehensive guide thru the complexities of government involvement in today's business environments. Extremely well organized, it is useful and I would personally recommend it for any business large or small."

Thomas V. Jones
Owner of Moraga Vineyards and retired CEO of Northrop Corp.

"Entrepreneurs often have lamented the negative impact of governmental regulations on their businesses without always recognizing their positive aspects. Unless they have spent years studying public policy and governmental regulations entrepreneurs have lacked a comprehensive framework with which to understand such regulations. Professor Truitt has provided a unique resource to entrepreneurs, governmental officials, and professional service providers to better understanding how U.S. firms function within regulatory frameworks and how regulations can be used for the firm's advantage."

Alan L. Carsrud, Ph.D
Executive Director
Clinical Professor of Management
Professor of Industrial & Systems Engineering
Global Enterprise Center
Florida International University

"Dr. Truitt has created a superb resource, taking the reader through the history of government's impact on American business and presenting a practical guide for the entrepreneur to understand government regulations and programs needed to successfully operate their company. Dr. Truitt provides an historical view of how and why regulations governing business exist today, and he delivers a practical guide for today's entrepreneur. If I would have had this background when I started my business 13 years ago, I could have taken years off my learning curve. If you are contemplating starting a business, this guide will provide you with the history of government regulations in America and offers modern day practical knowledge needed by any true entrepreneur. Dr. Truitt provides the entrepreneur the foundation to understand how government impacts business and provides the resource for a business owner to comply with government regulations and take advantage of government programs to help create and grow their business."

Mardi Norman  
President and CEO  
Dynamic Systems, Inc.

"Every entrepreneur learns that managing through the regulatory hurdles is critical to success. In this book, Wes Truitt provides the 'how to' and 'how not to' guidelines and perspectives pertaining to government regulations. A must reference for entrepreneurs!"

Bruce G. Willison  
Dean  
The John E. Anderson Graduate School of Management at UCLA

# What Entrepreneurs Need to Know about Government

## *A Guide to Rules and Regulations*

WESLEY B. TRUITT

Westport, Connecticut
London

**Library of Congress Cataloging-in-Publication Data**

Truitt, Wesley B., 1939–
    What entrepreneurs need to know about government : a guide to rules and regulations /
Wesley B. Truitt.
        p. cm.
    Includes bibliographical references and index.
    ISBN 0–275–98195–9 (alk. paper)
        1. Trade regulation—United States.   2. Industries—Government policy—United States.
I. Title.
    KF1600.T78  2004
    343.73′07—dc22        2004045937

British Library Cataloguing in Publication Data is available.

Library of Congress Catalog Card Number: 2004045937
ISBN: 0–275–98195–9

First published in 2004

Praeger Publishers, 88 Post Road West, Westport, CT 06881
An imprint of Greenwood Publishing Group, Inc.
www.praeger.com

Printed in the United States of America

The paper used in this book complies with the
Permanent Paper Standard issued by the National
Information Standards Organization (Z39.48–1984).

10  9  8  7  6  5  4  3  2  1

# Contents

# Tables

# Preface

No business in the United States today operates purely on the basis of market forces. Every business is impacted to one degree or another by government—federal, state, and local. Government is one of the most vital factors in a business' external environment. This is a fact of life in twenty-first-century America. It is not a temporary condition. It is permanent. The realities of this fact need to be well understood by leaders of businesses, small and large.

The purpose of this book is to improve the business' understanding of the critical role government plays in its daily life of a business. This will be especially useful for entrepreneurs because, in addition to examining the overall role government plays in shaping the business environment, it provides guidelines for governmental approvals needed by start-up and growing firms and checklists of regulations with which they must comply. Federal laws and policies are featured, along with representative samplings from state and local government, using California as the principal example because it is a worst-case situation.

Middle-size and large companies will find this analysis helpful to gain a deeper understanding of how government impacts their operations both positively and negatively, sometimes with great suddenness. Firms that know how to use government understand that it can perform indispensable services on their behalf.

No ideological preferences for more or less government find their way into this work. We are dealing here with facts and with the consequences of those facts on our businesses. Industry's angst about government's intrusiveness or bureaucratic biases against the profit motive are mid-twentieth-century issues that have become irrelevant by the reality of events. It is time to make business strategy and day-to-day operating decisions from a basis of fact—

government is deeply and permanently imbedded in the life of the private sector to an extent that is rarely understood or appreciated. Business strategies must be based on this fact to succeed.

For the private sector, the government's role in its external environment presents numerous opportunities. From a macroeconomic perspective, government sets the tone and pace of the overall economy through fiscal (taxing and spending) and monetary policy (interest rates). Government represents the chief opportunity for many businesses: selling to it, buying from it, having it protect an industry, having it represent industry in international discussions, having it grant, lend, or guarantee loans, and so forth.

Government is also an external threat to many companies. It regulates their operations and prices, taxes their profits, can change policy to harm a company's standing in the marketplace, can deregulate an industry throwing it into a competitive maelstrom, and it can take away key personnel during a reserve call-up.

Therefore, it is essential that business understand government to take advantage of the opportunities it represents and to mitigate the threats and risks it poses to a company's operations and well-being. No start-up company can hope to succeed without a clear understanding of and compliance with governmental rules. No established company can sustain successful operations without knowing how to evaluate policy trends to recast company strategy and how to intervene into the government policymaking process to use government for its own purposes.

This book is intended to help guide companies to do a better job of dealing with the critical realities of government's impacts on their business. To achieve this goal, the book is organized into four parts.

"Part I: Government Impacts on the Business Environment" has three chapters that discuss why and how the federal government has become the most important shaper of the environment external to the firm. It looks specifically at the development of its regulatory role, positive and negative impacts of it on business, and the levers of power the federal government has over the economy. This part ends with a chapter on state and local governments' impacts on the external environment, focusing on the ways states have of affecting macro business and economic conditions.

"Part II: Compliance: What Government Makes Business Do" has four chapters, each of which addresses what the federal government requires of a business during every phase of its life: start-up, ongoing operations, expansion, and liquidation. Rules and regulations on hiring, workplace, product safety, Environmental Protection Agency standards, financial reporting, antitrust, discrimination, ERISA pension requirements, and the like are presented. This part concludes with a chapter that summarizes state and local regulatory requirements.

"Part III: Assistance: What Government Can Do to Help Business" looks at the other side of the coin—ways government can assist business. One chapter deals with federal financial assistance (grants, loans, loan guarantees, R&D funding, export financing, and insurance, etc.) and another with federal marketing assistance (contracting policies, assistance to women and minorities, counseling, foreign export sales, etc.). The final chapter in this part looks at what state and local governments do to assist business—enterprise zones, tax incentives, training, infrastructure, and promotion of business in Washington, D.C.

"Part IV: Business/Government Interaction" has one chapter that addresses various strategies companies can use to encourage government to support their interests.

Business strategies must be based on data, hard facts, not on wishful thinking. Data itself, facts and figures, while interesting, are insufficient. The entrepreneur must make sense of data by aggregating it and putting it into a context that enables it to be used in crafting strategies for success. Analysis without data is groundless; data without analysis is pointless. In this book you will find plenty of data, and you will also find analysis that puts data into a meaningful framework from which you can deduce business strategy.

This book is the result of a number of experiences. As a corporate executive for twenty-six years, the author faced the challenge of dealing with a full range of governmental policies, rules, and regulations affecting his company—local, state, federal, and foreign. As a company lobbyist, he worked with governmental entities to effect favorable change and gain funding and approvals. He was an employee of five federal government agencies and served on Department of Defense advisory boards. As an adjunct professor at the Anderson Graduate School of Management at UCLA and at the Drucker Graduate School of Management at Claremont, he developed and taught courses dealing with these issues.

At Loyola Marymount University's business school, where the author is executive-in-residence, he developed an MBA course on business/ government relations. He is principal of Truitt Consulting, a firm that helps businesses with planning and government issues, and he consults with the nonprofit RAND Corporation on a variety of government topics. In addition, the author earned a Ph.D. in public law and government at Columbia University.

This book is intended to be a useful, practical guide to the entrepreneur in all phases of the life of your business, to enable you to deal appropriately and effectively with all the layers of government that have jurisdiction over your enterprise.

# Acknowledgments

The author thanks Sassan Parandeh for providing information and arranging appointments at the city of Long Beach, California, and also thanks the following officials: Robert S. Torrez, chief financial officer/director, Department of Financial Management; Dr. James A. Goodwin, business services officer; Eugene Fong, treasury operations officer–revenue; and Melanie S. Fallon, director, Department of Community Development.

Much gratitude is expressed to my colleagues, Fred Kiesner and Donald DePamphilis, for their close reading of the entire manuscript and for making valuable suggestions for its improvement.

Any remaining errors of omission or commission are the responsibility of the author.

# — PART I —

# Government Impacts on the Business Environment

This first part of this book provides the entrepreneur with an understanding of the ways and means by which government affects the business environment within which the firm must operate. This is the macro business environment—the economic and regulatory powers government has over the life of American business.

Chapter 1 provides a quick summary of how and why government took on its present-day regulatory role and describes the nature of today's system: the Constitutional bases for that role, its historical development, reasons for a federal regulatory role, the nature and type of federal regulations, and critical features of the current regulatory arrangement. Chapter 2 summarizes positive and negative impacts of the federal government's regulatory activities on business and provides information on the size and cost of that role. Chapter 3 identifies and examines thirteen levers of power in the hands of the federal government that affect the macro economy of the United States. Finally, chapter 4 summarizes ways by which state and local governments affect the macro business environment in their areas.

These four chapters provide a foundation for an entrepreneur's understanding of how and why our American regulatory system works the way it does today.

# — CHAPTER 1 —

# Growth of Government Involvement in Business

Before you start or expand a business, you have to understand the environment around you. This is best done in your business plan, where the pressures of external forces are put in the context of your business' mission, goals, and strategy.[1]

The external business environment contains a number of forces and factors that vitally affect your business: macroeconomic, sociocultural, technological, political, legal, regulatory, competitive, and others.[2] It is the thesis of this book that, other than direct competition from rivals, the external factor that affects a business the most is government.

It is the entrepreneur's task to understand the role government plays in shaping the environment within which he or she will be operating before starting or expanding a business. Government provides the "rules of the game" for a start-up, for ongoing operations, and expansion.

## EVOLUTION OF GOVERNMENT INVOLVEMENT IN BUSINESS

The growth of government activity in the U.S. economy has been a function of the country's economic growth and industrialization. Government and the economy are linked, and this interactive relationship causes each to be affected by and respond to changes in the other. This means that government not only affects the economy, but also that the economy affects government, which, like any social institution, responds to changes in its external environment.[3]

Government's extensive involvement in the life of business today is the result of an evolution that has been under way since the Civil War.[4] Before the 1860s, business and government were led by the same people: business leaders served in government as mayors, governors, and senators, and public service was considered an honorable duty by planters in the South, farmers and ranchers in the West, and business owners and merchants in the East. In 1840, the total number of civilian employees working in Washington, D.C., was 1,014; in the private sector, few industrial and transportation companies employed more than a handful of full-time salaried workers (often only one).

## Industrial Revolution

After 1865, America rapidly industrialized, and business enterprises such as railroads, steel, oil, and textiles emerged as large-scale, complex industries requiring permanent management. A new class of business leaders emerged: full-time, salaried managers making a lifelong career of climbing up the company's managerial ranks. It took more than a half century (to the Great Depression in the 1930s and World War II) for comparable administrative hierarchies to emerge in the federal government.

America is the only country in which the business-sector managerial/administrative class emerged before a comparable governmental administrative hierarchy.

By the 1890s, the U.S. railroad industry had become the largest business in the world, employing over 100,000 workers, but the civilian workforce in Washington was only 20,000. In 1929, the total number of civilian workers (non–post office) in Washington, 68,000, was smaller than the number employed by either the United States Steel Corporation or General Motors.

## New Deal and After

With the Great Depression, the New Deal, and the anticipation of World War II, the scene changed dramatically in Washington. In 1940, the federal government employed one million civilians, and by 1970 the number had nearly tripled. In 2001, the federal civilian workforce numbered 2.7 million. Thus, the dramatic growth of the federal bureaucracy is a fairly recent phenomenon, beginning in the late first half of the twentieth century.

## Adversarial Relationship

Why is there an adversarial relationship between the public and private sectors in the United States? "Because," explains Alfred Chandler, "two sets of administrative hierarchies grew at different periods for different reasons to carry out different objectives, two quite different cultures were the result."[5] The attitude of the federal civil bureaucracy was formed before the creation of a professional class of public administrators, and this preprofessional group developed their role and attitude toward business during the period of perceived business excesses.

During the 1880s and 1890s, under pressure from the populist movement that represented the economic and social interests of farmers and blue-collar labor, the federal government accepted the role of regulating big business. This was the era of freewheeling *laissez-faire* capitalism and the so-called railroad "robber barons." The legislative bases for this new regulatory role began with the Interstate Commerce Act of 1887 and the Sherman Antitrust Act of 1890, and it was reinforced in 1914 by the Clayton Antitrust Act and the Federal Trade Commission Act.[6]

Aggressive enforcement of these laws began with Theodore Roosevelt's "trust busting" activities, continued with William Howard Taft's even more aggressive antitrust enforcement, and culminated in Woodrow Wilson's Progressive Era economic reforms. These were the major activities that embedded into the American political culture government's role as the defender of non-big business. The public perceived that the biggest industries of that day—railroads, steel, and oil—threatened other, smaller companies and individuals, and these largest of enterprises had to be reigned in. The only force powerful enough and capable of doing so within the American system was the federal government.

It was during this formative period in the late nineteenth and early twentieth centuries that "the standard American response to complex economic problems was to pass laws creating regulatory commissions to monitor the activities of businesses."[7] This standard procedure was repeated in the 1930s when perceived greed and ineptitude of big business was accused of largely causing the Great Depression, and it was repeated again in the 1960s and 1970s when big business was blamed for pollution and the depletion of resources that resulted from the enormous output of our gigantic industrial economy.[8]

The adversarial relationship of government versus big business is more than one hundred years old. It is a firmly embedded feature in the domestic political culture. The hallmark of this relationship is the public's fear of business monopolies and the abuses that firms having them might perpetrate against the public's best interest, which is secured by an open, competitive marketplace policed by the federal government.

## CONSTITUTIONAL BASIS OF GOVERNMENT'S INVOLVEMENT IN BUSINESS

What is the basis upon which government involves itself in America's business? As are most things in the United States, it is based on law. The fundamental law of the land is the U.S. Constitution established in 1789, and that document provides the legal footing for the legislation that Congress has enacted and presidents have signed and enforced to intervene in the economy and regulate business. Let us identify the key clauses of the Constitution that address what the Framers at Philadelphia considered important to protect private property rights and commercial freedoms, the two factors they clearly viewed as the vital foundations of an open, democratic economic and political system.[9]

### Article I, Sections 8 and 9

Article I of the Constitution establishes the legislative power in the Congress. Two key sections of this article provide ample authority for Congress to pass laws governing the economy. Most of these powers are based on Section 8, which gives Congress the power "to regulate Commerce with foreign Nations and among the several states."

This is the famous "commerce clause," the fundamental legal basis for federal regulation of the domestic economy. Since 1789, Congress has used this power to establish and preserve a single economy among and between the states in the Union, making the United States one economy—as opposed to the Articles of Confederation era preceding it that preserved the sovereign power of each state to tax and regulate trade.

The second key provision in Article I is Section 9. It provides that "no Tax or Duty shall be laid on Articles exported from any State. No preference shall be given by any Regulation of Commerce or Revenue to the Ports of one State over those of another; nor shall Vessels bound to, or from, one State, be obliged to enter, clear, or pay Duties in another."

This section establishes the fundamental principle of federal supremacy (vs. state supremacy) in the regulation of commerce among the states and between states and foreign nations. It also establishes the principle of equality of the states ("No preference shall be given . . . "). More than anything, Sections 8 and 9 are responsible for establishing a "common market" throughout the entire United States—initially thirteen states, and now a continental-sized country of fifty states plus the District of Columbia.

### Sanctity of Contracts and Private Property

With respect to the sanctity of contracts, the Constitution restricts Congress and the states from interfering in them. The key restriction is in Article I, Section 10, which states, "No State . . . shall pass any Law impairing the Obligation of contracts." The famous American expression "a contract is a contract" owes its origin to this Constitutional provision—once signed, a contract is binding and no one, not even a governmental entity, can overturn it. The rights of citizens to freely engage in commercial activities, virtually all of which require contacts, are thus solidly anchored in the Constitution and upheld by an early Supreme Court ruling.[10]

Regarding the sanctity of private property, two amendments to the Constitution establish this fundamental precondition for a thriving free market economy. The Fifth Amendment states in part, "nor shall private property be taken for public use, without just compensation." This is known as the "takings clause" of the Constitution, and it is part of the first ten amendments known as the Bill of Rights. It has always been a principle of English common law that government could seize private property for some legitimate public purpose, for example, building a road, but that such taking, known as "eminent domain," requires the government to fairly compensate the owner of the property.

This key principle of just compensation was expanded in 1987 by a U.S. Supreme Court ruling that a property owner must be compensated even when his ownership of the property is retained but his use of the property is restricted. Government land-use regulations, such as those protecting environmentally endangered species or forests, deny the owner full use of property, and the Court has therefore put this further limit on government's power to control private-sector resources.[11]

The Fourteenth Amendment to the Constitution states in part, "nor shall any State deprive any person of life, liberty, or property, without due process of law." With this provision, the Constitution empowers the federal government to establish the "rules of the game" uniformly throughout all of the states, but it restricts the national government from exercising governmental power over citizens' lives and property arbitrarily ("without due process of law"). Knowing that every citizen has fundamental rights of due process, even against the government, establishes a solid footing for the private sector to function without fear of governmental caprice.

Additional sections of Article I of the Constitution give "the legislative power" to the Congress to enact laws regulating business and the economy. Congress is given the power to levy and collect taxes, borrow money, establish bankruptcy laws, promote science and useful arts by granting patents, provide for the common defense, promote the general welfare, and to "make all Laws which shall be necessary and proper for carrying into Execution the foregoing Powers, and all other Powers vested by this Constitution in the Government of the United States, or in any Department or Officer thereof." The Article I, Section 8 phrase, to "promote the general Welfare," has been one of the major bases enabling expansion of the federal government's power in the economy and the entire domestic society.

The Supreme Court broadly interpreted these various provisions of the Constitution during most of the post–Civil War period to expand the federal government's role in business, the economy, and society in general.[12]

## GROWTH OF FEDERAL REGULATION OF BUSINESS

The first instance of the federal government's regulation of business was not the enactment of a law, but a decision of the Supreme Court. In 1876, in a landmark case *Munn v. Illinois*, the court ruled that the government (the state of Illinois in this instance) has the power to set a maximum price to store grain in warehouses. The basis of the ruling is this: "When private property is devoted to a public use, it is subject to public regulation."[13] A decade later, in 1887, Congress established the first federal regulatory agency, the Interstate Commerce Commission, to regulate railroad routes and rates. This began the first wave of federal regulatory intervention in private business.

### Populist and Progressive Era

In the early twentieth century, the pace of federal regulatory action accelerated. In 1903, the Antitrust Division of the Department of Justice was established to enforce the Sherman Antitrust Act. Using the Justice Department, Presidents Theodore Roosevelt and William Howard Taft, both Republicans, aggressively prosecuted and broke up some of the country's largest businesses that they alleged were monopolies—the Standard Oil Company and the American Tobacco Company.[14] Roosevelt alone initiated forty-three antitrust proceedings during his administration.[15]

In addition to antitrust activity, the federal government initiated regulations governing specific industries and areas of the economy. For example, in 1906 the Pure Food and Drug Act and the Meat Inspection Act were passed to protect consumers, to establish standards of purity in those industries, and provide for governmental enforcement. The Hours of Service Act (1907) and the Employers' Liability Act (1908) were passed and, though they affected only railway workers, established the foundation for national labor regulation.[16]

Under President Wilson, a Democrat, in 1913 the Federal Reserve System was established to regulate the country's commercial banking system, the Federal Trade Commission was enacted the next year to supplement the enforcement of the Clayton Antitrust Act by promoting competition, and in 1920 the Federal Power Commission (now the Federal Energy Regulatory Commission) was established to regulate interstate transmission of electrical and other forms of energy.

This new regulatory regime reflected a bipartisan response to the fact of life that the United States had transitioned from an agrarian economy to an industrial economy that needed to develop new governmental "rules of the road" for its mammoth industrial sector. The fact is that by the early twentieth century, the United States had become the world's largest industrial economy. This fact was not ignored by America's rivals on the world stage, all of whom adjusted to the nation's new economic might between the Spanish-American War in 1898 and America's entry into World War I in 1917.

## New Deal and After—Industry Regulation

The next wave of federal government agencies and regulatory commissions came about during the New Deal of the 1930s on an industry-by-industry basis. These agencies were established to stimulate economic activity to pull the country out of the Great Depression and to create new "rules of the road" to prevent a repeat of perceived business abuses of the past that many believed partially caused the Depression. President Franklin Roosevelt's new agencies included the following:

- Federal Home Loan Bank Board, 1932—to provide low cost, low interest mortgages to marginally qualified borrowers to purchase homes (actually started before Roosevelt's inauguration);
- Federal Deposit Insurance Corporation, 1933—to ensure banks against failures, and thus to insure their depositors' funds;
- Federal Communications Commission, 1934—to regulate the growing use of the public airways for broadcasting on radio and later television;
- Securities and Exchange Commission, 1934—to regulate the securities industry;
- National Labor Relations Board, 1935—to regulate labor practices and to provide intermediary and arbitration services between organized labor and management;
- Social Security Administration, 1935—to administer the Social Security Act, providing a method of enforced savings for working people;
- Civil Aeronautics Board, 1938—to regulate the growing commercial airline industry (the CAB was abolished in 1984, and its remaining duties fell to the Federal Aviation Administration).

With the establishment of this plethora of new commissions, agencies, and other laws that regulated even more aspects of business, the federal government's intervention into the very workings of the nation's now highly industrial economy became permanent. These agencies dealt at a basic level with activities at the heart of the life of a modern industrial economy.

## Growth of Social Regulation

Later, in the 1960s and 1970s, a deeper penetration by the federal government into the fabric of our now more advanced, complex economy began. This was the era of social regulation—adjusting behavior within society to benefit the public in general. New agencies were established and many existing ones were expanded and given new powers. During the late 1960s and 1970s, the regulated share of the American economy expanded from one-tenth to almost one-fourth of the gross national product.

Among the new agencies established during this period were the following:

- Environmental Protection Agency, 1970—to protect the natural environment by regulating air, water, and other types of pollution from factory, auto, truck, and other sources of emission;

- National Highway Traffic Safety Administration, 1970—charged with setting standards for motor vehicle safety, fuel economy, and standards for state highway safety programs;
- Occupational Safety and Health Administration, 1970—to establish rules for the workplace that ensure workers are safe from hazardous conditions and are provided minimum standards of health;
- Consumer Product Safety Commission, 1972—tasked with protecting the public from unreasonable risks of injury from consumer products;
- Mine Safety and Health Administration, 1977—to establish and enforce mine safety regulations.

By 1979, these five agencies had 19,000 employees.[17] They all share three features: (1) they promulgate rules and regulations regarding the specific area they are chartered to serve, (2) they provide an administrative forum for presentation of complaints by the public against specific companies and industries, and (3) they have enforcement powers they can impose on companies that violate their regulations.

During this period, much of the growth of federal social regulation was in the area of environmental protection. The landmark legislation was enacted in 1969: the National Environmental Policy Act. This law laid the foundation for the environmental "revolution" by requiring environmental impact statements for projects needing federal permits. This act also established the Council on Environmental Quality. Established by law in 1970, the Environmental Protection Agency (EPA) became the organization that administered environmental legislation, of which there was plenty during the next decade, as Table 1.1 illustrates.[18]

By the late 1990s, there were fifty-three major federal regulatory agencies and commissions that established rules and regulations for virtually every facet of American business activity and provided for their enforcement. The cost to operate these agencies was $17 billion in 1998, approximately twice the cost of a decade earlier. The head count of all federal regulatory agencies in 1998 (near the all-time high) was 126,147 people.[19] This is a vast public workforce imposing a significant "government overhead" cost on private business.

## Professional Administrators: Public vs. Private Sector

Along with the massive increase of federal regulations and the bureaucracy that administers them, there has been a corresponding change in the way the private sector has adjusted to this intervention by the public sector.

In the late nineteenth century during the first wave of federal regulations, the private sector gradually developed full-time professional managers to administer America's growing industrial economy. In 1881, the world's first business school, the Wharton School at the University of Pennsylvania, was established to train professional managers for America's businesses. This trend

**Table 1.1**
**A Decade of Environmental Laws**

| Year | Act (or Amendment) | Purpose of Legislation |
|------|--------------------|------------------------|
| 1969 | National Environmental Policy | Required environmental impact statements |
| 1970 | Clean Air Act Amendments | EPA to set national air quality standards |
| 1972 | Water Pollution Control Act | Established guidelines for states |
| 1972 | Coastal Zone Management | Control shore development; provided funds |
| 1972 | Federal Insecticide, Fungicide, and Rodenticide Act Amendments | Improved labeling and premarket testing of new products for adverse health effects |
| 1973 | Endangered Species Act | Habitat protection for endangered species |
| 1974 | Safe Drinking Water Act | Set federal standards for safe drinking water |
| 1976 | Federal Land Policy and Management Act 473 | Ended policy of seeling public land to private owners; million acres put under Interior Dept. |
| 1976 | National Forest Management Act | Forest Service to ensure sustained-yield timber harvesting in perpetuity |
| 1976 | Toxic Substances Control Act | Federal control over chemicals that endanger human health or the environment |
| 1976 | Resource Conservation and Recovery Act | Federal/state control over hazardous waste from point of generation to final disposal |
| 1977 | Surface Mining Control and Reclamation Act | Set standards to control disturbance of land from coal mining and assure reclamation |
| 1977 | Clean Air Act Amendments | Set tougher standards for clean air; set earlier deadlines for meeting standards |

continued and accelerated through the early twentieth century—the professionalization of management and administration in corporate America.[20]

A half-century later, World War II, an entirely new class of civil servants became a permanent and growing feature of government at all levels. These government employees were the opposite-number managers and administrators of those who populated corporate offices throughout the country. Most recently, corporations have sought to reduce their bureaucracies to cut overhead cost but find it difficult to do so because compliance with rules and regulations, especially filing periodic government-required compliance reports, necessitates having large administrative staffs to perform these duties.

## UNDERLYING REASONS FOR GOVERNMENT REGULATION

There are two broad underlying circumstances arguing for governmental regulation of private business: (1) when flaws appear in the marketplace that produce undesirable consequences, and (2) when adequate social, political, or other reasons exist.[21] Flaws in the market mechanism were the principal reason for governmental intervention in business for the first 175 years of the country. Since the mid-1960s, regulations have been introduced largely for sociopolitical reasons.

### Market Mechanism Flaws

A competitive market mechanism is an efficient allocator of resources in a society when it works well. When it functions perfectly, it produces the goods and services demanded by consumers when they want them, where they want them, and at a price they are willing to pay. An open market is often linked with an open, democratic society because neither is under the control of a central governmental authority. Occasionally, the market mechanism develops flaws and sometime cannot or is not allowed to function perfectly.

There are five major flaws that can develop in the market mechanism:

1. *Natural Monopoly*—If one company can supply all the demand for a particular product or service within an economy more efficiently and cheaply than a combination of firms, a natural monopoly exists. Competition can be wasteful of resources under these circumstances. Public utilities are the classic example, and government has long regulated them to prevent consumer abuse. Many local utilities are being deregulated today largely because advancements in technology have enabled competitive forces to erode the once natural monopoly.

2. *Natural Resource Regulation*—Exploitation or overuse of natural resources can result from monopolistic practices and can cause undesirable consequences. For instance, overproduction of oil from a particular oil field could reduce pressure

in the field, lower oil yields, and too quickly deplete the subterranean oil pool. Government regulates the number of wells that industry can drill in any one particular field to prevent these unwanted consequences. In another example, public airwaves, if left unregulated, could produce a cacophony of sound if government did not allocate particular bandwidths to particular broadcasters through its licensing mechanism—thus producing an orderly use of radio wavelengths.

3. *Destructive Competition*—When a few companies dominate an industry and the barriers to entry are high, they may exercise their market power by cutting prices to force out their competitors and then raise prices once the competition has been reduced. They may also exercise their market power by underproducing or limiting consumer choices regarding quality and service. If a few companies in an industry conspire to fix prices, they are engaging in an illegal act and can be prosecuted by the Justice Department.

4. *Externalities*—These are costs of production that are borne by society as a whole and not by the company that causes them. If a company dumps toxic waste and pollutes a river, society, not the company, pays the cost of cleanup (unless the company is successfully prosecuted). If the factory invests in equipment to prevent polluting the river, that company's costs may be driven up to the point where it is noncompetitive with rival firms that do not invest in such equipment. Therefore, government levels the playing field by imposing the same regulations on all firms in an industry with respect to environmental protection, safety practices, health hazards, jet noise, and so forth.

5. *Inadequate Information*—Competition in the marketplace requires that consumers have adequate information upon which to base an informed decision. If the information is not available, government regulations can require that it be provided. Facts for consumers are required regarding product quality, contents, and warranties, while data concerning work hazards must be made available for workers. The Securities and Exchange Commission requires disclosure of financial information for investors.

## Sociopolitical Regulations

Social and political reasons for governmental regulations are the major factor for governmental intervention into the private sector since the New Deal. There are products and services for which there is a demand in society, but for which no private company is able or willing to provide them under normal market conditions. Thus, government takes action to supply these "public goods." Typical examples are police protection, public parks, highways, and clean air and water. Also, government regulates some valuable or scarce natural resources, such as energy and fresh water resources.

There are five categories of sociopolitical regulation:

1. *Protecting Individual Rights and Privacy*—Unethical or immoral activities of businesses are a reason for regulation—to protect the public from future Enrons and WorldComs. "Helping individuals" as a category of governmental action has expanded to include regulations for safe working conditions, safer products for

consumers (especially children), elimination of discrimination in employment, improving health care, and so forth.

2. *Resolution of National and Global Problems*—Examples abound where the federal government has regulated key industries in the nation: railroads, air traffic, financial institutions, food, product safety, and so on. On an international scale, the federal government negotiates favorable conditions for American export products (lowering tariffs and other import restrictions abroad), protects U.S. workers from foreign competition with import restrictions and anti-dumping regulations (foreigners selling products in the United States at prices under cost), and generally reduces the barriers to trade in the belief that American farms and factories can meet or beat the foreign competition if the playing field is level.

3. *Regulation to Benefit Special Groups*—Some laws and regulations are enacted to favor one group over others. Economists refer to this as "rent seeking," the process by which interest groups seek to influence legislative and regulatory bodies for favorable treatment. This is not government at its loftiest, but at its most political—favoring special interest groups that are politically or economically powerful. Much regulation is or has been on the books protecting special interests, such as steel and cane sugar, in the United States against foreign competition.

4. *Conservation of Resources*—Governmental regulations conserve national resources for use by future generations, such as forests, lakes, and clean water. This is an example of government supplying "public goods."

5. *Limitations on Ownership and Control*—Laws and regulations pertaining to ownership rights or operating control are focused on particular industries. The complexity of these regulations is illustrated by Federal Communications Commission (FCC) rules that bar any one company from dominating media outlets (radio stations, TV stations, and newspapers) in major cities. FCC also prohibits foreign interests from directly owning more than 20 percent (or indirectly owning more than 25 percent) of a U.S. broadcasting company. These regulations are reviewed periodically as market and technology conditions change.

   Previous FCC rules prevented cross-ownership of television stations and newspapers in the same market, imposed a limit of two TV stations per market, and prohibited a single company from owning TV stations that reach more than 35 percent of the nation's households. Chicago-based Tribune Company owns the *Los Angeles Times* newspaper and KTLA television station—both in Los Angeles—and lobbied to kill the newspaper/TV rule rather than have to divest one of its properties.[22] News Corporation's problem was worse; it owns two TV stations and one newspaper in New York City. The FCC ruled to raise the 35 percent ceiling to 45 percent and eliminate restrictions on cross-ownership of newspapers and TV stations. A federal court later stayed this ruling, while Congress considered rollback legislation. In the end, Congress raised the ceiling to 39 percent, leaving the FCC's cross-owndership rule in place.[23]

   Other regulations forbid foreign-owned companies from owning or having operating control over certain industries deemed critical for national security, such as defense contractors performing highly classified work. Many other nations totally forbid foreign ownership, even minority ownership, of broadcasting, telecommunications, and defense companies.

**Consequences of Regulations**

Owing to the fact that regulations can help or harm particular industries or particular companies within an industry, there clearly is a need to evaluate the consequences before issuing them. Regulations, like tariffs, can protect certain industries from competition. For example, Major League Baseball benefits from an antitrust waiver permitting it to operate as a monopoly in that sport. Other potential entrants into the sport are denied access, protecting Major League Baseball and its teams from having to compete for fans.

An opposite type of example is the trucking industry, on which deregulation had a major, immediate impact, completely transforming it within months with new players. The Motor Carrier Act of 1980 initiated a process of deregulation of the trucking industry and opened it to anyone "fit, willing, and able" to carry freight from one state to another. Prior to 1980, 17,000 regulated trucking firms held a near monopoly on that $108 billion industry, based on the fact that Interstate Commerce Commission licenses (also known as "operating rights") exclusively authorized their trucks to travel certain routes and carry certain types of cargo. These licenses could be bought and sold, often were used as collateral for loans, and were a major intangible asset on the books of the companies holding them, having an estimated industry value of $748 million. The day the Motor Carrier Act went into effect ending the monopolies, the asset value of ICC licenses dropped by at least one-third.[24]

In all cases of regulation and deregulation, it is the public's interests that are supposed to be served by increasing or diminishing competition. Yet, there are occasions when regulations are established or struck down to protect friends and political allies and harm political rivals. This is an old political game that undermines the stewardship role of government "to promote the general welfare," not the particular welfare.

## TYPES OF REGULATIONS AND ENFORCEMENT

There are two types of regulations government agencies use to implement and enforce laws: rule making and adjudication. When Congress passes a law establishing particular standards, such as the Clean Air Act, it then becomes the role of the appropriate regulatory agency, in this example the Environmental Protection Agency (EPA), to establish specific rules or regulations to implement the principles of that act. This is rule making. It is essentially an extension of the legislative function of government in that the agency enunciates policy statements and additional, detailed requirements for industry compliance.

Adjudication is essentially a judicial function of the rule-making agency, in which the agency establishes enforceable orders that are backed by civil or criminal penalties, and the agency decides specific disputes brought to it, much like a court.

## Rule Making

How do agencies establish rules? All regulatory agency rules are based on laws, that is, Acts of Congress approved by the president. Once a law is passed pertaining to a particular industry (e.g., all commercial airlines) or circumstance (e.g., all smoke emissions from factory chimneys), the appropriate rule-making agency or agencies (in these examples, the Federal Aviation Administration and EPA, respectively) are given the responsibility and authority to establish rules to implement the law—to actually put the law into force.

The law typically contains language directing the rule-making agency's approach to enforcement (e.g., establish standards and/or issue permits) and establishing a timetable for implementing specific features of the act, while leaving detailed execution to the agency's discretion. Frequently, new laws amend existing ones, and the regulatory agencies having oversight need to amend old rules to conform to the new law.

The procedure the rule-making agencies follow to accomplish this is also established by law—the Administrative Procedures Act of 1946. This act prescribes a general procedure all rule-making agencies follow, but each agency has developed its own specialized system.[25] Once a new law is enacted, the appropriate agency publishes a notice of proposed rule making in the *Federal Register*, the official communication journal of the federal government. This notice declares the intention of the agency to establish rules on this particular subject, invites the public to comment, and establishes a timetable for these activities. If, however, the new rule makes very minor changes to an existing practice, it can be published without prior notice and without public comment.

Public comments can be limited to specific features of the proposed new rule or they can address the entire rule. Agencies can conduct public hearings where their staff members or the head of the agency hear these comments. Typically, the "public" that presents comments consists of companies in industries affected by the proposed new rule and trade associations representing those companies. Executives from these companies and associations usually work directly with agency members informally to make their views known and even offer draft language for the new rule.

Each year approximately 4,500 new rules are proposed and noticed in the *Register*. Of these, about six hundred are projected to have effects of sufficient magnitude to warrant their review by the president's Office of Management and Budget (OMB). Between fifty and one hundred of these proposed rules meet the criteria to be designated "economically significant," meaning that they are likely to create annual benefits or costs worth more than $100 million. Recent General Accounting Office (GAO) studies indicate that the OMB receives input from parties outside of government on nearly half of the rules it reviews and on which it makes its own input to initiating agencies.[26] Such "economically significant" proposed rules must undergo a formal analysis by the initiating agency of the rule's likely benefits and costs.[27]

The initiating agency is required to take into account all comments and other information it receives, in addition to that which is developed from its own research, during this formative phase of the rule-making process. This is required to make as certain as possible that the new rule will serve the public interest, take into account industry concerns with respect to implementation, and be enforceable as law. This process takes time—typically a few months for a fairly straightforward rule, to a few years for one that is complex and far-reaching.

Once the process ends, the agency publishes its final rule in the *Federal Register*, making it effective usually thirty days after publication. The final rule is then published in the *Code of Federal Regulations*, making it law. The *Code* contains the regulations of all federal agencies.

### Adjudication

There are two types of adjudication—informal and formal—but most are informal. This process pertains to companies seeking permits or licenses to operate in an industry or activity governed by the issuing agency. For example, a company seeking to establish a radio station in a community not now served will apply for a license from the Federal Communications Commission (FCC). The FCC will review the company's application and adjudicate it—that is, decide whether or not to issue the license. In informal proceedings, agencies also set rates and make determinations regarding civil and criminal enforcement. The agency's decision at the conclusion of this informal process is called an "order."

Formal adjudication is similar to a trial. In this instance, a company charged by an agency with violation of a rule is brought before the agency for a hearing. If the company wishes to do so, it can appear before an administrative law judge of the agency bringing the charge. This quasi-judicial proceeding has many of the trappings of a courtroom—attorneys argue the case, call witnesses, keep a record of the proceedings, and so forth. The outcome of the hearing or the administrative law proceeding is also called an "order." If it disagrees with the order, the company may appeal to a federal court. A federal court will not hear the appeal unless it believes the agency's order is arbitrary, capricious, or clearly contrary to the intent of the underlying statute.[28] All orders are enforceable under the law with civil and/or criminal penalties.

## CONCLUSION

The body of laws, regulations, and administrative rulings affecting businesses in the United States is quite extensive and is the result of a long evolution of political forces and economic factors unique to this country's industrial development and to its political culture based on the Constitution. Today, this regulatory environment appears to be widely supported by dominant special interests and the public at large, and it appears to be permanent.

# — CHAPTER 2 —

# Impacts of Federal Regulations on Business

T he federal government impacts American business in two ways: positively and negatively. How this is done, who does it, and why are key factors the entrepreneur needs to understand to successfully launch a start-up or to expand a business. The process of establishing federal regulations provides both opportunities and threats for start-ups, small businesses, and major corporations.

## INTRODUCTION

There are two basic approaches to regulation: command-and-control and performance-based. Until quite recently, command-and-control had been the prevailing type use. Under this system the government's coercive power enforces its intervention in the marketplace by setting prices, quantities, standards, and barriers to entry or exit. A newer approach that is beginning to come into use is performance-based regulation, which uses market forces to achieve the same goals. Under this system, government affects industry behavior through taxes, subsidies, and quotas. This is results-oriented, as opposed to command-and-control's process and penalty approach. Outcomes, not processes, are emphasized, permitting regulated industries greater leeway and efficiencies to meet specific performance requirements through market incentives.

Regardless of which type is used, there are enormous impacts on business from the regulatory process. See appendix 2.1 for a typical corporation organization chart showing the impacts particular federal agencies have on specific departments of a notional company,[1] and appendix 2.2 for a glossary of acronyms used.

First, the most important benefits to business produced by the regulatory process are examined, then its negative impacts are covered, followed by a discussion of deregulation.

## POSITIVE IMPACTS OF FEDERAL REGULATIONS ON BUSINESS

There are six positive impacts on business stemming from the regulatory process. First, having briefly summarized in chapter 1 the process regulatory agencies use to make rules and issue orders, it is apparent that the process is open to business to make its input. No regulatory agency capriciously issues a rule governing an industry without it being backed by an Act of Congress and without it having been open to all types of public input, including formal hearings and informal presentations to the agency's staff via working papers and suggestions.

The rule-making process is supposed to be transparent, and it is. Any company or trade association representing a company has the opportunity to input its views at numerous steps along the way, beginning with the legislation while it is being drafted, as it is being considered in House and Senate committees, and when it is on the two chambers' floors. After the bill is enacted, industry can lobby the Executive Branch to request approval or a presidential veto. Finally, companies can lobby the administrative agency given oversight by the statute, as well as the Office of Management and Budget, which has the power to review agencies' rules while in draft and can return them to the drafting agency for revision. No new rule should come as a surprise to industry.

Second, companies benefit from rules because they establish uniform standards within an industry. All rules pertain to all companies within an industry or with respect to a particular issue, such as emissions from smokestacks, no matter who owns them. This leveling of the playing field, giving no unfair advantage to one firm over others, is a vital principle of our competition-based open market system. If a firm finds it is being injured by a rule that unfairly provides a rival with an advantage, it has recourse through the adjudication process or ultimately through the federal courts.

Third, many businesses benefit from governmental assistance, typically in the form of federal subsidies,[2] which are provided to small business through Small Business Administration (SBA) loans. Federal subsidies are provided to numerous specific industry activities: agricultural products, timber industry for road construction in forests, shipping companies, international companies to insure against risks of foreign investments, and so forth. Assistance is also provided in the form of preferences, loans, loan guarantees, and tax benefits for minority businesses, women-owned businesses, exporting businesses (those creating jobs in the United States), and those facing stiff foreign competition (U.S. steel industry).

Fourth, society as a whole benefits from having rules and regulations, especially because government can improve the way companies perform their business. For example, higher manufacturing quality standards (International Organization for Standardization, ISO 9000) have helped American firms compete against foreign producers having similar or lower quality standards. Clean air and water benefit everyone in our society. Safety on highways, in factories, and offices is improved by higher standards for construction, handling hazardous materials, and improved conditions in the workplace generally. Social benefits have resulted from rules regarding nondiscriminatory employment practices, health services for the poor and elderly, control of diseases through heightened health standards, and so on.

Fifth, small business benefits directly from numerous rules. One in particular stems from the Regulatory Flexibility Act of 1980, which mandates that regulatory agencies certify that any new rule should not have a significant adverse impact on small businesses. This mandate, coupled with another law (Unfunded Mandates Reform Act of 1995) and an Executive Order (No. 12866), requires that agencies assess costs and benefits of alternative regulations before selecting the rule that provides maximum benefit at least cost. A reasonable number of alternatives must be considered. This cost/benefit review is mandatory if the regulation will likely result in required expenditures over $100 million.[3]

Sixth, given that there is a regulatory environment in the United States, efforts to focus and restrain it can be viewed as benefits. A major step in that direction was taken in 1993 with the enactment of the Government Performance and Results Act, which requires that "public benefits" stemming from agencies' actions be linked to the federal budget. "In practice this means federal agencies must set a limited number of achievable outcome-oriented goals and make clear how those strategic goals improve or protect the lives of the American public."[4] The Environmental Protection Agency (EPA) provides an example of the effects of this requirement. EPA shifted its measure of success from how many enforcement actions and fines it imposes per year to a broader strategic measure—is the environment better off after EPA publishes a rule or takes an action?

## NEGATIVE IMPACTS OF FEDERAL REGULATIONS ON BUSINESS

All of the benefits cited above come with costs. These costs are both general and specific, being borne by society as a whole and by individual firms, industries, and consumers.

### Quantity of Regulations

One of the most important negative impacts of regulation is the sheer quantity of it. Each day, the *Federal Register* publishes hundreds of new proposed rules and hundreds of final rules ("orders") requiring industry compliance. Keeping up with the immense volume of these regulations is a major challenge for large companies and a near impossible task for small businesses. One estimate is that in 2000, a business would have needed 2.5 people full-time to keep track of new federal regulations; in 2001, owing to a reduction in new rules, the number dropped to two people.[5] Companies have to decide which proposed rules to fight, which ones to accept, and in some instances, which orders to ignore—and hope you are not found out.

One of the most useful roles of trade associations is they usually provide as a service to their members the tracking of proposed rules being developed in the regulatory agencies appropriate to their industry. These associations also frequently provide the leadership for organizing their industry's position on these measures, and they interface with the agencies' staffs to make their undustry's views known. Trade associations provide useful political "cover" for individual companies that do not want to appear to be too outspoken on a particular subject.

For example, no auto manufacturer would want to gain publicity for lobbying against a new child-safety device (presumably because of the cost and complexity of designing and installing it in passenger vehicles), so the American Automobile Manufacturers Association would take the lead in making the case on behalf of the whole industry, diffusing the negative publicity that might result.

### Costs of Compliance

Each proposed rule has a dollar cost of compliance. The staff of the agency proposing the rule makes a best estimate of the cost of compliance and publishes it with the notice of the proposed rule. These estimated dollar costs range from negligible to gigantic, depending on the rule and how far-reaching it is expected to be. Companies need to take action to comply with rules ranging from alterations in their processes (to not use certain dyes thought to have health consequences) or labeling (to name the ingredients contained in a package) to enormously costly installations of pollution control devices (such as scrubbers in chimneys or catalytic converters in autos).

An example is the steel industry. In 1977, according to the Iron and Steel Institute, EPA's first seven years of clean air rules actually cost the steel industry $20 for each ton of steel produced or $45 million for each 1 percent reduction in airborne pollution. EPA's estimate had been $14 per ton of steel.[6] To go from 96 percent compliance to 100 percent would have cost an additional $1.2 billion over five years, according to the industry.[7]

Figuring out the aggregated dollar cost of compliance to business of all the rules and those that are proposed is indeed a challenge. One pioneering study in 1976 calculated the costs as follows: each $3 billion of appropriated funds to operate the regulatory agencies costs $60 billion (or twenty times as much) for business to comply with regulations, including $25 billion for paperwork alone. A 1980 study using the 20/1 ratio showed that the total compliance cost had doubled—to $126 billion.[8] By fiscal year 2002, using this ratio, the cost of compliance for EPA regulations alone was $156.8 billion.[9]

The National Association of Manufacturers conducted a survey of its members to assess the cost of compliance with just one type of regulation workplace rules. They found that U.S. manufacturers spend an average of $2.2 million to comply with these regulations. This cost represented 1.6 percent of a typical company's gross receipts and was 75 percent higher than previous government or academic estimates.[10]

According to a study by the General Accounting Office (GAO) of fifteen large corporations, not one company could identify all the regulations with which it was supposed to comply, much less provide cost data for compliance. How are small businesses supposed to calculate their costs of compliance? The short answer is they cannot.

In 1995, the SBA's Office of the Chief Counsel for Advocacy published a first-of-its-kind report measuring regulatory costs and looking at their impacts on small versus larger businesses.[11] The study concluded that for firms with fewer than five hundred employees, the average annual cost of regulation, paperwork, and tax compliance was about $5,000 per employee, compared with approximately $3,400 per employee for larger firms more than five hundred employees. Thus, small businesses, which employ 53 percent of the workforce, shoulder 63 percent of the total business regulatory burden.[12]

According to the SBA study, the total national dollar regulatory cost for firms with fewer than five hundred employees was $247 billion and for larger firms, it was $148 billion. Thus, small business carried 67 percent of the total cost burden of regulation, paperwork, and tax compliance. The SBA concluded, "this indicates that the burden is too heavy on the smaller firms."[13]

Another aspect of the cost of compliance is the impact on companies' net worth caused by a change in accounting regulations mandated in 2001 by the Securities and Exchange Commission (SEC) and the Financial Accounting Standards Board. Under the old rules, corporations could record expenses each quarter for as long as forty years to write off "goodwill," an accounting term for the amount that an acquiring company overpaid (amount paid above fair market value) for an acquired firm. Under the new rules, acquiring firms must immediately and fully write off the goodwill amounts. In 2002, with the falling stock market depressing the value of many acquisitions, hundreds of American corporations that had recently made acquisitions with inflated shares had to write off an estimated $750 billion for goodwill, a figure more than 10 percent greater than Canada's gross domestic product (GDP).

In 2002, AOL Time Warner recorded goodwill expenses of $99.7 billion to reflect the plunge in value following AOL's acquisition of Time Warner, creating a net loss for the year of $98.7 billion, the largest in corporate history. Other major firms making large goodwill write-offs were AT&T, Quest Communications, and WorldCom, which filed for bankruptcy.[14] The cost of compliance can be fatal.

### Costs of Noncompliance

Another dollar cost is that of noncompliance. If a company fails to comply with a rule, the rule-making agency has the power to fine the company usually in an amount equal to the savings from not complying. For EPA, the maximum civil penalty during the early years of its existence was $25,000 a day per violation with no ceiling. For the years 1974–80, through its enforcement of the Clean Air Act and Clean Water Act, EPA cited 340 violations and settled or imposed penalties totaling $55.2 million, more than half of which was paid by steel companies.[15]

Over time, the dollar cost of noncompliance with regulations of all types grew considerably. Federal and state prosecutors' indictments for fraud, violations of accounting standards, tax evasion, obstruction of justice, and numerous other criminal charges against executives at Enron, Arthur Anderson, WorldCom, Tyco International, Adelphia Communications, Rite Aid Drug, Global Crossings, HealthSouth, and ImClone Systems have resulted in bankruptcies and prosecutions, convictions and settlements totaling in hundreds of millions of dollars, plus, in some instances, jail time.[16]

The ultimate price for noncompliance by a company was paid by the once-respected accounting firm Arthur Anderson, which, following its federal felony conviction, ceased business operations.[17] The ultimate price for an individual was paid by Rite Aid's chief executive officer, Martin Grass, who became the first CEO of a major company to be held criminally accountable on thirty-five counts for accounting fraud, paid the ultimate price for an individual and faces fines and at least eight years in federal prison.[18]

The largest settlement was for $1.4 billion between federal regulators and ten of the largest Wall Street securities firms including J.P. Morgan Chase, Merrill Lynch, and Citigroup's Salomon Smith Barney. These firms were accused of dozens of conflict-of-interest activities, including issuing fraudulent, overly optimistic stock research reports to investors on companies whose investment banking services they coveted.[19]

The Federal Communications Commission's largest single fine ever was $6 million against SBC Communications for "willfully and repeatedly" breaking a merger condition by restricting local telephone competitors from using its network to carry toll calls. SBC paid a total of $66 million in fines to the FCC, plus hundreds of millions in fines to various state regulators.[20]

Firms conducting international business are also affected. For example, federal charges against Boeing and Hughes Aircraft for violations of U.S. export laws by providing China with sensitive rocket technology resulted in a $32 million settlement.[21]

On the domestic side, another penalty against Boeing was the Air Force's withdrawal of $1 billion in rocket contracts that the government accused Boeing of winning with the aid of proprietary information illegally obtained from its archrival Lockheed Martin, giving the contracts to Lockheed. Boeing was also suspended from future Air Force rocket work. According to the Air Force, this was among the harshest penalties ever imposed on a defense contractor for "serious and substantial violations of federal law said the Air Force."[22]

## Opportunity Cost

Another type of decrement is opportunity cost. If managers spend their time reviewing and working to comply with rules, that time is denied them for performing other duties more central to conducting their business. The SEC filed 24 percent more enforcement actions in fiscal year (FY) 2002 (598) than in the prior year (484), and the GAO reported that publicly traded companies had been making financial restatements for accounting irregularities more frequently, jumping 170 percent from 1997 to 2002.[23]

In 2002, in the wake of the Enron, Arthur Anderson, and WorldCom scandals, Congress enacted the Sarbanes-Oxley Act, which charged the SEC with issuing a host of new regulations for publicly traded companies. These affect their financial reporting standards, codes of ethics for senior executives, financial expertise on audit committees, stock trading during pension fund blackout periods, retention of audit records, independence of auditors, conflicts of interest among stock analysts, and more.

One stunning feature of these new rules is that CEOs and CFOs of publicly traded companies are required to personally review financial reports and sign them, certifying that the data they contain were properly collected, recorded, reviewed, and are accurate. Signing up to phony numbers could bring criminal penalties as much as twenty years in jail and $5 million in fines for each person. A year after filing the first financial reports under the new rules, only one company was sanctioned by regulators—HealthSouth Corporation—despite the fact that a number of companies failed to comply with the rules.[24]

The SEC estimated the "time cost" of compliance by CEOs and CFOs would be five hours of company time each quarter. The vice president and corporate secretary at Intel, the giant computer chip maker, stated, "we think they're wrong by 100 times and maybe an even larger order of magnitude. It's hard to figure how they [SEC] came up with that number."[25] One attorney in private practice who works with corporations stated that since the passage of Sarbanes-Oxley, "he's been doing 90% Sarbanes-Oxley and 10% everything else."[26] When the CEO and CFO have to personally certify their company's numbers, all senior executives in the firm are brought into the process, and all their time that is necessary to provide the top executive with assurance that the numbers are real will be spent on this task. This begs the question, "Who is running the store?"[27]

## Cost to Society

The cost of compliance by industry, whatever it is and however it is measured, is also a cost borne by society as a whole. The growing number of rules is largely based on the growth of social, as opposed to industry-specific, regulation. General, broad-based rules affecting the entire society or large segments of it—like workers' minimum wage and safe working conditions, standards for fair employment and nondiscrimination, and environmental protection—represent the types of rules that are mostly issued today.

Another type of social cost of rule making in the post-Enron era could result from imprecision of or changes in normative procedures resulting from a rule. For example, the SEC's new rule on "audit fee" disclosure may be sufficiently loose to permit accounting firms to charge clients for what was traditionally an audit, as well as for what had been consulting services and tax work, thus undermining the SEC's objective of gaining transparency in accounting firms' fees.[28] A second example is the SEC requirement, mandated by the Sarbanes-Oxley Act, that attorneys become whistle-blowers on their clients, even in-house lawyers working for corporations, if they observe financial misconduct. Such a requirement strikes at the heart of attorney-client confidentiality, thus undermining a sacred social norm.[29]

A classic example of the regulatory burden imposed by the government on a prime contractor is the cost of administering its subcontractors. During one fifteen-month period in 1981–82, the Hughes Aircraft Company prepared 325 subcontract plans and had to negotiate seventy-four additional plans with subcontractors. Two laws mandated this work: Truth in Negotiations Act of 1962 and the Small Business Act of 1950. These subcontract plans cost $921,000 to produce; each plan weighed one pound, 11 ounces.[30]

## Cost to the Economy—Taxes and Debt

Operating the federal government represents a cost in the form of taxes paid by individuals and businesses, other revenue sources, and borrowing. For fiscal year 2002, total receipts by the federal government were $1.853 trillion; total outlays were $2.011 trillion, leaving a deficit of approximately $150 billion. Receipts represented 17.9 percent of gross domestic product, and outlays were 19.5 percent.[31]

The sources of this $1,853 billion in FY-2002 revenues were as follows: $858 billion from individual income taxes, $701 billion from social insurance and retirement receipts, $148 from corporation income taxes, and $146 billion from other sources.[32] Thus, corporations accounted for less than 8 percent of total federal revenues, while the individual income tax continues to be the single largest revenue source for the federal government, as it has since World War II.[33]

For FY- 2003, the cost to operate all of the sixty-one federal independent agencies and government corporations, plus the sixty-four smaller federal boards and commissions, was $30.1 billion, an all-time high. (See appendix 2.3 for a list.) According to one study, "hidden taxes" caused by compliance with regulations on goods and services cost Americans $843 billion a year, roughly $8,000 per household, in addition to the average tax paid per household of $19,613.[34]

The cost to operate the fifteen departments of the Executive Branch was $1,209 billion in FY-2003; the total number of employees was 3,952,940, including active military.[35] Table 2.1 provides a summary of the fifteen departments of the federal government.

Owing to the fact that the government's revenue has typically been insufficient to pay for its spending, the government runs deficits. These are financed through borrowings by the Treasury Department, mostly called T-bills; as of FY-2002, the federal debt held by the public totaled $3,540

Table 2.1
**Departments of the Federal Government**

| Department | FY-2003 Budget ($ in Billions) | Employees (000) |
|---|---|---|
| Agriculture | 77 | 131 |
| Commerce | 6 | 37 |
| Defense (Civilian & Military) | 331 | 2,967 |
| Education | 48 | 4 |
| Energy | 19 | 15 |
| Health & Human Services | 459 | 65 |
| Homeland Security | 38 | 170 |
| Housing & Urban Develop. | 31 | 10 |
| Interior | 10 | 69 |
| Justice | 23 | 129 |
| Labor | 59 | 17 |
| State | 16 | 28 |
| Transportation | 61 | 118 |
| Treasury | 17 | 150 |
| Veterans Affairs | 52 | 207 |

billion.[36] Another type of debt amassed by the government is off-budget debt or "agency debt," the sums borrowed by individual agencies, like the SBA. Most of this debt is financed by the Federal Financing Bank (FFB), an agency of the Treasury Department, finances most of this debt. As of FY-2002, the FFB held $6,198 billion in government accounts, the largest being trust fund surpluses of Social Security. Agency debts include those of the Farm Credit System, HUD, and the Tennessee Valley Authority.[37]

All these debts are, in the end, financed with borrowings by the Treasury from the public, making the U.S. Treasury the largest competitor in the world's capital market. As the Treasury competes for credit, it may have the effect of "crowding out" private borrowers from available capital or cause interest rates to rise if the demand for capital exceeds supply. If these phenomena occur, they could produce indirect costs to the economy and to other borrowers.[38]

In March 2003, the newest federal department came into being—the Department of Homeland Security, headed by its first secretary, Thomas Ridge. This department employs 170,000 federal workers and had a budget of $38 billion for its first year. The establishment of this giant organization was the result of terrorist attacks on the United States and the government's response to the need for heightened security within our borders.

The department is essentially a rearrangement of activities and agencies previously organized within eight other, existing departments; as a result, some of the dollar and employee data shown in Table 2.1 are duplicative. As examples, the new department received the Secret Service from Treasury, the Coast Guard from Transportation, Immigration and Naturalization Service from Justice, Office of Emergency Preparedness from Health and Human Services, and National Communications System from Defense.[39]

### Summary of Costs

In sum, all these regulations and those who make them represent costs— for enactment, compliance, and enforcement. These costs are paid in the form of taxes by individuals, smallbusinesses, and corporations. They are paid in the form of federal debt that grows as the Treasury's deficit grows to finance these activities, causing the government to compete for funds against private borrowers in the nation's capital markets. They are paid in the form of higher prices for goods and services because the cost of compliance is passed from the firm to the consumer. They are paid in the form of loss of sales by domestic companies that comply with regulations versus many foreign companies producing competing products in nations where such regulations are absent, minimal, or not enforced. They are paid in "opportunity cost"— managers taking time away from core duties to administer regulations.

And this represents only the federal burden; there is also the state and local burden to pay for regulatory agency activities at those levels. This is a social overhead cost that is rarely mentioned, except during election campaign speeches.

## DEREGULATION

Deregulation of business began during the mid-1970s in the Ford administration and continued industry-by-industry to the end of the twentieth century. It was a feature of every administration during that period: Ford, Carter, Reagan, Bush, and Clinton. Deregulation was a major bipartisan force in American politics for almost twenty-five years.

The motivation for deregulation was to increase competition and thereby lower prices to consumers.[40] Regulations began to be perceived as a hidden tax on the consumer, and a consensus of support grew to let more efficient market forces set prices and the scope of specific businesses instead of federal regulators.

### Industry-by-Industry Deregulation

The energy industry was the first to be partially deregulated by statute, with the passage of the Energy Policy and Conservation Act in 1975; this act mandated the decontrol of petroleum products within six years. Next, in 1978, was the partial decontrol of the airline industry mandated in the Airline Deregulation Act, and over time that industry was fully deregulated; even its regulatory agency, the Civil Aeronautics Board, was itself abolished in 1985.[41] Next was trucking, with the enactment of the Motor Carrier Act of 1980, discussed above. Coupled with this industry's deregulation was the gradual phasing out of its regulatory agency, the Interstate Commerce Commission; the ICC completely disappeared in 1996, having had a life span of more than one hundred years.

Over time, the railroad, financial services, and telecommunications industries have been partially or fully deregulated—telecommunications with the Telecommunications Act of 1996,[42] and financial services with the Financial Services Modernization Act of 1999, which repealed many provisions of the Glass-Steagall Act of 1933.[43] Broadcasting and public utilities, such as electric power generating companies, have been progressively deregulated only partially. Public utilities are still regulated by their state public utilities commissions.

### Consequences of Deregulation—Prices

As a consequence of deregulation, it is debatable on an industry-by-industry basis how much cost savings consumers have gained through increased competition and whether, due to industry consolidations, shareholder values of acquiring companies have increased. Lower cost and better service certainly resulted from deregulation in trucking, and lower cost but not better service have resulted from railroad, airline, and telecommunications deregulation.[44] Price and service benefits to consumers are still in question in financial services and broadcasting as these industries continue to consolidate.

Prices to consumers have been reduced by deregulation in certain industries. On average, according to one study, price savings from deregulation are at $40–60 billion a year.[45] Airfares fell approximately 40 percent (inflation-adjusted) from 1977 to 1996, saving passengers $14.8 billion (in 2000 dollars) annually. Increased competition is partially responsible; in 1978, there were only fifteen domestic carriers compared with thirty-two flying scheduled service in 2002. Railroad shipping rates fell steadily after deregulation; by 1999, rates were half their 1984 level. Trucking rates also fell following deregulation, and shipping price reductions for truck and rail have saved U.S. industry between $38 and $54 billion annually.[46]

### Consequences of Deregulation—Industry Consolidations

Another consequence of the deregulated environment is that shakeouts, bankruptcies, and mergers and acquisitions within deregulated industries have been rampant. Industry consolidations occurred in each of these businesses for years following their deregulation. Why do companies acquire others? Once the government permits consolidations within an industry, acquiring companies seek synergies with acquired companies, hoping to achieve cost reduction by elimination of redundant activities, improved operations, and growth of market share. Occasionally antitrust considerations have prevented an acquisition or required partial divestiture of assets by the acquiring company.[47]

As an example, let us take a closer look at deregulation's immediate impacts on railroads. The Staggers Act of 1980 sharply reduced federal regulation of this industry. It freed freight-carrying companies to set rates (many of which increased immediately[48]), increase or decrease service, sign long-term contracts with shippers, acquire other railroad companies, and to downsize—all activities that previously required years of review by the ICC. Within just three years of deregulation, the number of large rail companies had been reduced through mergers from thirteen to seven, the workforce was slashed by one-third, excess track was abandoned, and investment in modern facilities and equipment doubled. All this was to reduce cost and increase competition between railroads and between rail and other shippers, especially trucks.

Between 1980 and 1982, the now fewer Class I railroads (the companies carrying almost all rail freight) did as much business as the whole industry before deregulation, and they did it with 4 percent fewer locomotives, 24 percent fewer railcars, 16 percent less track, and 22 percent fewer employees. They made more than twice as much money, even during these recession years. These companies recorded $4.4 billion in net income over those three years—a figure that was half a billion dollars more than all railroads made in the entire decade of the 1970s under regulation.[49]

## Size of Government

With deregulation, has the size of government decreased? The short answer is no. Net total employment in the independent agencies remained roughly the same from 1990 to 2001—999,894 people in 1990 and 1,040,657 in 2001. During this time, some agencies made reductions in personnel and budget, and others grew. For example, the Nuclear Regulatory Commission dropped nearly 15 percent of its employees, while the Federal Communications Commission grew by about 14 percent.

The entire federal civilian workforce has also remained fairly steady over a longer period, despite expansion in the late 1980s and early 1990s. In 1975, it totaled 2,877,000 people; in 2001, it totaled 2,704,000. The payroll for these people has of course grown: $39 billion in 1975 to $131 billion in 2001.[50] Only in a few deregulated industries is the "government overhead" cost lower.

Will there be more deregulation in the near future? Under current conditions, it is unlikely, absent a major change in governmental philosophy. Episodes of market instability in certain key industries, coupled with poorly designed reductions in their regulation, have stimulated a reticence for further deregulation. The California energy crisis in 2000–2001 and the savings and loan industry crisis in the 1980s are two leading examples. Significant economic benefits from deregulation are being balanced against the post-9/11 need for greater security in the nation's economic activity. These heightened security requirements have dramatically increased the cost of transacting business and appear to have lessened the near-term likelihood of further deregulation. Indeed, the reverse may be the case.

## Impacts of Terrorism: Return to Regulation?

The U.S. economy was in a "mild" recession during the first three quarters of 2001.[51] Unemployment was growing, as were claims for unemployment benefits. Consumer confidence was declining. Business investment in equipment and software was also in decline.[52] And the stock market had been relentlessly bearish since early 2000. Against this sluggish economic backdrop, terrorists attacked on Monday, September 11, 2001. The Bush administration's response was immediate: wage war on terrorism at home and abroad, first in Afghanistan and later in Iraq.

With the nation now on a semipermanent war footing, what were the economic consequences? The immediate impacts were stark. By the close of the week following the terror attacks, the New York Stock Exchange had dropped 1,369 points, or 14.3 percent—its worst week since 1933. The stock market decline continued, as did other economic bad news: the government estimated that $15 billion in new building projects and 300,000 potential jobs were lost in the year following the terror attacks on the United States. During that year, federal government spending spiked: an additional $40 billion on homeland security, plus $355 billion on defense, of which $100 billion went for the worldwide war on terrorism.[53] In 2003, Congress approved an emergency supplemental bill of $79 billion for the war in Iraq, homeland security, foreign aid to Afghanistan, and an airline industry bailout.[54]

For longer-term consequences, analysts predicted continuing growth in federal defense and security spending, sharply reversing the trend of the 1990s when defense spending shrank from 5.2 percent of GDP in 1990 to less than 3 percent in 2000. Some analysts predicted at least partial reregulation of some industries because they saw the federal government, "whose role waned in the last decade, returning with a vengeance as warrior, regulator, economic manager, big spender."[55]

Many industries were hard hit by the dramatic economic turndown, which over time began to appear to be a change in lifestyle for the country, if not the world. Hardest hit was the hospitality industry and air transportation. Discretionary air travel appeared to have died. Domestic airlines lost $7.7 billion in 2001—$4.2 of it after September 11—and they lost another $8 billion in 2002, half for extra security.

Major air carriers, already in trouble from the continuing economic slump, are still reeling. During the eighteen months following September 11, 2001, two of the six major carriers, United and US Airways, filed for Chapter 11 protection while they cut costs. The world's largest carrier, American Airlines, threatened bankruptcy to wring the same type of cost concessions from its unions, lenders, and aircraft lessors. The Air Transport Association (ATA) pleaded for federal help in a March 2003 report citing a "perfect economic storm" had hit the industry: "terrorism, war, higher fuel prices, higher security costs, deflation, and a weak economy."

All this was putting the industry on course to lose another $10.7 billion in 2003. (Not mentioned in the ATA report was the fact that United and US Airways' expenses were more than 11 cents per seat mile versus 7.4 cents for Southwest and 6.3 cents for JetBlue.)[56] Some reregulation of the major carriers might be in the offing, but the profitable carriers—Southwest and JetBlue—will doubtless resist it, as will be the case with profitable performers in other industries.

## CONCLUSION

The federal government's impacts on American business and society are both positive and negative. Even the positive impacts come at great cost—to business and to society as a whole. In recent years, these costs and economic inefficiencies sparked a move to both lessen command-and-control regulation in favor of a performance-based approach and to deregulate or partially deregulate certain key industries: energy, airlines, trucking, railroads, finance, and telecommunications.

An open question is whether or not the impacts of the semipermanent antiterrorism war will stimulate a reverse process and reregulate portions of some of these industries, particularly the hard-hit airline industry.

In the next chapter, the federal government's levers of power over the American economy are presented. By exercising these levers, the government has enormous influence on the environment external to the firm in the most vital area—the economy.

## APPENDIX 2.1

### Federal Agency Impacts on Departments of a Notional Corporation

**Board of Directors**
Justice Dept., SEC, FTC, FASB

**Chief Executive Officer**
Justice Dept., SEC, FASB
FTC, Sarbanes-Oxley

| Finance Resources | Human | Marketing | Operations | R&D |
|---|---|---|---|---|
| SEC | HHS | FTC | EPA | Patent Office |
| Fed. Reserve | EEOC | FDA | Energy Dept. | Defense Dept. |
| GCAS | NLRB | USDA | HSD | NSF |
| Treasury/IRS | ERISA | DOC | OSHA | SBA |
| SBA | Wage/Hour | Defense Dept. | NRC | NASA |
| FASB | Standards | GSA | Commerce Dept. | USDA |
| Justice Dept. | HSD | FHSA | CPSC | DOT |
| | Labor Dept. | State Dept. | EPA | NIH |

| Planning | Government Legal | Inbound/Outbound Relations | Logistics |
|---|---|---|---|
| DOC-Census | Justice Dept. | White House | Energy Dept. |
| State Dept. | FTC | Exec. Branch Depts. | HSD |
| Fed. Reserve | SEC | Congress | EPA |
| White House | EPA | Regulatory Agencies | FHSA |

| Government Planning | Inbound/Outbound Legal | Relations | Logistics |
|---|---|---|---|
| Congress | Courts | FEC | FAA |
| Regulatory Agencies | Reg. Agencies | Foreign Embassies | NTSB |

| Security | Contracts & Purchasing | International Relations | Shareholder |
|---|---|---|---|
| HSD | FAR/DAR | Commerce, State | Justice Dept. |
| FBI | FTC | Treasury, Defense | Treasury Dept. |
| CIA/NSA | Defense Dept. | OPIC/STR | SEC |
| Defense Dept. | Justice Dept. | CIA/NSA | USPS |
| | OFCC | Intl. Trade Comm. | FASB |
| | Courts | U.S. Embassies | |
| | | Export-Import Bank | |

## APPENDIX 2.2

### Glossary of Acronyms

| | |
|---|---|
| CIA | Central Intelligence Agency |
| CPSC | Consumer Product Safety Commission |
| DOC | Department of Commerce/Census Bureau |
| DOT | Department of Transportation |
| EEOC | Equal Employment Opportunity Commission |
| EPA | Environmental Protection Agency |
| ERISA | Employee Retirement Income Security Act |
| FAA | Federal Aviation Administration |
| FAR/DAR Regulations | Federal Acquisition Regulations/Defense Acquisition |
| FASB | Financial Accounting Standards Board |
| FBI | Federal Bureau of Investigation |
| FCC | Federal Communications Commission |
| FDA | Food and Drug Administration |
| FEC | Federal Election Commission |
| FHSA | Federal Highway Safety Administration |
| FTC | Federal Trade Commission |
| GCAS | Government Cost Accounting Standards |
| GSA | General Services Administration |
| HHS | Health & Human Services Dept. |
| HSD | Homeland Security Dept. |
| IRS | Internal Revenue Service |
| ITC | International Trade Commission |
| NASA | National Aeronautics and Space Administration |
| NIH | National Institutes of Health |

| NLRB | National Labor Relations Board |
| NRC | Nuclear Regulatory Commission |
| NSA | National Security Agency |
| NSF | National Science Foundation |
| NTSB | National Transportation Safety Board |
| OFCC | Office of Federal Contract Compliance |
| OHSA | Occupational Health and Safety Administration |
| OPIC | Overseas Private Investment Corporation |
| Sarbanes-Oxley Law financial reports | Requires CEOs and CFOs to certify accuracy of |
| SBA | Small Business Administration |
| SEC | Securities and Exchange Commission |
| STR | Special Trade Representative |
| USDA | U.S. Department of Agriculture |
| USPS | U.S. Postal Service |

## APPENDIX 2.3

**Federal Independent Agencies and Government Corporations**[57]

AMTRAK

Broadcasting Board of Governors

Central Intelligence Agency

Commission on Civil Rights

Commodity Futures Trading Commission

Consumer Product Safety Commission

Corp. for National & Community Service

Defense Nuclear Facilities Safety Board

Environmental Protection Agency

Equal Employment Opportunity Commission

Export-Import Bank of the United States

Farm Credit Administration

Federal Communications Commission

National Capital Planning Commission

National Council on Disability

National Credit Union Administration

National Endowment for the Arts

Federal Emergency Management Agency

Federal Housing Finance Board

Federal Labor Relations Authority

Federal Maritime Commission

Federal Mediation & Conciliation Service

Federal Mine Safety & Health Review Comm.

Federal Reserve System

Federal Retirement Thrift Investment Board

Federal Trade Commission

General Services Administration

Institute of Museum and Library Services

Inter-American Foundation

International Broadcasting Bureau

Merit Systems Protection Board

National Aeronautics & Space Admin.

National Archives & Records Administration

Overseas Private Investment Corporation

National Endowment for the
  Humanities
National Labor Relations Board
National Mediation Board
National Science Foundation
National Transportation Safety
  Board
Nuclear Regulatory Commission
Occupational Safety & Health
  Review Comm.
Office of Compliance
Office of Government Ethics
Office of Personnel Management
Office of Special Counsel
Federal Deposit Insurance
  Corporation
Federal Election Commission

Panama Canal Commission

Peace Corps
Pension Benefit Guaranty Corporation
Postal Rate Commission
Railroad Retirement Board

Securities and Exchange Commission
Selective Service System

Small Business Administration
Social Security Administration
Tennessee Valley Authority
Trade and Development Agency
U.S. Agency for International
  Development
U.S. International Trade Commission
U.S. Postal Service

— CHAPTER 3 —

# Levers of Federal Economic Power

When surveying the environment external to the firm, the entrepreneur instantly recognizes that the condition of the economy is one of the most critical features in the environment that affects the company. Whether the economy is robust and growing, sluggish, stagnating, or in recession are conditions that greatly impact the ability of the business to succeed.

Why is this important to the entrepreneur? Inflation rates, interest rates, tax rates, unemployment rates, depreciation schedules, levels of consumer confidence, and the like are economic factors hugely influenced by actions of the federal government, which impact a business at virtually every level. The firm's market grows or shrinks due to macroeconomic policy. Fiscal policy impacts the cost of operating the business by raising or lowering taxes, monetary policy raises or lowers the cost of money, and operating costs are impacted by complying with regulations that in turn affect its profits.

This chapter briefly summarizes ways that the federal government influences the performance of the U.S. economy, directly impacts businesses through the economy, and stimulates social change. Also briefly examined is the federal government's ability to influence international business conditions, which in turn affect the domestic business climate because of our participation in the global economy.

## INTRODUCTION

The United States government is the single largest and most powerful organization in the country and probably the world. It employs more people than any other entity, public or private. It has the largest payroll, makes the most purchases, and owns the most property. It has the power to tax, print money, and set interest rates for the world's largest economy. It has the largest debt. It regulates the private sector and enforces those regulations. It has a monopoly of force and physical power within the society. It officially speaks for everyone in the country on any issue outside the country. And, given that America is the only superpower, it has more ways and means to influence events on this planet than any other entity. Nothing on earth compares with the power of the U.S. government.

The federal government's macroeconomic policy is its major mechanism for influencing the performance of the domestic economy. This policy has two components: fiscal policy, set by the Executive Branch and Congress, and monetary policy, set by the Federal Reserve. Macroeconomic policy affects the key components of aggregate demand that largely power the economy: consumption, investment, government purchases, and net exports (exports minus imports). Generally speaking, the government adjusts these control levers with the goal of achieving moderate, steady growth in the nation's gross domestic product (GDP) without significant inflation and deflation and without high unemployment.

What are the specific levers of power that this mighty entity has to influence the performance and condition of the domestic economy? There are thirteen levers of federal economic power that can be grouped into three categories, as follows:[1]

A.  Normal Government Operating Levers
    1. Employment and Payroll
    2. Government Purchases

B.  Policy Levers Intended to Affect the Macro Economy
    3. Fiscal Policy
    4. Monetary Policy
    5. Wage and Price Controls
    6. International Trade and Finance

C.  Policy Levers Intended to Affect Social Change or Specific Industry Segments
    7. Transfer Payments
    8. Subsidies
    9. Credits
    10. Programs
    11. Tariffs and Other Import Barriers
    12. Excise Taxes
    13. Miscellaneous Programs

Each of these levers is addressed below:

## EMPLOYMENT AND PAYROLL

The first "normal" operating lever is employment and payroll. These are normal activities because the government has to have employees to perform its work and it has to pay them. Yet, this power lever is far from normal, given its size.

The payroll of the federal government is enormous. The civilian workforce in 2001 was 2,704,000 people (excluding uniformed military), with a payroll $131.9 billion.[2] This is the same dollar value as 2002 revenue at General Electric, the nation's fifth largest company, $131.6 billion.[3] The active duty military in the same year numbered 1,385,000 people, and its payroll totaled $74 billion.[4] IBM's 2002 sales were $83 billion, for comparison.

Civilians are paid every two weeks and most of the military once a month. These funds enter into the circuit flow of a community like lifeblood. Each federal worker typically deposits his/her check in a local bank or credit union, and those institutions immediately put the money to work.

### Federally Impacted Communities

No community is more dependent on this process than Washington, D.C., and its suburbs because that city, naturally, has the highest concentration of federal workers. Indeed, locals like to call it the "recession-proof" economy because government checks come out regular as clockwork, regardless of the overall economy. In 2001, there were 181,000 federal civilian employees living in Washington, D.C., which was the second largest number after California with the most at 248,000 employees. In FY-2001, total federal disbursements in Washington, D.C., were $30.9 billion, with a per capita value of $54,000—by far the largest in the nation. California was the largest dollar recipient of federal disbursements: $188 billion with per capita of $5,500.[5]

For communities having large-scale government installations, such as a major U.S. Army or Navy base, the military payroll is a vital feature of their local economy. No wonder congressmen and senators fight so fiercely when the Defense Department names their local base to be closed.

Expansions or contractions in the federal payroll, base closures, and decisions to locate a major federal facility in a community are all immensely important factors for local economies. These payrolls often are the most significant source of revenue for these communities, and they are the main baseline factor for the local job "multiplier," that is, how may additional jobs in the community are generated by each government job or each government contract's dollar value.

## GOVERNMENT PURCHASES

The other normal activity of government is making purchases. Because of its sheer size and the way it makes procurements, the purchasing lever of power is also a major weapon in government's arsenal to achieve particular economic objectives and social change.

## Size of Federal Procurements

The federal government is the largest buyer of goods and services in the American economy. In 2001, its purchases from the private sector totaled $893 billion.[6] By accelerating or reducing its procurements, the government can stimulate overall economic activity or dampen it, increase employment or reduce it, encourage development and growth of certain types of industries, favor one company over others by buying its products, and provide financial stimulus and technical assistance to firms from whom it procures products or services.

All government agencies make purchases from the private sector. Very few items are not outsourced. One of a few examples of "make" not "buy" is the making of our currency: the Treasury Department's Bureau of Engraving and Printing makes all paper money, and the department's two mints make all coins, using purchased equipment and supplies. The currency is then issued by Federal Reserve banks, representing about 46 percent of the media of exchange in the United States (checks represent the bulk of the rest).[7] Another example is military training, which is conducted by the armed services at training bases or at sea.

Outlays in FY-2002 by the General Services Administration, which procures routine office items like paper clips, personal computers, and telephone systems for government offices, totaled $600 million. Procurements by the Defense Department totaled $59.6 billion in the same year, buying everything from aircraft carriers and tanks to parachutes, aspirin, and boots. NASA's outlays that year were $14.5 billion, sustaining an entire sector of the American economy.[8]

## Achieving Economic Objectives

Examples abound of government achieving particular objectives through its procurement power. To stimulate the development of American industry, in 1802, the army bought black powder for guns from a little start-up company near the Delaware River, thus ensuring a customer base for E. I. du Pont de Nemours & Company, which of course is still in business as one of the world's leading chemical companies with 2002 sales of $24 billion.[9]

Later in that century, the government sought to bind the country together with railroads linking the East and West Coasts. To encourage railroad building, the government gave federal land to railroad companies for their rights of way and to pay for supplies. More recently, to keep certain aircraft production lines open, the U.S. Air Force has purchased quantities of airliners for its own use as transports, for executive travel and possibly for air-refueling tankers.[10]

The war on terrorism increased federal purchases, beginning with an FY-2002 supplemental appropriation of $27.1 billion. Half of this amount was for Defense Department and intelligence agency use, and most of the remainder was for homeland security and rebuilding in New York City. These activities contributed to a sharp increase of 6.4 percent in the annual growth rate of real federal purchases in 2002. State and local government purchases rose at a more normal 1.7 percent annual rate that year.[11]

## Government Sets Standards

One of the most important ways government has impacted the economy and made social change through its purchases is by setting standards. It not only stipulates specifications for particular products and services it is buying, but also as part of the contract for those products, it sets specifications for its contractors' workplace conditions. For example, government contractors may not discriminate in hiring practices, must adhere to rules on environmental discharges, and must meet workplace standards for employee health and safety. Federal standards for the workplace are now universal throughout the private sector.

Regarding product specifications, government standards have established commercial baselines for a host of industries: medical instruments, space satellites, communications equipment, and military equipment. An example is flat-panel television. It came about as a result of a U.S. Air Force requirement for high resolution, flat, electronic displays (such as radar) in the limited space of a jet fighter's cockpit. Once this technology was proven for military use, it became commercially available.

## Government as Customer

The government is a very good customer. It never defaults on a payment, its checks never bounce, it provides technical support and assistance, it buys in bulk so production runs can usually be based on solid forecasts, and it provides financing. The fact that the government pays "progress payments" for its large-scale purchases enables companies to have significant cost savings by paying for the work while it is in progress—without having to borrow these funds from banks at prevailing interest rates. Having had the government as a customer is a bit like having a *"Good Housekeeping* Seal of Approval" for your company—it adds credibility for you and confidence for your other customers. Chapter 11 discusses how to sell to the federal government.

## FISCAL POLICY

The major power levers the government has in its arsenal to affect the macro economy are fiscal policy and monetary policy. Two others will also be discussed: wage and price controls and international trade and finance policy.

Fiscal policy is a catchall term describing the government's power to tax and spend. This power is shared jointly between the president and Congress and implemented through the Treasury Department. The president initiates the process by proposing an annual budget delineating how much money is needed (taxes) for spending (appropriations) on activities and programs he deems important. Congress then considers the president's budget request. The House Ways and Means Committee initiates the tax legislation, and the various authorizing committees consider the spending requests under an umbrella figure approved by the budget committees. The House and Senate Appropriations Committees recommend the actual spending amounts. The various authorization and appropriations bills are enacted by the two houses and are sent to the president for his signature and execution.[12]

## Tax Policy

The Constitution empowers the Congress to "lay and collect Taxes, Duties, Imposts and Excises" and to appropriate these funds for public purposes (such as "pay the Debts and provide for the common Defense and general Welfare of the United States").[13]

In making decisions relating to taxation, Congress and the president also decide who to tax (individuals, corporations, imports, etc.), at what rate to tax them (marginal tax rate), how long to tax them (temporary, permanent), what kind of taxes to impose (personal, corporate, inheritance, value-added, user, tariffs, etc.), and how to collect them (annual, quarterly, payroll withholding, transaction/sales, etc.). These decisions and the process by which they are made are the very essence of America's democratic political system.

For example, in 2001, the Economic Growth and Tax Relief Reconciliation Act was passed. It featured a broad-based cut in marginal tax rates, largely to encourage entrepreneurship and risk taking, which high marginal tax rates discourage. The act also provided rebate checks to most taxpayers to stimulate demand, resulting in the creation of 800,000 private-sector jobs and raising the GDP by a half percentage point within a year.[14]

Individuals pay a variety of taxes each year to the federal government, the largest categories being individual income, Social Security, Medicare, excise, and inheritance. In addition, they pay state taxes on individual income and property. There are also county and city taxes: income, property, and use taxes (usually for utilities). Totaling up all these changing federal, state, and local taxes (omitting sales taxes, fees, and licenses), the effective tax rate for a typical individual is 30 percent of his/her income, which takes the average person 101 to 109 days of work to pay—or until April 19, 2003 and April 11, 2004—the earliest since 1967. Taxes are the single largest component of a typical person's budget—exceeding food, clothing, and shelter combined.[15] Business and sales taxes are, of course, in addition to these.

One government fiscal year (October 1 to September 30) is examined below as a snapshot of federal revenue. In FY-2001, the federal government's $2,019 billion of revenue, representing 20 percent of the U.S. gross domestic product of $10.08 trillion,[16] came from the sources shown in Table 3.1:[17]

In 2002, after four years of surpluses, the government recorded a deficit of $158 billion, representing about 1.5 percent of GDP. Revenues that year were $1.853 trillion, 7 percent below 2001 levels. The deficit was attributed to four factors: lingering aftereffects of the prior year's recession, the stock market plunge, and increased federal expenditures for the war on terrorism and for homeland security.[19] As discussed in chapter 2, deficits are financed by Treasury Department borrowings from the public, which currently holds in excess of $3.5 trillion in government instruments.

An important long-term trend is this: since 1956, as a percentage of total federal revenues, social insurance payroll taxes have increased substantially (half of which are paid by employers), corporate income taxes have declined, and individual income taxes have remained roughly constant as the largest contributor.

Decisions regarding who to tax and by how much have immense influence on the way the economy performs and on how individuals and businesses conduct their affairs—adjusting their activities to take advantage of or to mitigate against "tax consequences." For example, the federal tax deduction for home mortgage interest payments has been a leading reason individuals have bought homes on credit, increasing the home ownership rate in America to its highest levels in history—68 percent in 2002.[20]

A negative example is the so-called Death Tax, inheritance taxes collected by both the federal and state governments. According to one study, as many

Table 3.1
Sources of Federal Revenue, FY-2001

| Revenue Source | Dollars in Billions | % of Fed. Budget | % of U.S. GDP |
|---|---|---|---|
| Individual Income Taxes | 972 | 48 | 9.7 |
| Social Insurance Payroll Taxes[18] | 682 | 34 | 6.8 |
| Corporate Income Taxes | 195 | 9.6 | 1.9 |
| Excise Taxes | 77 | 3.8 | .7 |
| Estate and Gift Taxes | 32 | 1.6 | .3 |
| Customs Duties (Tariffs) | 21 | 1 | .2 |
| Miscellaneous Revenues | 40 | 2 | .4 |
| Total | $2,019 | 100.0 | 20.0 |

as one-quarter of all successful small companies will be forced to close if the temporary suspension of the Death Tax is reinstated because the tax is a larger amount than the heirs can pay without selling the business.[21]

### Job Creation and Worker Assistance Act

Another important example for businesses is a tax law enacted in 2002 that provides help as an economic stimulus primarily for small businesses. This is the Job Creation and Worker Assistance Act (JCWAA).[22] It provides federal tax relief in three categories: depreciation, net operating losses, and retirement plan changes. The act also promotes investment to stimulate growth by allowing businesses to immediately write off (by expensing) 30 percent of the value of qualified investments in the year of purchase (up to September 11, 2004). Expensing lowers the amount of taxable income and improves after-tax cash flow. Many state laws do not yet conform to these new federal rules.

JCWAA changed existing law on depreciation in two ways: the annual amount is increased to $25,000 effective in 2003, and any business assets purchased from September 11, 2001 to September 10, 2004 qualify for a "bonus" depreciation, allowing the business to immediately write off 30 percent of the asset's cost, plus a percentage of the remaining amount depending on the term of depreciation. The result is that business assets can be depreciated from 33 percent to 100 percent in the first year the asset is put into service—as opposed to as long as thirty-nine years under former rules. Depreciation can cut a business' taxes by reducing its taxable income.

Rules on net operating losses were changed by JCWAA to permit companies having losses in 2002 to retroactively apply them to past tax returns, allowing recovery of taxes paid up to five years earlier. This may provide an immediate refund. Retirement plan changes affect companies with fewer than one hundred employees, allowing these companies to claim a credit equal to 50 percent of the cost of starting or maintaining an employee retirement plan. The limits are a ceiling of $1,000 on costs and a maximum of three years per company. All three of these measures can directly improve cash flow and quickly benefit the bottom line of a small business.

### Spending Policy

In making decisions relating to spending, Congress and the president also make decisions regarding what role government will play in society in general and in the economy in particular. In other words, will government play a passive role in the economy (like it did in most of the nineteenth century) or an activist role—as it has since the New Deal in the 1930s? As a basis of or justification for spending, the Constitution provides Congress the power to provide for "the common defense" and to "borrow Money on the credit of the United States," "coin Money, regulate the Value thereof, and of foreign Coin," "declare War," "raise and support Armies," "provide and maintain a Navy," "promote the Progress of Science and Useful Arts," and "make all Laws which shall be necessary and proper for carrying into Execution the foregoing Powers, and all other Powers vested by this Constitution in the Government of the United States."[23]

Those who are "strict constructionists" argue that the Constitution provides only limited powers to the federal government—to enable it to perform only specific "enumerated" activities and duties, such as those quoted above. Providing for the "common defense" and protecting life and property are government's primary roles.

Others take a more liberal interpretation of these constitutionally granted powers, largely basing their interpretation on the "necessary and proper" clause. They argue that in an advanced industrial society, government should undertake a wider role in society and the economy, and that the enumerated powers are only suggestive of the types of actions the government should undertake. By the twenty-first century, this argument is somewhat moot, given the now long-standing precedent of an activist federal role in the economy and society.[24]

The major categories of federal expenditures are shown in Table 3.2, using FY-2001 as an example:[25]

Total outlays in FY-2001 were $1.835 trillion. "Nondefense Discretionary" spending includes education, training, science, technology, housing, transportation, and foreign aid. "Other Entitlements" include such means-tested programs as food stamps, supplemental security income, child nutrition, veterans' pensions, earned income tax credit, and food aid to Puerto Rico. "Other Mandatory Entitlements" include federal retirement and insurance programs, unemployment insurance, payments to farmers, and the like. Not all federal spending programs are included in the unified budget. FY-2001 was the last year of a surplus.

Table 3.2
Federal Spending Categories, FY-2001

| Program | Dollars in Billions | % of Federal Budget |
|---|---|---|
| Social Security | 422 | 23 |
| Nondefense Discretionary | 355 | 19 |
| Medicare/Medicaid | 342 | 19 |
| National Defense | 292 | 16 |
| Net Interest Payments | 208 | 11 |
| Other Entitlements | 111 | 6 |
| Other Mandatory Entitlements | 117 | 6 |

Looking at these numbers, it is apparent that social programs accounted for 54 percent of federal spending that year, and this is the portion of the budget that is growing at the fastest rate. Defense and nondefense discretionary spending together totaled 35 percent.

## MONETARY POLICY

Monetary policy is the activity of government that affects the economy's performance largely through its controls over the currency and the banking system. This seemingly narrow mandate has far-reaching implications for the entire economy through the government's regulation of the nation's money supply, interest rates, and bank reserve requirements. The Fed's (Federal Reserve System) goal for the past half century has been a stable economy having moderate growth with low inflation. But the day may come, as has happened in Japan for more than a decade, when it will have to wrestle with a new nemesis, deflation—a substantial reduction in aggregate demand and persistent declining prices throughout most sectors of the economy.[26]

### The Federal Reserve System

The monetary policy lever is in the hands of the Federal Reserve System, headed by the Federal Reserve Board of Governors consisting of seven members appointed by the president for fourteen-year terms. The Board of Governors, together with twelve district Federal Reserve Banks, is the central bank of the United States. Known as "the Fed," this agency is technically independent of the Executive Branch, but presidents have strongly influenced its policies though the power of appointment to the Federal Reserve System and through persuasion. Coordinating monetary and fiscal policies to achieve a consistent economic impact is sometime a tough assignment, given that these levers are in different hands.

The Federal Reserve System, established in 1913, consists of the Federal Reserve Board of Governors, headquartered in Washington, D.C., and led by a chairman, and twelve district Federal Reserve Banks located in major commercial centers of the country.[27] Alan Greenspan and his predecessor, Paul Volker, exercised great influence on the economy by their activist roles as chairmen.[28] Each of the district banks monitor economic activities in their geographic area of responsibility and regularly report to the Board of Governors their assessments of the economy's performance, making recommendations for adjustments in the Fed's policies.

### The Fed's Powers

What specific powers enable the Fed to have immense influence on the economy? The Federal Open Market Committee, consisting of the Board of Governors plus the presidents of five of the district Federal Reserve Banks, has the power to do the following:

- Set reserve requirements at commercial banks, which determines the portion of available funds member banks of the Federal Reserve System must retain in their vaults or in the regional Federal Reserve bank;
- Set the discount rate, which is the rate the Fed charges member banks when they borrow reserves from the Federal Reserve System;
- Set the federal funds rate, which is the rate charged by one bank to another to borrow (usually overnight) some of its reserves in excess of those required by the Fed;
- Decide to purchase or sell treasury securities (U.S. government bonds) to affect money supply growth, which expands or contracts economic activity; and
- Charter and supervise (with the Comptroller of the Currency) the operation of certain types of banks.

Through these major levers, the Fed is able to greatly influence interest rates, the availability and cost of credit, inflation rates, the stock of money, and the overall performance of the economy.

Fed decisions regarding the federal funds rate are perhaps the most well known. During 2001, to stimulate economic growth in the face of a recession, corporate scandals, a significant loss of stock market wealth, and terrorist attacks, the Fed reduced the federal funds rate eleven times, from 6.5 percent to 1.75 percent. It held the rate steady throughout 2002 until November, when it reduced it another half percent to 1.25 percent. In June 2003, citing deflation concerns, the Fed cut the rate again by a quarter point to a forty-five-year low of 1 percent, indicating it will remain there for quite a while.[29]

As the Council of Economic Advisors stated, "[a] lowering of interest rates stimulates demand through four main channels: encouraging consumption (particularly of durables), stimulating business investment (by lowering the cost of capital), promoting residential investment (as seen from the booming housing sector), and lowering the foreign exchange value of the dollar (which tends to raise exports and lower imports)."[30]

Regarding the stock of money, in late 2002, there was $620 billion of U.S. currency in circulation, of which more than half—between $340 and $370 billion—was circulating outside the United States. These so-called Eurodollars (because they are mostly held in Europe) form a large portion of many countries' reserves.[31]

In 2003, with a persistent sluggish economy, personal bankruptcies reaching a new high, and the percentage of U.S. home loans in foreclosure hitting a record high, the Fed decided for the first time in its history to initiate a public education campaign about how to manage money, called "There's a lot to learn about money." The Fed chairman himself made television spot commercials and visited schools to help the public learn how to better handle its finances.[32] This is an entirely new role for the Fed.

## WAGE AND PRICE CONTROLS

During normal economic times, the government does not control prices. Prices are subject to market forces, having supply and demand as the key variables. If supply exceeds demand, prices tend to go down. If demand exceeds supply, prices tend to rise. When there is equilibrium between supply and demand of goods and services, prices are generally stable. Government does not control these market forces (except in the few remaining "command" economies in the world—Cuba, North Korea—where the government sets both prices and supply), but it routinely influences them and reserves the right to intervene directly if needed.

During periods of great economic stress, such as wartime or severe recession, the federal government has intervened in the economy to control wages and prices. This technique is generally considered ineffective in the long run, especially to control inflation, as President Nixon's experience with it demonstrated during the recession of 1970–71. The key to successful wage/price controls is their coordination with monetary policy, making certain that the Fed reduces the rate of growth of the money supply at the same time the president places legal constraints on wages and prices.[33] To work, these two activities, under the control of two different parts of the government, must be complementary—not in conflict.

During World War II, the government not only had wage/price controls in place, it also controlled the supply of goods to the civilian economy and, through rationing, limited the demand for goods. Such controls are highly artificial and cannot last indefinitely without causing serious disruption to market forces. Such measures also stimulate a black market for highly prized controlled goods—gasoline and tobacco were World War II favorites. The high water mark of government economic control was during World War I, when the government operated the railroads and imposed wage/price controls and some rationing.

Other tools of direct intervention include releasing scarce materials from federal stockpiles (e.g., oil from the Federal Petroleum Reserve) and seizing and operating key industries (such as the railroads during World War I). These measures, together with wage/price controls, are viewed as "blunt instruments" and have serious side effects, making them rarely used. Yet, these real powers are there, and they underlay the credibility of the government's persuasive power.

## INTERNATIONAL TRADE AND FINANCE

The final macro lever affecting the domestic economy is the federal government's ability to influence international trade and investment, both outbound and inbound. These activities include encouraging international capital flows (foreign direct investment), having a liberal trade policy to stimulate international commerce, and stabilization of exchange rates.

This lever is increasingly important as the percentage of U.S. GDP generated by international commerce increases; by 2000, it represented approximately 20 percent. During the last half century, world exports grew twenty-fold, while world output grew sevenfold. By 2002, world trade amounted to 24 percent of global output. These data are solid indicators of our global economic interdependence.[34]

### Foreign Direct Investment

The United States would not have developed as rapidly as it did in the nineteenth century without massive amounts of foreign investment. European investors put their money at risk to help finance the building of the American railroad system and other major industries such as steel, oil, and electric power. And overseas investments by U.S. firms are a major part of many firms' asset base. In 2002, General Electric's assets in Europe were approximately $25 billion, an amount equal to the total sales of the company when Jack Welch became CEO twenty years earlier.

Foreign investment in the United States has always been attractive due to usually good returns, few restrictions on foreign investments, and because America is viewed as one of the lowest risk areas of the world from a "stability" standpoint. One major restriction is in the Trade Act of 1988 (Exon-Florio procedure), requiring foreign mergers and acquisitions of American firms that might affect U.S. national security to be reviewed by a government committee that has veto power over the intended merger or acquisition.[35]

Foreign direct investment in the United States in 2000 totaled $1.238 trillion, with the top five sources being Britain, Japan, the Netherlands, Germany, and France, in that order. American law and policy have always encouraged foreign investment here, and by example it encourages Americans to invest abroad to generate wealth for U.S. business owners and to stimulate the growth of other economies—making them better customers for American-made goods. In 2000, U.S. direct investment abroad totaled $1.244 trillion, with the top five recipients being Britain, Canada, the Netherlands, Japan, and Switzerland, in that order.[36]

Various federal programs encourage Americans to invest abroad in the expectation that this will generate domestic employment, increase tax revenue at home, and develop or stabilize foreign economies. One policy is transferability of funds. Some foreign governments place severe restrictions on the movement of funds out of their economies, but the United States has always had a liberal policy on this, with only occasional periods or amounts of restriction.

Another policy is tax credit for U.S. exports and foreign investment if domestic jobs or technology will be benefited. The Domestic International Sales Corporation procedure that allowed taxes on foreign profits to be deferred was supplemented by. the Extraterritorial Income Exclusion provision of the tax code that provides a tax break for U.S. multinational firms for their exports to offset the lighter tax burdens of European competitors when they operate overseas. The World Trade Organization (WTO) labeled this tax break an export subsidy because it rewards overseas production and has declared it illegal.[37]

Finally, the government offers insurance against political and social risk to American companies that invest abroad. This is done through the Overseas Private Investment Corporation, which insures overseas investments by U.S.-based firms. See chapter 10 for a discussion

### Liberal Trade Policy

America has long been a champion of liberal international trade policy. After World War II, the General Agreement on Tariffs and Trade (GATT) was negotiated with more than two dozen countries to open up trade around the world by reducing tariffs and other trade barriers. These barriers have continued to be reduced, and in 1995, the World Trade Organization replaced GATT as the multinational vehicle for achieving this goal. More than 130 countries are now WTO members, including China.

By stimulating trade and international investment, the government seeks to generate higher levels of performance in the domestic economy. The Council of Economic Advisors explains how trade creates benefits:

> Imports provide U.S. firms with a wider variety of low-cost inputs, and consumers with a wide variety and lower prices for goods. Moreover, competition from international producers induces domestic firms to raise their productivity, which raises incomes in the long run. Trade therefore boosts consumer satisfaction at home and ensures that American producers remain competitive, by increasing the size of the market in which they operate.[38]

The economic theory of comparative advantage is at work here. This is the idea that countries should work at the tasks in which they have a comparative advantage (based on skills, national resources, existing infrastructure, cost of production, etc.) and not engage in those they do not. The general belief behind the United States' open trade policy is that if barriers to entry are lowered or removed, American firms that have a comparative advantage in numerous product areas and will be able to compete successfully on a level playing field with anybody.

Today, labor unions and others call into question this basic principle, arguing that foreign governments and their protected industries do not and will not compete fairly, costing American companies and their employees lost business and jobs. Demonstrations against the perceived negative effects of globalization are now a fairly standard feature at international conferences.

In 2001, the United States had total goods exports of $731 billion and total goods imports of $1,141, leaving a negative balance of $410 billion. The largest "goods" component by far of our exports and imports is manufactured goods. America's five largest export customers are Canada, Mexico, Japan, United Kingdom, and Germany. Our largest import suppliers are Canada, Mexico, Japan, China, and Germany.[39]

### Exchange Rate Stabilization

The federal government also promotes trade and investment by working to maintain stable exchange rates between the U.S. dollar and other major convertible currencies, especially the euro, pound sterling, and the yen. This is done to reduce risks in international transactions stemming from potential sharp increases or declines in value of one currency against another.

Since the 1970s, when the United States discontinued "fixed" exchange rates (fixed parity of the dollar to gold) and began a system of "managed float" with market conditions, the U.S. government (represented by the New York Federal Reserve Bank) and the central banks of our major trading partners (European Central Bank, Bank of England, Bank of Japan, etc.), have intervened in the world's major currency markets to buy or sell one another's currencies in an effort to prevent major disequilibriums in their exchange rate relationships. International businesses still take their own actions, such as currency hedging, to mitigate against exchange rate risks, especially on long-term agreements.[40]

### TRANSFER PAYMENTS

Let us now turn to a discussion of the various policy levers the government has to affect. social change or to affect specific industry segments. The first of these is transfer payments.

The federal government provides money directly to millions of individual American citizens and to companies and institutions. This is done through transfer payments. Politicians refer to them as entitlements. The largest such program is Social Security, followed by Medicare payments to individuals, hospitals, and health-care providers. In fiscal year 2001, Social Security payments to over 45 million retired and disabled workers, their dependents, and survivors totaled $422 billion. That year, Medicare payments to over 40 million elderly and disabled people and Medicaid payments to 34 million poor, disabled, and elderly in nursing homes totaled $342 billion. Means-tested entitlement transfer payments, such as Supplemental Security Income, Child Nutrition, and Food Stamps, totaled $111 billion.[41]

## Social Security and Medicare

The funds disbursed by the federal government for the two largest programs are generated by their own special taxes—Social Security and Medicare. These taxes are paid by employers and their employees on a matching basis through withholdings from their salaries or, in the case of self-employed individuals, through their own direct payments. Self-employed individuals pay the full amount because there is no employer to split the tax with.

Federal transfer payments are a major lever on the economy affecting social change. The rising number of senior citizens, both in absolute numbers and in proportion to the total population due to improved diet, exercise, and health care, means that Social Security payments will be an increasingly larger portion of the American economy. In 2000, 12.4 percent of the U.S. population was sixty-five years old and older. That percentage will rise dramatically as successive waves of baby boomers enter the post–sixty-five demographic.[42]

Medicare is a vital funding vehicle for many hospitals, nursing homes, hospices, individual medical practitioners, and private health-care providers. Changes in the level of payments or additions/deletions of types of coverage provided by Medicare instantly impact the health-care industry and its range of services. Communities with large percentages of senior citizens dependent on Medicare, as well as Social Security, are especially impacted by such changes.

## FEDERAL SUBSIDIES

What are subsidies? There are various techniques the government uses to stimulate the production of goods and services in specific industries like steel, geographic areas such as agricultural, and commodities like sugar. Subsidies include tax benefits, direct payments, credits (direct loans and loan guarantees), price supports, funding for new construction, funding to support ongoing operations, and so forth. Funding for these activities comes from revenue paid by taxpayers that Congress has decided should be used to benefit particular interests and from government agencies extending the guarantee of the "full faith and credit" of the United States without a congressional appropriation. Credits are such a large and important form of subsidy, they are addressed in the next section.

Numerous tax benefits are provided in the Internal Revenue Code for a variety of purposes. Companies are stimulated to engage in research and development by writing off portions of these costs. For example, the mining industry greatly benefits from tax relief for developing new mines— especially for exotic metals needed for national defense. Companies large and small can itemize losses to cushion a bad year's balance sheet. Taxes in the form of tariffs can protect domestic producers against lower-priced foreign imports.

Direct payments by the government to companies in the nuclear industry absorb the cost of new product development. Direct payments to boat builders ensure there is a domestic fishing industry. Direct payments to defense companies fund research and development of new weapon systems.

## Price Supports

Price supports are endemic in agriculture. Many crops are grown in the United States at a higher cost than in foreign locations having lower land and labor costs. To insure a domestic industry for such commodities, Congress funds the Agriculture Department to pay price supports for such corps, equalizing their price in the open market with foreign imports. Such crops include cane sugar, coffee, pineapples, and tobacco.

Members of Congress and senators representing areas of the country where such crops are grown are the principal champions of these price supports. Representatives from other areas, whose constituents are paying for these supports by paying higher prices for the items in their stores, go along with the champions because they have their own special interests. Trade-off voting is a time-honored practice on Capitol Hill.

## Construction

Funding for new construction is another way government impacts the economy. The Interstate Highway System, begun in 1955, would never have been build without federal funding at an average of 90 percent of the cost, with state and local match of 10 percent. Funding for harbors, navigable rivers, dams, flood-control barriers, aqueducts, and forest preserve roads all depend on federal support. Development of new types of vehicles, such as a transit bus designed for urban transit authorities, depends on federal funds being appropriated by Congress and administered by the Transportation Department, typically on an 80/20 federal/local government match.[43]

## Purchases and Operations

Federal funds subsidize the purchase of new buses and trolleys by cities, and they fund a major portion of day-to-day operations of such transit systems. Other transportation systems depend on federal subsidies: Amtrak and Conrail would shut down without massive government support, most U.S.-based shipping lines depend on federal subsidies of various kinds, and the airline industry was vitally dependent on government support of operations through carrying the mail (which was discontinued after September 11, 2001). Low cost public housing would be nonexistent without federal subsidies of various types—federal financing of the initial cost of construction, tax benefits, and direct payments to individual owners or tenants.

## FEDERAL CREDIT

A low-profile lever of tremendous power on the economy affecting specific industry segments is the ability of the federal government to extend credit. Federal credit subsidizes specific activities in the private sector, making up the difference between the true cost of an activity and the price paid by a consumer. A classic example is farm price supports, where the Agriculture Department pays farmers more for a crop than the open market would pay. This unique subsidy is also rather stealthy, because most of the funds involved do not appear in the unified federal budget and most are not appropriated by Congress for a specific lending situation.

### Size of Federal Credit

The dollar amounts are staggering.[44] By FY-2002, the federal government had made direct loans totaling $193 billion, guaranteed private loans totaling $1,750 billion, and quasi-government agencies (like Fannie Mae and Freddie Mac) had extended $3,798 billion in credit to private borrowers. All told, the federal government's direct loans, guaranteed loans, and loans issued by government-sponsored agencies were $5.741 trillion, a sum far greater than the national debt held by the U.S. Treasury ($3.5 trillion in FY-2002). Indeed, they totaled an amount equal to approximately half of the nation's GDP.

Federal credit programs greatly benefit their recipients. Direct or guaranteed loans are more attractive than those found in the commercial marketplace because their interest rates are usually lower, maturities are longer, and less or no collateral is needed.

More than a dozen federal or quasi-governmental agencies issue credit. These include the Department of Housing and Urban Development (HUD), Small Business Administration (SBA), the Export-Import Bank (ExIm Bank), the Federal Home Loan Mortgage Corporation (Freddie Mac), and the Federal National Mortgage Association (Fannie Mae). The overwhelming majority of federal direct and guaranteed loans involve the housing industry, making Fannie Mae and Freddie Mac the largest financial institutions in the country.

### Major Bailouts

The extensions of credit to New York City and the Chrysler Corporation, where the government made direct loans and pledged the "full faith and credit" of the United States to guarantee bank loans to these two entities, are the most high-profile examples of a federal bailout.[45] Certainly they were the single largest such bailouts up to their time, eclipsing an earlier example—the bailout of Lockheed Corporation with $250 million in federal loan guarantees during 1971–74, when that major defense contractor overextended itself with a failing commercial aircraft program (the L-1011). In all three of these bailouts, the borrowers repaid the loans with interest and the two companies and the city were saved from bankruptcy.

These extensions of credit fall into a pattern established during the New Deal when the government provided direct loans to companies to stimulate the economy and prevent bankruptcies. The Reconstruction Finance Corporation (RFC) was the Depression-era federal institution performing this role. After World War II, legislation was enacted restricting the RFC's activities: requiring maximum ten-year limits on loan maturities, sufficient collateral by the borrower, and mandating that the RFC not compete with private credit sources. The RFC was abolished in 1952.

Other major examples of federal loans and loan guarantees are Conrail (freight carrier in the Northeast), which received $3 billion in federal aid, and Continental-Illinois Bank of Chicago, which in 1984 received Federal Deposit Insurance Corporation (FDIC) direct funding of $1.5 billion and sold its loan portfolio to the FDIC for $3.5 billion. The largest bailout of all time was the savings and loan crisis in the late 1980s and early 1990s, which cost the federal government a total of $180 billion.[46]

### Cost of Credit

Are there costs to the government and to the economy for these federal credit programs? Indeed, there is no free lunch. The costs fall into three categories:[47]

1. Economic Costs—Because government credit programs do not increase the supply of investment funds and they deny credit to other, more credit-worthy borrowers.
2. Initial Fiscal Cost—Since such programs increase the total size of government borrowings, this expansion of the government's credit volume causes higher interest rates, and the fiscal cost to the government rises because that portion of higher interest rates servicing the public debt is a direct, though unseen, charge to the federal budget.
3. Ultimate Fiscal Cost—If borrowers holding government-guaranteed credit default, the Treasury bears the cost. Ultimately, taxpayers pay off the loans. In 2001, the federal government wrote off $6.1 billion defaulted direct loans and $1.1 billion defaulted guaranteed loans. By the end of FY-2002, the government held $32 billion defaulted loans it had guaranteed to private borrowers.[48]

A real, though intangible, cost is the "opportunity cost" of these federal credit programs, another way of describing "economic cost." Funds provided or guaranteed to borrowers through these credit programs at subsidized interest rates, longer repayment terms, and typically with low or no collateral are funds that are not available to other, more credit-worthy borrowers whose positive contributions to the economy may well be greater than those of the marginal, subsidized borrower receiving government credit.

## GOVERNMENT PROGRAMS

The federal government influences the economy and thereby affects social change or specific industry segments by starting, accelerating, or occasionally terminating programs. These programs are activities that use funds authorized by Congress, are administered by a federal department or agency, and are undertaken purportedly to achieve some useful public purpose.

During the Great Depression, President Roosevelt initiated numerous federal programs for the underlying purpose of putting people to work to stimulate the economy. These programs built roads, bridges, dams, public buildings, and the like. They had names like the Civilian Conservation Corps and the Works Projects Administration. Roosevelt also established Social Security, which is today the government's largest program by far.

In the 1950s, President Eisenhower established the largest road-building program in history, the Interstate Highway System, and the space program, administered by NASA. President Kennedy founded the Peace Corps, to provide poor nations with American experience in improving the lives of their people. President Johnson's Great Society started numerous programs to help the poor, children, minorities, and the elderly to gain equal education opportunities and health care. The Head Start Program and Medicare are two of these programs.

### Cost of Programs

All programs have costs. The specific dollar cost of performing these particular tasks is one cost; the lost opportunity of using those same funds for other purposes is another. The option of leaving these funds in the pockets of taxpayers is a specific opportunity cost. Once programs are established, they take on a life of their own—having their own bureaucracies, their own congressional supporters and defenders, and their own constituencies within the larger society. President Reagan once remarked that you can drive a stake into the heart of a federal program, but you cannot kill it; it will pop up again somewhere else under a new name.

The budget for individual federal programs is often difficult to calculate because most of them are imbedded in the fifteen departments of the Executive Branch. One of thousands of examples is federal funding support for elementary and secondary education. In FY-2002, this activity had a budget authority of $21 billion out of the total Department of Education budget authority of $56.7 billion.[49]

## TARIFFS AND OTHER IMPORT BARRIERS

A lever of federal power intended to affect the economy and specific industry segments is tariffs and other import barriers. By raising or lowering such barriers, the government harms or benefits particular industries and activities from foreign competition, which in turn affects the overall economy.

Tariffs are a tax imposed by the federal government on goods imported into the United States. Unlike some nations, the United States does not charge transit tariffs (a tax on goods crossing the border for a foreign destination) or export tariffs (taxes on goods being exported). The Constitution explicitly for bids export tariffs. All tariffs are either *ad valorem*, meaning they are a percentage added to the value of the item being imported, or a per-unit specific fee. The Constitution specifically empowers the federal government, not states, which had been the case under the Articles of Confederation, to impose tariffs. The federal government also has the power to impose nontariff restrictions on imports, such as limiting the tonnage of steel or the number of autos imported.

Tariffs have been used both as a revenue measure and as a mechanism to achieve domestic economic goals, such as protecting domestic producers of goods competing with foreign producers. Sometimes they are used as a diplomatic tool to retaliate against a foreign government's import duties, which may be injuring a U.S. exporter. They may also be used as a diplomatic lever to stimulate a foreign government to reduce tariffs on some unrelated commodity, such as imposing a high tariff on imported bicycles as a lever to open up exports of certain U.S. agricultural products.

As a revenue source, tariffs have become a very small factor in the federal government's income, less than 1 percent. Today, they are primarily used as a bargaining chip to achieve advancements in the basic U.S. philosophy of expanding trade to promote economic growth and employment. Indeed, since shortly before World War II, the United States has pursued this liberal trade philosophy by negotiating reciprocal trade agreements both bilaterally and multilaterally, the latter usually through the General Agreement on Tariffs and Trade, which, in 1995, morphed into the World Trade Organization (WTO). Accordingly, over the past half century, America's tariffs have dropped dramatically and now represent a small fraction of the cost to consumers of imported goods.

Tariffs can be an important economic policy instrument. A good example is steel. Over the past decades, many American steel producers failed to keep pace with their foreign rivals in technology upgrades and in lowering production costs. As a result, more than thirty steel companies went into bankruptcy. President George W. Bush, having had political support from steel-making states, vowed to help them.

In March 2002, he imposed tariffs for three years up to 30 percent on imported steel to provide U.S. companies an opportunity to retool by investing in new technology, consolidating, negotiating more favorable terms with unions, and thereby becoming more competitive.[50] For the first six months of 2003, steel imports were down by 20 percent as compared with the same period in the previous year. In July 2003, imports plunged a whopping 34.8 percent from the prior July.[51] These data suggest the tariffs were having their intended effect. The downside was that the European Union threatened retaliation by raising tariffs on U.S. exports. President Bush lifted the steel tariff in December, 2003.

Because tariffs are now so low on most commodities, nontariff import restrictions are far more important as a tool of foreign policy. The most important of these is quantitative restrictions, usually in the form of quotas. For example, a few presidents have asked foreign automobile manufacturers to voluntarily restrict exports to the United States of their lower priced cars to allow U.S.-based companies to compete with them on price and quality.

Additional nontariff barriers include the following:

- subsidies, where the price of an exported product is lowered by a government subsidy;
- requirements to buy locally, such as "Buy America" restrictions on government purchases;
- standards, setting labeling and testing standards in a way to benefit local producers;
- product purity inspections that are delayed and take weeks to clear a shipload of fruit and vegetables at a port; and
- administrative delays, simply not having customs inspectors or stevedores available for weeks to process imports—as in South Korea, where it typically takes thirty days for merchandise to clear customs, causing spoilage and inventory cost.

Other examples are from the European Union: subsidies on Airbus Industrie commercial jetliners, 20 percent quotas reserved for domestically based companies importing bananas, and standards against genetically modified agricultural products, denying imports of U.S.-produced corn.

A number of "free trade" regions have been established over the past few decades. The earliest and largest is the European Union (EU), whose origins were in the 1956 Treaty of Rome, which established the European Economic Community—basically a nascent common market consisting initially of six continental nations. By 2004, the EU had grown to twenty-five member nations, ranging from Ireland and Portugal on the west to Finland and Cyprus on the east. There are essentially no tariffs or other trade barriers between these nations.

Another major tariff-free zone is the North American Free Trade Area (NAFTA), consisting of Canada, the United States, and Mexico. This was established in 1994 to promote North American trade. Other, less comprehensive, trade zones are in the Caribbean, Central America, portions of South America and Africa, and in Southeast Asia.

## EXCISE TAXES

Excise taxes are levied by all levels of government on various commodities, such as cigarettes, gasoline, and alcoholic beverages, to raise revenue and to achieve social objectives, like reducing smoking by having a high tax on tobacco products. Federal excise tax on cigarettes rose from $4 per thousand in 1964 to $17 in 2000; over the same period pipe tobacco rose from $.10 per pound to $.95 per pound.

This is one of the oldest forms of taxation, beginning in England during the 1600s. One of the galvanizing factors leading up to the American Revolution in 1776 was the British government's tea tax. In 1791, the newly established U.S. government imposed a tax on whiskey to raise revenue to finance the new government; this sparked the Whiskey Rebellion in which President Washington put down the rebels and collected the tax, using federal armed force for the first time to exforce an Act of Congress.

Like tariffs, there are two types of excise taxes: a per-unit tax (e.g., a tax per gallon of gasoline) and *ad valorem* tax, a percentage of the price of the item. In both cases, people purchasing these commodities pay the tax at the time of purchase.

During World War II, the federal government raised virtually all excise taxes between 5 and 20 percent to generate revenue to pay for the war and to dampen consumer demand for products, especially gasoline, to prevent inflation and to redirect the items for military use. In 1965, Congress overhauled the type and size of excise taxes, eliminating many consumption types of taxes on consumer products and entertainment admissions and adopting more user-type taxes, especially on gasoline, to help fund construction of the Interstate Highway System and airports.

Today, excise taxes are a small portion of federal government revenue, less than 4 percent. They represent a much more important source of state revenue, accounting for roughly 10 percent. States also use excise taxes on certain commodities for social change purposes, for example, imposing high sales taxes on cigarettes to discourage their use for health reasons.

## MISCELLANEOUS PROGRAMS

Over the years, the federal government has established specific programs, activities, and agencies to achieve specific economic or social goals or to affect specific economic activities or industry segments. There are numerous examples: the land-grant college system providing mass higher education for our youth, the Army Corps of Engineers flood control projects, the former Civilian Conservation Corps scenic highways, the Peace Corps overseas projects for education and construction, and the largest of all—the Tennessee Valley Authority (TVA).

An Act of Congress established TVA in 1933, as a government corporation. Its initial funding came from appropriations, administered by a three-person board. Its purpose was to build dams on the Tennessee River and some of its tributaries, mainly in Tennessee, Kentucky, northern Alabama, and northwest Georgia to control flooding, make the river navigable, generate electricity, boost the region's economy, and establish recreational areas. Altogether, fifty dams were built, of which twenty-nine generate electric power, and the other goals of the program have been met.

Today, TVA's capital construction activities are financed by government bonds, notes, and by lease/leaseback arrangements, all of which are under a statutory cap of $30 billion. In FY-2004, TVA's public debt totaled $25.7 billion, which represented 94 percent of total federal agency debt. The next largest agency debt was that of the Farm Credit System at $325 million. Total federal nonagency debt held by the public in FY-2002 was $3,540 billion.[52]

## CONCLUSION

The federal government has thirteen major levers of power, described above, to influence the performance of the U.S. economy. By exercising these levers, blending them in varying proportions, increasing some or decreasing others, the federal government has more influence on the performance of the world's largest economy than any other entity. And through its economic levers, it has the power to achieve social change and affect specific economic and industry segments of our society.

Entrepreneurs and small business owners are impacted by the use of these government levers in myriad ways. They need to constantly scan their external environment to monitor the economy's performance and the government's policies and activities that impact it, and adjust their business plans to take advantage of them or take direct action with their elected representatives to seek redress or relief.

# — CHAPTER 4 —

# State and Local Government
# Impacts on Business

S tate and local governmental impacts on the external environment
of a business are numerous and must be taken into consideration
by start-ups and small businesses, as well as by large corporations. State
and some local governments have considerable power to foster positive business conditions or to sour them for companies operating within their jurisdictions.

Entrepreneurs need to have a clear picture of their state and local government situation before launching a new venture or taking the risk of
expanding an ongoing operation. In this chapter, the macro factors affected
by these governments are discussed. Micro factors are discussed in chapter 9.

## INTRODUCTION

State and local (meaning counties, cities, and other municipalities) governments impact the business environment at the macro level, but not even
the largest state government has the muscle to shape the economy and other
vital external conditions within its borders like the federal government. The
power that states and cities have is the ability to encourage or discourage
business by taxing it more or less and by imposing rules and regulations that
exceed federal requirements.

States and municipalities, like businesses, are themselves impacted by and
must react to changes in their external environments influenced by the federal government, especially its fiscal and monetary policies. Cities and states
are highly dependent on federal grants, subsidies for particular activities (like
operating city transit authorities), and for transfer payments directly to their
citizens, forming a key component of the local economic base. With few
exceptions, state and local governments must comply with federal laws and
regulatory rules, just like businesses.

Moreover, laws and regulations enacted by states and municipalities must at a minimum conform to federal statutes and rules, or a court might strike them down. Thus, most state and local regulations governing business largely mirror prevailing federal standards, and in some instances, exceed them to address particular local conditions. For example, the South Coast Air Quality Management District in the greater Los Angeles area has stricter air emission standards than the federal Clean Air Act because of unique geographic and atmospheric conditions in the Los Angeles basin.

Therefore, the general rule is this: If there is a federal law or regulation governing a particular activity, state and local rules and regulations will be the same or possibly greater in impact on a business.

Before turning to a discussion of state and local governments' abilities to affect macro external business conditions, a few facts about the size and economic importance of state and local governments are summarized below.

## PROFILE OF STATE AND LOCAL GOVERNMENTS

America has a lot of government, and each governmental unit has costs associated with it. Owing to our continental size and federal system, which provides layer upon layer of governmental units, we have more government than any other industrial nation except China. In 2002, the United States had 87,901 governmental units, as shown in Table 4.1.[1]

Special districts usually do not have taxation power, but all the other units do. All can impose rules and regulations governing activities within their jurisdictions.

Which states have the most government units? Illinois has the most governmental units with 6,835, Pennsylvania is second with 5,070, Texas is third with 4,700, California is fourth with 4,607, and Kansas is fifth with 3,950. Hawaii is the smallest with 19.

Table 4.1
Governmental Units in the United States, 2002

|        |                                                          |
|-------:|----------------------------------------------------------|
| 1      | Federal government                                       |
| 51     | State governments, plus the District of Columbia         |
| 3,034  | County governments                                       |
| 19,431 | Municipal governments                                    |
| 16,506 | Towns and townships                                      |
| 13,522 | Independent school districts                             |
| 35,356 | Special districts (e.g., irrigation, power, and housing) |
| 87,901 | Total                                                    |

Many of these governmental units are also markets. For example, virtually all states have delegated—under state guidelines—to counties the operation and administration of public schools. Therefore, if you are a supplier of goods and services to schools K–12, you have 3,034 separate marketing targets for your textbooks, pencils, notebooks, desks, and chairs. If you were in France or Japan, you would have one target market, because all elementary and secondary education is centralized in a national education ministry.

## State and Local Taxes

State and local governments are tax collectors. In 2001, state and local governments' revenue totaled $1,293 billion. On a national basis, their largest revenue sources are shown in Table 4.2.[2]

Sales taxes, states' largest revenue source, are shared with municipalities, with states doing the collecting. Typically, 1 percent of sales taxes collected by states is transferred to counties, and another 1 percent goes to cities, both of which pay the state a collection fee. Sales tax revenues vary from year to year, depending on economic conditions.

Property tax is the third largest source of state and local revenue, following federal grants-in-aid. This tax is usually administered on the county level, with cities, villages, and other subunits sharing in the countywide tax pool. In some cases, both state government and counties administer property taxes. Valuations on land and buildings are made by county assessors and taxed at a rate determined by state law. When property valuations rise, so do property tax revenues; during recessions, when valuations decline, so does revenue.

In 1978, California voters adopted the famous Proposition 13, which established 1 percent as the tax rate on assessed value of property, with reassessments made only upon change of ownership. This law, upheld by the U.S. Supreme Court, means that California homeowners have a much lower property tax rate than homeowners in other states lacking this cap. Another key feature of Proposition 13 is that the allocation of property tax revenues—how much goes to the state, counties, and cities—is a decision made by the governor and the legislature; thus, counties and cities must lobby in

**Table 4.2**
**State and Local Government Revenue Sources, 2001 ($ Billions)**

| | | | |
|---|---|---|---|
| $337 | Sales taxes | $41 | Nontax income (e.g., user fees, licenses) |
| 274 | Federal grants-in-aid | 29 | Corporate income tax |
| 258 | Property taxes | 21 | Other income (e.g., park admission fees) |
| 234 | Personal income taxes | 11 | Social insurance contributions |

Sacramento for a share of the revenue. Before 1978, property taxes accounted for roughly 28 percent of California cities' general fund revenues, as compared to 14.5 percent in 2003—a loss of half.[3]

Personal income tax is the fourth largest tax source for most states. The state with the highest personal income tax bracket is Montana, at 11 percent on income above $76,200. Next is Vermont with 9.5 percent on income above $307,000, and third is California, where the top bracket is 9.3 percent on income above $38,291. State tax rates vary widely: states with low or no personal income tax make up for it with other sources of revenue such as higher property and/or sales taxes. Seven states have zero personal income tax: Alaska, Florida, Nevada, South Dakota, Texas, Washington, and Wyoming. Alaska, which has neither a personal income tax nor a sales tax, derives 30.7 percent of its revenue from corporate income tax; the bulk of its revenue comes from oil tax. Florida derives 60 percent of its revenue from sales tax.

"Nontax income" includes such items as licenses and permits (typically business licenses, building permits, and dog licenses), fines and penalties (mostly vehicle violations), and revenue from use of money and property. "Other income" is largely derived from utility user taxes for electricity, gas, telephone, and water. Typically, utility user taxes account for 10 to 15 percent of city revenue.

Corporate income tax accounted for just 2 percent of revenue. Five states have no corporate income tax: Nevada, Texas, South Dakota, Wyoming, and Washington, though Washington does have a sliding-scale gross receipts tax. Otherwise, Colorado has the lowest corporate income tax rate, at 4.63 percent. The state with the highest pure corporate income tax is Pennsylvania, at 9.99 percent, plus a capital stock and franchise tax. New York's corporate income tax is 7.5 percent, with a 2.5 percent surcharge, effectively making it the highest corporate income tax state at 10 percent.

Among the more complex corporate tax systems is California's, having a corporate income tax base rate of 8.84 percent, a tax rate on financial institutions of 10.84 percent, a 6.65 percent alternative minimum tax rate (2 percent for financial institutions), and a minimum tax on corporations of $800. Adding up all these various rates, the Tax Foundation concludes California has the highest corporate income tax rate in the nation.[4]

### Total Tax Burden

Which states have the highest and lowest overall taxes? In 2003, the nation's average state/local tax burden was 9.6 percent of residents' income. The highest was Maine's with 12.2 percent, and the lowest was Alaska's with 6.3 percent. New York's was 11.9 percent, and California's was 10.5 percent. In 2002 and 2003, it took seventy-four days of work to pay the average state tax, which was a decline from the high of eighty-four days in 2000.

Each year these state-by-state rankings change due to changes in states' tax laws. See www.taxfoundation.org for the latest data.

When the federal tax burden is added to state/local taxes, the totals come out somewhat differently because of divergent federal tax payments. On a federal/state/local combined basis in 2002, the average was 30 percent, which happened to be Wisconsin's. The highest tax burden was in Connecticut with 35.2 percent, followed by Massachusetts with 33.6 percent, and New York and California were tied with 32.7 percent. The lowest again was Alaska with 24.7 percent. In 2002 and 2003, it took 109 days of work to pay the average federal/state/local tax, which was a decline from the high of 120 days in 2000. In 2004, it declined another 3 days.[5]

To determine which states are the most and least "business friendly," the Tax Foundation, a nonpartisan and nonprofit organization, annually provides a report called the State Business Tax Climate Index, that gauges the economic impacts on business of states' taxes and the manner in which each state extracts these revenues. The ten most and least business-friendly states at the beginning of 2003 are shown in Table 4.3.[6] The most friendly is Wyoming and the least friendly is Mississippi.

Common characteristics of states scoring low on the index are complex, multirate corporate and individual tax codes with above-average tax rates, above-average sales tax rates with few business exemptions, high overall state tax burdens, revenues growing faster than citizens' incomes, and tax codes that impose considerable compliance costs on businesses.

The Tax Foundation's overall index is composed of five separate indexes, each a major feature of a state's tax system: the corporate income tax, individual income tax, sales or gross receipts tax, the state's fiscal balance, and

**Table 4.3**
**Ten Most and Least Business-Friendly States in 2003**

| Most Friendly | Least Friendly |
| --- | --- |
| Wyoming | Mississippi |
| New Hampshire | California |
| Nevada | Arkansas |
| Colorado | Ohio |
| Alaska | Nebraska |
| South Dakota | Hawaii |
| Florida | New York |
| Washington | Maine |
| Oregon | Minnesota |
| Tennessee | Louisiana |

the conformity of the state's tax system with other systems. Note that California scored forty-ninth in 2003.

### State and Local Expenditures

State and local expenditures in 2001 totaled $1,275 billion, leaving a surplus of $18 billion, which was the last. Beginning in the fourth quarter of 2001, state and local governments as a total were in deficit, with California's deficit in 2003 being the nation's largest at $38.2 billion, a figure larger than the revenue of thirty-six states.[7] The largest state and local government direct general expenditures by function, using 1999 as an example when the total was $1,399 billion, are shown in Table 4.4.[8]

Expenditures for salaries and wages of state and local government workers are aggregated into these figures; if shown separately, they would total $522 billion. Purchases are also aggregated; if shown separately, total state and local procurements in 2000 were $489 billion, which represented 57 percent of all government purchases in the United States that year.[9]

### Largest States, Counties, and Cities

The five largest states ranked by population are shown in Table 4.5.[10] Gross state product (GSP) is the sum of gross domestic income within a state, excluding compensation of federal employees and federal military consumption. Therefore, GSP is a somewhat smaller figure than gross domestic product (GDP), which includes federal data. In 2001, total U.S. GSP was $10,137 billion.

The next five largest states are Pennsylvania, Ohio, Michigan, New Jersey, and Georgia. Interestingly, because of the concentration of population in the largest states, it only takes these ten states plus one more, North Carolina, to elect a president through the electoral college. These eleven states have 271 electoral votes; 270 are needed to elect.

**Table 4.4**
**State and Local Government Expenditures, 1999 ($ Billions)**

| | | | |
|---|---|---|---|
| $340 | Elementary and secondary education | $48 | Health |
| 215 | Public welfare | 45 | Correction |
| 123 | Higher education | 43 | Sanitation and sewerage |
| 93 | Highways | 38 | Electric power system |
| 85 | Employee retirement | 34 | Water supply system |
| 71 | Hospitals | 28 | Transit system |
| 67 | Interest on general debt | 19 | Employee compensation |
| 53 | Police | 97 | Other |

Table 4.5
Five Largest States

| State | 2001 Population (Millions) | 2001 GSP ($ Billions) | 1999 Revenue ($ Billions) | 1999 Expenditures ($ Billions) |
|---|---|---|---|---|
| California | 34.5 | 1,359 | 242 | 218 |
| Texas | 21.3 | 764 | 117 | 100 |
| New York | 19.0 | 826 | 172 | 160 |
| Florida | 16.3 | 491 | 88 | 81 |
| Illinois | 12.4 | 476 | 74 | 69 |

In 2001, the top five exporters in dollar value were California, Texas, New York, Washington, and Michigan. These five states account for approximately 40 percent of the value of all U.S. exports.[11]

The five largest county governments in the United States are shown in Table 4.6.[12] Cook County's major city is Chicago, Harris County's is Houston, Maricopa's is Phoenix, and Orange County's is Anaheim.

The next five largest counties are San Diego; Kings (Brooklyn), NY; Miami-Dade; Dallas; and Queens, NY.

Finally, the five largest cities in the United States are shown in Table 4.7.[13]

The next five largest cities are Phoenix, San Diego, Dallas, San Antonio, and Detroit.

## ECONOMIC IMPORTANCE OF CALIFORNIA

As the above tables illustrate, California is by far the largest state in the Union in every sense of the word except geographic size, being third. In 2003, it had 35 million people, 12 percent of the total U.S. population of 285 million. It had the largest gross state product (GSP) with $1,359 billion

Table 4.6
Five Largest Counties in the United States

| County/State | 2000 Population (Millions) | 1999 Revenue ($ Billions) | 1999 Expenditures ($ Billions) |
|---|---|---|---|
| Los Angeles, CA | 9.806 | 15.7 | 13.2 |
| Cook, IL | 5.377 | 2.5 | 2.2 |
| Harris, TX | 3.557 | 1.9 | 1.9 |
| Maricopa, AZ | 3.303 | 1.7 | 1.6 |
| Orange, CA | 2.938 | 2.6 | 2.4 |

Table 4.7
Five Largest Cities in the United States

| City/State | 2000 Population (Millions) | 1999 Revenue ($ Billions) | 1999 Expenditures ($ Billions) |
|---|---|---|---|
| New York, NY | 8.008 | 56.6 | 54.1 |
| Los Angeles, CA | 3.694 | 9.6 | 8.1 |
| Chicago, IL | 2.896 | 5.7 | 5.4 |
| Houston, TX | 1.953 | 2.8 | 2.7 |
| Philadelphia, PA | 1.517 | 5.6 | 5.2 |

(2001), representing 13.5 percent of the total U.S. GDP of $10,019 billion that year. If California were an independent nation, in 2001, it would have ranked fifth in the world in GDP equivalent, after Britain and ahead of France.[14]

California is the nation's largest exporter and importer and has the country's largest port—Los Angeles/Long Beach.[15] It has the nation's largest output of agricultural products,[16] is its largest manufacturer,[17] and has its largest state revenues and expenditures, the largest deficit, and ranks next to last in business friendliness regarding taxes. California also has the nation's most ethnically diverse population and the most populous county, Los Angeles County, with approximately 10 million people. That county has for some years been the largest manufacturing county in the nation.

This study, therefore, uses the Golden State as its primary example, not only because of its size and economic importance, but also because in key respects it is typical of large states: it has a mixed urban/suburban/rural population, a mixed manufacturing/services/agricultural economy, is heavily dependent on federal grants-in-aid, is deeply engaged in international trade, and its state and local governmental structures are typical of most states. It is also a worst case example from a business owner's perspective regarding taxes and regulations. Table 4.8 summarizes national and California data.[18]

California is the home to more small businesses than any other state.[19] In 1999, 99.1 percent of the businesses in California were small (500 employees or less). In 2001, employer small businesses numbered 985,800, and 1,489,000 individuals were self-employed. Small companies employed a total of 6,565,000 people, representing 53.1 percent of the state's 12.3 million employees in 1999. Proprietors' income totaled $127 billion in 2001, an increase of 5.6 percent over 2000. Women-owned businesses generated $121 billion in revenue in 1997, and the same year, minorities owned 738,000 of the state's businesses. The number of new small business employer firms is growing: the state had 128,885 such firms in 2001, up 22.8 percent over 2000.

**Table 4.8**
**Summary Data for the United States, California, and Los Angeles County**

|  | United States | California | Los Angeles County |
|---|---|---|---|
| Population (millions), 2001 | 285 | 34.5 | 9.6 |
| Households (millions), 2000 | 105 | 11.5 | 3.1 |
| Median household income (thousands), 1999 | $41.9 | $47.9 | $42.1 |
| Median value of housing units (thousands), 2000 | $119.6 | $211.5 | $209.3 |
| Private nonfarm establishments (millions), 1999 | 7.0 | 0.785 | 0.222 |
| Private nonfarm employment (millions), 1999 | 111.0 | 12.3 | 3.7 |
| Nonemployer establishments (millions), 1999 | 16.1 | 2.0 | 0.635 |
| Manufacturing shipments (billions), 1997 | $3,842 | $379 | $106 |
| Retail sales (billions), 1997 | $2,460 | $262 | $69 |
| Minority-owned firms (%), 1997 | 14.6 | 28.8 | 37.2 |
| Women-owned firms (%), 1997 | 26.0 | 27.3 | 25.8 |
| Government employment (millions), 1997 | 10.2 | 1.1 | 0.341 |

## STATE AND LOCAL IMPACTS ON THE
## MACRO ENVIRONMENT

In what areas do state and local governments impact business at the macro level? States and municipalities can affect the general business environment in negative ways through taxes, environmental laws, and regulations regarding business operations.

They can impact business conditions in positive ways: providing physical infrastructure (roads, airports, energy); providing social infrastructure (education, public health); and promoting business activity by offering investment incentives, export promotion, and representing state interests in Washington, D.C. If government fails to provide these positive features, they become negatives because other states will offer them in today's highly competitive environment for investments and jobs.

For example, among the reasons Boeing moved its corporate headquarters from Seattle to Chicago in 2001 was high state and local taxes, overall deteriorating business climate and infrastructure in the Pacific Northwest, and an incentive package offered by the state of Illinois and the city of Chicago.[20]

### States and Their Economies

The national economy is of course composed of the economies of the fifty states. When you read reports from the U.S. Commerce or Labor Departments about U.S. GDP performance and employment, those data are mirrored in most states as a general rule.

There are some state-by-state exceptions to these national macro performance measures. Some states' economies do grow because of local conditions, even when national data show decline. For example, oil- and natural gas-rich states (Alaska, Texas, Louisiana) may prosper even though the rest of the country's economy is sluggish. The reverse may also be the case. When the national economy is performing well, certain states dependent on particular commodities (like mining of certain natural resources such as copper or iron ore) may be hurting if demand for these commodities slows.

Beginning in the first quarter of 2001, the U.S. economy entered a mild recession that lasted for three quarters. For the next two years, the national economy remained sluggish, growing at a modest pace with unemployment creeping up to 6.4 percent in mid-2003, despite strong fiscal and monetary stimuli—two tax cuts and interest rates plummeting to historic lows.[21]

This sluggish performance was reflected in every state, with modest variations owing to local conditions. States dependent on tourism (Florida, California, New York) were especially hard-hit because of consumers' reluctance to spend for vacations. New York's situation was exacerbated by 9/11. States dependent on capital goods manufacturing (Illinois, Michigan, Washington) faced slow growth due to business' reluctance to invest in new plant and equipment pending stronger demand for finished goods. The critical driver in the U.S. economy is, of course, consumer spending, accounting for roughly two-thirds of GDP growth.

Therefore, the entrepreneur needs to examine national economic data, data regarding his/her own state, and also trend data in your particular industry. National and industry data is available online from the Commerce and Labor Departments, as well as from industry trade associations. State data is available from state government offices of finance and commerce.

Getting data from independent sources—such as universities, private forecasting services, banks, and econometric modeling companies—is usually desirable, to provide balance to what might be optimistic projections by state officials. The UCLA Anderson School Forecast is an example.

## California's Economy

In 2001, California was in recession, along with the rest of the nation. California's recession was exacerbated by a variety of factors: continuing decline in high-tech manufacturing, loss of high-pay technology jobs, especially in Silicon Valley (Santa Clara County lost 18.1 percent of its jobs from December 2000 to June 2003), the overall effects of the dot.com bubble burst, and steep declines in tourism. Statewide unemployment was at 6.7 percent in mid-2003, 0.3 percent above the national average.

Certain California revenue sources shrank along with employment. In 2000, at the height of the technology boom, one-quarter of the state's general fund revenue came from taxes on capital gains, stock options, and bonus income; this amount was $80 billion, which dropped to $20 billion in 2002.[22] Personal income in 2000 rose by 10.5 percent; in 2002, it rose by 0.9 percent. For a state that heavily relies on personal income taxes to fund state services, this was a mighty blow. Sales taxes, the largest source of state revenue, rose 12 percent in 2000, were flat in 2001, and declined by 1.3 percent in 2002. The one bright spot in the economy was continued strong building construction fueled by robust residential real estate sales.[23]

*Energy cost.* Other factors contributing to the deterioration of California's business friendliness were skyrocketing energy costs and workers' compensation taxes. Manufacturers saw their energy costs double from 10 to 20 percent of their operating costs over a three-year period (2000–2003), according to the California Manufacturers and Technology Association. During that period, gasoline prices were more than $.20 per gallon higher in California than the national average and ranged as high as $.30 to $.40 per gallon higher in 2004.[24]

*Workers' compensation.* In 2003, businesses of all types paid $5.25 of every $100 of employees' wages for workers' compensation premiums, the highest in the nation, compared with the U.S. average of $2.50, according to the California Chamber of Commerce. The legislature raised the maximum benefit by 71 percent, from $490 per week in 2002 to $840 in 2005. Companies in California pay four to five times more in workers' comp per employee than in Texas, a low-cost state to which many firms have moved.[25] A recent study of twelve large states found the average cost of workers' comp claims in California was 33 percent above the median.[26]

Employers' workers' comp costs ballooned from $9 billion in 1995 to $29 billion in 2003, according to a report filed by the state's independent auditor. The report blamed state officials for failing to set caps on what insurers pay for medical services or on the number of visits injured workers are allowed to make to doctors, physical therapists, chiropractors, and others. Injured workers have 49 percent more visits with doctors and 100 percent more visits with chiropractors than workers in other states, according to a study by the Workers' Compensation Research Institute.

Costco Wholesale Corp. operates in thirty-six states, and 79 percent of its workers' comp costs come from California, even though only one-third of its workers are in the state. Costco labeled the California system "bad, unjust and corrupt." California's insurance commissioner said, "the system is totally out of control. It ranges from an outright disaster to a serious job-creation issue." Governor Schwarzenegger declared fixing the state's worker's comp to be among his top priorities, calling it "the poisen of our economy."[27]

Workers' comp and other high-cost factors place California at number forty-six on the national Cost of Doing Business Index, ahead of only Connecticut, New Jersey, Massachusetts, and, most costly, Hawaii.[28]

### Taxes

State and local tax laws impact business conditions either by promoting or stifling business growth. "Tax competition among states is an unpleasant reality for state revenue raisers," wrote the Tax Foundation, "but competition is a godsend to taxpayers. The most effective restraint on state taxes is the knowledge that business will take jobs and prosperity out of state if taxes become unmanageable."[29]

Most states have an array of taxes: sales, property, personal income, corporate profit, unemployment insurance, workers' compensation, and estate tax. Additionally, state fees or user permits are often thought of as disguised taxes—business licenses, permits, and operating fees. The higher and more complex these taxes and fees, the greater the burden on the bottom line of the business and the less business friendly the state becomes.[30]

Five states also have Disability Insurance (DI)—a payroll tax that provides partial wage-replacement payment to workers who suffer job loss when they are unable to work due to nonwork-related illness or injury or medical disability, including pregnancy or childbirth. These five states are California, Hawaii, New Jersey, New York, and Rhode Island. Twelve million California employees pay this tax through payroll deductions at the rate of 0.9 percent of pay, capped at $56,916 annually, and are covered for up to fifty-two weeks of benefits.[31]

In 2004, California's first-in-the-nation Family Temporary Disability Insurance Act was added to its DI program. This new program's purpose is to provide disability compensation to cover individuals who take time off from work to care for a seriously ill child, spouse, parent, or domestic partner, or to bond with a new child. This is a mandatory program, administered through payroll withholding, and will cost employees an additional 8 percent of the taxable wage limit (or $55.06 in 2004), whether they take time off or not.[32] "We'll spend a lot more [time and money] training replacement workers," predicted Tim McCallion, Verizon's top executive in California, commenting on this program, "and our productivity will decline because of all the absenteeism."[33]

In 2003, California's Domestic Partner Act was enacted, extending most of the rights and benefits accorded a spouse to a same-sex partner, placing the state just behind Vermont in same-sex friendliness. Vermont is the only state that recognizes gay "civil unions," and it is the leader in granting civil protections and services to same-sex couples.[34] The Family Temporary Disability Insurance Act now includes time-off provisions for same-sex families.

Two days before he was recalled as California's governor, Gray Davis signed into law another first-in-the-nation act that would require small businesses to provide health insurance to the working poor and their families. Employers with two hundred or more employees would be required to provide health coverage on January 1, 2006, or pay into a state fund to provide coverage, businesses with fifty to 199 employees would have another year to provide coverage, and employers with twenty or fewer workers would be exempt until the state provided a tax credit subsidy to help offset the insurance cost. Employers would pay 80 percent of the cost and employees 20 percent. To be eligible, an employee must work at least one hundred hours per month and have been employed at the same company for at least three months. The president of the California Chamber of Commerce called the law a "job killer."[35]

High-tax states like California, Connecticut, Maine, New York, and Rhode Island have difficulty attracting businesses to move there or to start there, unless there is some special market, operational, or personal reason for doing so. In 2003, as a percent of income, California's state and local tax burden is eighth highest in the nation.[36]

The sources of California's tax revenue of $90.4 billion in 2001 were as follows:[37]

| Percent | Tax |
|---------|-----|
| 43.8 | personal income |
| 25.9 | sales |
| 15.3 | other |
| 7.3 | corporate income |
| 4.3 | licenses |
| 3.4 | motor fuel |

Regarding personal income tax, in 2000, 54 percent of that revenue came from taxpayers who earned $300,000 or more, due to California's steeply progressive tax code. Almost 38 percent was paid by millionaires, who file less than one-third of 1 percent of tax returns.[38] The stock market nosedive and dot.com bubble burst came home to roost in Sacramento that year.

Most states offer some type of incentives for businesses to establish themselves or expand in their state. These usually include low taxes or specific tax deductions such as tax "holidays" for new factories (no or low taxes for a certain number of years), special no or low tax areas ("enterprise zones"), and tax credits to offset the cost of new equipment to increase capacity and create more jobs. State incentives are discussed in chapter 12.

A job is not a job from a revenue standpoint. High-paying jobs result in state tax revenues; low-paying jobs do not. In California, for example, the difference between a manufacturing job and a service-sector job is more than $25,000 annually. The vast majority of service-wage jobs do not meet the state income tax threshold, meaning they produce not a single cent in state tax revenue.[39]

## BUDGET GROWTH AND DEFICITS

If state and local governments are well managed, this is a plus for business. It is especially important with respect to finances. If governments operate with a balanced budget (as required by every state except Vermont), their management is usually given high marks. The reverse is true for states and municipalities that run deficits and/or fail to provide essential services for business and individuals. States with large surpluses are viewed as overtaxing.

In 2003, *USA Today* conducted a study of the fifty states' financial management skills and concluded that Georgia performed best as a money manager and California performed fiftieth. The analysis concluded that California was "in a league of its own in matters of failing to exercise restraint in the good times and making the tough decisions in the bad times."[40] The Tax Foundation summed it up this way: "statistically speaking, every aspect of California's tax system is antagonistic to business development and economic growth."[41]

From 2000 to at least 2004, on a national basis, state and local governments were in their worst fiscal crisis since World War II, according to the National Governors Association.[42] These annual deficits mean that from one fiscal year to the next (most states' fiscal years are July 1 to June 30) revenue is below spending, requiring either spending cuts, revenue increases through new or higher taxes or borrowing, or a combination of spending cuts, higher taxes, and borrowing. The ten states with the worst business tax climates accounted for 60 percent of total state deficits in FY-2004.[43]

Why were so many states running deficits? During the economic boom years of the late 1990s, most state and local governments dramatically ramped up spending, taking advantage of the flood tide of revenue poring into their treasuries. Annual spending grew on national average by 3.5 percent in 1997 and by 8 percent in 1999–2001. In California, spending increased 38 percent over a two-fiscal-year period, 1999–2001.[44]

In 2000–2001, with the burst of the dot.com bubble, the recession, and the persistent bear stock market, revenues slowed, causing deficits of growing proportions. In 2001, state and local deficits on a national basis ranged from $20 to $40 billion, and by 2003, they averaged approximately $50 billion.[45] Table 4.9 shows the dozen largest states' revenue shortfall as a percent of state general fund budgets for fiscal year 2004.[46]

Approximately half the dollar amount of all states' total budget shortfall is concentrated in just two states—New York and California. In New York in 2003, the legislature passed the 2004 budget that increased sales tax by a quarter-cent and imposed an income tax surcharge for upper-income residents. Republican governor George Pataki vetoed the budget, which the Democratically controlled legislature then overrode, requiring a bipartisan effort. The legislature also overrode Governor Pataki's veto to permit New York City to raise income and sales taxes by $2.7 billion.

Table 4.9
States' Revenue Shortfall as Percent of General Fund Budget, 2004

| State | Percent | State | Percent |
| --- | --- | --- | --- |
| Alaska | 25.0 | Colorado | 15.0 |
| Arizona | 25.0 | North Carolina | 14.0 |
| New York | 24.0 | Illinois | 13.6 |
| California | 20.6 | Nebraska | 13.6 |
| Oregon | 17.0 | Texas | 12.0 |
| Minnesota | 15.5 | Massachusetts | 10.8 |

New York City's projected 2004 budget deficit was $6.4 billion. Republican mayor Michael Bloomberg and the Democratically controlled City Council had months of acrimonious debate and high drama on how to balance it. In the end, they agreed to a $44.5 billion budget, which included spending cuts of $3.2 billion (e.g., closing six firehouses and laying off 5,600 city workers) and raising property taxes by 18.5 percent, the highest jump in history, along with increases approved by the state in personal income and sales taxes. The 2005 budget was estimated to have a $1.8 billion deficit.[47]

### California's Deficit

California is the extreme case, with a deficit in 2003 of $38.2 billion. Early in 2003, the Democratic governor, Gray Davis, stated he found "no good choices" for cutting the budget, and the budget debate with the Democratically controlled legislature lurched along for months, while spending pressures grew and state revenues failed to keep pace.[48] One of those spending pressures was the enlarged state payroll; between 1997 and 2001, state government employment grew by 13.6 percent, twice as fast as the state population.[49]

A major reason for delay in approving the budget is that California law, like that in only two other states, requires a two-thirds majority of the legislature to pass a budget. This gives the Republican minority a political lever denied them on all other issues. Instead of compromise, Democrats and Republicans spent their time accusing each other of "treachery and stupidity."[50] Another part of the political context was a petition drive to recall Governor Davis, whose job disapproval rating had climbed to an historic high of 72 percent;[51] the petition was successful, requiring a vote on the governor's fate in a special election the following October, which Davis lost and Arnold Schwarzenegger was elected governor.

One consequence of the budget impasse and political turmoil was a lower rating for state bonds and higher interest and fees to sell them, digging the budget hole even deeper. In June 2003, California sold $11.6 billion in short-term warrants to keep the state solvent for two months. To get the deal done, the state paid $110 to $170 million in extra interest and fees to investment banks to provide a type of insurance for the warrants.[52] The state's bond rating dropped to "A," the lowest among the states.[53]

The situation worsened the following month, when Standard & Poor's (S&P) reduced the rating on California's $26.8 billion in general obligation debt by a surprising three notches, from A to BBB, immediately triggering a penalty payment of $33.6 million to the banks that held the $11.6 billion in warrants floated the previous month. Only one state's debt rating (Massachusetts) had ever been this low in the forty-seven years S&P had tracked state-issued bonds.[54]

Governor Davis unilaterally tripled the state's auto registration fee, already among the highest in the nation, to raise $4 billion in revenue.[55] Tuition and fees at the University of California and California State University systems were raised 30 percent, and community college fees were raised even more.[56]

Finally, in late July 2003, after nearly eight months of deadlock, the legislature passed a $99.1 billion budget that rejected Davis' earlier proposal to raise income, sales, and tobacco taxes. Instead, the new budget raised state fees, reduced some spending, adopted a complicated accounting scheme swapping state sales taxes and county property taxes, and planned to float two new bonds: $1.9 billion to pay into the unfunded state employee pension fund and $14 billion to fund a major portion of the next year's operations and pay off the prior year's deficit-balancing bonds, putting off the day of reckoning. As the governor said when he signed it, the budget "isn't pretty."[57]

Moody's Investors Service agreed. They immediately downgraded the state's general obligation bonds from A2 to A3, one notch above junk status; the state's lease-revenue bonds were downgraded to junk, from A3 to Baa1.[58]

Governor Schwarzenegger's first priority was to balance the state's budget without violating his campaign pledge of no new taxes. He did so with two massive bond measures adapted in a 2004 referrendum that sidelined the state legislature.

### Other States' Deficits

In Michigan, with a deficit smaller than most states—$158 million in 2003 and growing to $1.7 billion the following year—the new Democratic governor, Jennifer Granholm, and the legislature took a tough approach. No new taxes were proposed. Instead, they cut spending across the board by 20 percent: police, prisons, universities, K–12 education, and so forth. Granholm declared the use of "every sheet of stationery in existence, even if my predecessor's name is on them."[59]

In South Carolina, the Republican governor, Mark Sanford, a wealthy man known for his frugality, set a personal example to help close the budget shortfall of $340 million in 2003. He announced he would close the governor's mansion to save $100,000 a year in operating costs, and he, his wife, and four young sons would live in an upstairs apartment, doing their own cooking and laundry. Local businesspeople offered the money to keep the mansion open as a draw to bring investors to the state. Sanford accepted, saying he would use prison labor to operate the house and would invite people for breakfast (not dinner) because it is cheaper. A local firm is supplying the grits gratis.[60]

Delaware represents a success story of bipartisan cooperation. In 2003, the Democratic governor and Republican-dominated legislature approved a $145 million tax increase proposed by the governor, using a process developed in the late 1970s. At that time, Delaware had a divisive budget crisis that undermined the state's credit rating. To prevent a reoccurrence, the legislature established an economic forecasting committee and a joint House-Senate finance committee to develop budgets in a cooperative atmosphere. As the cochairman of the finance committee stated, "Even though we might yell and scream, we do recognize we've got to come out of this with something that represents a balanced budget."[61] Delaware scores high marks for fiscal responsibility.

And finally there is the bizarre case of Nevada. In 2003, Republican governor Kenny Guinn signed a budget raising state spending by more than 25 percent, but the Republican minority in both houses of the legislature refused to raise taxes by the amount necessary to balance the governor's budget. Fifteen Assembly republicans deadlocked the situation because Nevada law requires a two-thirds majority in both houses to raise taxes. The governor then filed suit in the Nevada Supreme Court against the legislature on the grounds that it failed to meet the constitutionally mandated requirement to begin the fiscal year with a balanced budget and to fund education. The court ruled six to one to override the constitution and permit the tax increase with a simple majority.[62] Nevada's brothels were exempted from the new 10 percent "live entertainment tax."[63]

### Budget Deficits—Cities

City governments are facing the same fiscal challenges as states. Revenues are not keeping pace with spending that rose to new heights in the boom years of the late 1990s. New York City has already been discussed.

*Los Angeles.* Mayor James Hahn's 2003–2004 budget proposal was released in April 2003, and immediately confronted stiff opposition from his City Council, which had a majority of his fellow Democratic Party members. His budget proposed $5.1 billion in spending, an increase in fees (sewer, trash collection, zoo admissions) to pay for hiring 320 more police, and left a deficit of $280 million. The council voted eleven to four to delay police hires, and the budget debate raged for months.[64]

A large cost driver was Workers' Compensation. As is the case with businesses, cities, counties, transit authorities, and other governmental units across California faced spiraling costs of their workers' comp taxes, covering half the workers in the state. Between 1999 and 2004, workers' comp costs for the city of Los Angeles nearly doubled, from $76 million to $142 million. The workers' comp budget for Los Angeles County jumped from $157 million to $352 million over the same period. The state insurance commissioner said the workers' comp system "will drive the [state's] economy further into the tank."[65]

*San Francisco.* The City by the Bay faced even more dire conditions.[66] The dot.com bubble's epicenter was San Francisco, and with its burst, the post-9/11 tourism slump, and the national economic slowdown, the impacts on San Francisco were severe—the worst in the state. These impacts were threefold: loss of personal income tax revenue resulting from massive business bankruptcies and layoffs, loss of tourism tax dollars, and loss of property tax revenues resultingfrom downward reassessments of property value, as allowed by Proposition 13.

The municipal budget for the city of San Francisco in 2004 was $5 billion with a $347 million deficit. Property taxes are a major part of the revenue base. The dot.com crash emptied huge swaths of the city's marginal business districts, including Multimedia Gulch, the bay-front area where hundreds of Internet start-ups were housed; it's just a gulch now. The vacancy rate varies widely—from more than 40 percent in the dot.com districts to less than 10 percent in the Class A buildings in the more stable downtown financial district. Where the vacancies are low, so are the rents, plunging from $90 per square foot in 2000 to $25 in 2003, the same as a decade earlier.

Building owners asserted their property declined in value from 2000 to 2003 by roughly one-half, and so should their property taxes. Take the example of a landmark building, the Transamerica pyramid. Its owners claimed the property lost half its value over those three years; their assessment was lowered in 2001, from $236 million to $187.5 million, and the owners pressed for a further reduction to $97 million for 2002. With citywide reassessments slashing values on commercial property by $8 billion (more than one-third), the city deficit is exacerbated by an additional $90 million of revenue loss.

*Data mining.* Desperate for any source of funding, cities have begun "data mining" to find additional revenue. State laws have been passed at urging by cities to authorize them to obtain information from residents' state income tax returns to see if they are avoiding payments for business license fees and permits, sales taxes, and fees for other municipal services. For example, the city of Los Angeles now obtains state tax return information on every city resident to see if they should have paid a city business license fee. Privacy is openly vitiated by law.

### Fiscal Dilemma—Pensions

Across America, cities, counties, and states face the same "perfect storm" of slowing revenues and fixed increases in entitlements. One of the highest cost items is pensions. During the late 1990s, flush with surplus funds from the halcyon-level stock market producing a flood tide of tax revenues, state and local governments put into law generous pension plans for state and local workers, especially police and firefighters.

In 1999, the state of California passed a law increasing pensions for most state employees at a cost of $400 million more per year. Formulas for pensions were adjusted to favor the employee: retirement at age fifty-five instead of sixty, with 2.5 percent versus 2 percent of compensation for each year of service. Police and fire employees were given age fifty with 3 percent, versus age fifty-five at 2.5 percent. These formulas were made permanent.[67]

Orange County, California, which was bankrupt in 1995, passed a law boosting police and fire employees' pensions even more—to 100 percent versus 90 percent of last year's salary. The city of Orange in that county did the same, raising pension costs from $624,000 to $2.4 million in one year.[68] The city of San Diego, having adopted a similar program, had a $720 million pension fund deficit; the City Council put off full payments to the pension fund until 2009, when the annual pension bill will be $214 million.[69]

As a result of these generous pension programs, retirements accelerated, ballooning costs as employees rushed to take advantage of them, and cities, counties, and the state now face a long-term dilemma. These fixed costs will have to be paid at the expense of other government programs or services or by increased taxes and fees because pension contracts have priority over other governmental obligations—educating children, public safety salaries, road building, or health care for the poor. This fiscal condition scores low marks for any governmental units so affected.

### Unemployment Insurance

States are required to collect unemployment insurance from employers to pay out these funds in the event of unemployment. Owing to persistent sluggish economic conditions resulting in job layoffs, U.S. unemployment rose to a nine-year high of 6.4 percent in mid-2003. Nationally, more than 2.6 million workers lost their jobs between March 2001 and June 2003, putting continuing pressure on states' unemployment insurance funds.

Taking California as an example, by January 2004, the state's unemployment insurance program was projected to run out of funds to pay jobless workers, unless employer premiums (i.e., taxes) were raised again, as they were in early 2003. About half of the state's 1.1 million unemployed workers receive cash benefits, and the number is growing, with the prolonged sluggish economy throwing more people out of work. At current projected rates, the state's unemployment fund could be $1.1 billion in deficit by the end of 2004, unless taxes are raised again, further eroding California's already poor business climate for employers.[70]

## STATE AND LOCAL INFRASTRUCTURE

Business-friendly states also have excellent infrastructures. This is a key macro area where states and municipalities can make a difference by providing a positive business environment. There are two types of infrastructure—physical and social.

- *Physical*—If the state, county, and city have excellent roads, airports, parks, and other physical assets necessary for modern society, then they are viewed as responsible and are desirable places to do business—as well as for their employees to live. If the state has adequate, reliable, and affordable supplies of water and energy—electric power and fuel for vehicles—it is viewed as a desirable location.
- *Social*—A key component of social infrastructure is public education in secondary schools and colleges and universities. If public education is rated high, then the state is viewed as meeting its obligation to provide a steady supply of skilled labor and to help industry attract and retain employees with families. For high-tech firms, being located near a major research university is a distinct plus—to draw on the intellectual capital locally available. It is no accident that Silicon Valley includes Stanford. If the state has excellent health care, emergency facilities, and hospitals with well-trained staffs, this, too, is important—to attract and retain employees.

If a state lacks any one of these key infrastructure items, much less several of them, it will rank low on the list. Some states that score low on one or more of these key factors seek to offset deficiencies with other desirable features—low wage rates, low taxes, no requirement for unionization (right-to-work laws), secure physical environment (strong community culture against crime coupled with a well-trained police force), and strong work ethic, plus specific incentives to attract investment.

### California's Education Infrastructure

As the twenty-first century dawned, California had a mixed bag of infrastructure grades. Looking first at education, the state scored very high with its public university system—the eleven-campus University of California system is arguably one of the finest in the world. Asymmetrically, however, the state scored well below national performance standards with respect to public primary and secondary education. Only 48 percent of the state's classes are taught by "highly qualified" teachers according to the U.S. Education Department's criteria. As the Pacific Research Institute put it, "our schools rank near the bottom among the 50 states."[71]

Looking at the "3Rs," in 1998, California's fourth and eighth graders had reading skills that scored 52 and 36 percent "below basic," respectively. For writing, eighth graders ranked 24 percent "below basic." And for mathematics, in 2000, 48 percent of fourth and eighth graders ranked "below basic." Only 4 percent or fewer of fourth and eighth graders scored in the highest category, "advanced."[72]

In 2002, for reading skills only, 79 percent of California's fourth graders, 69 percent of eighth graders, and 64 percent of its twelfth graders scored "below reading proficiency," ranking the state thirty-eighth in reading skills on the 2002 National Assessment of Educational Progress test. These scores put California in the same cluster as Mississippi, District of Columbia, Louisiana, and Hawaii, of the states that administered the test.[73]

This abysmally substandard performance in the public secondary schools of California persists, despite the fact that education is the largest portion of the state's budget, the state budget has been increased by $10 billion since 1995 to lower class size to twenty pupils from kindergarten to third grade, the California lottery provides supplementary funding for K–12 schools, and despite billions of federal funds coming to the state over the years. Indeed, more than $6 billion in federal assistance for California's secondary schools was included in President Bush's FY-2004 budget—an increase of $1.4 billion over 2001 levels.[74]

One plan to improve students' performance and accountability in secondary schools was to introduce a statewide proficiency examination, modeled somewhat on the New York Regents' Exam, that students must pass before being allowed to graduate from high school. Florida has a similar exam, which 13,000 of its graduating seniors failed—and received no diplomas.

Under California's plan, all twelfth graders would take a nine-hour test spread over two days. The level of competency is geared to ninth grade in math and tenth grade in English. Fearing a large number of failures (estimated at 20 percent) and political backlash from parents, the state postponed the introduction of the test for at least two years. Postponement "leads to more cynicism that this too shall pass, like a number of other California education reforms," said a former president of the state's Board of Education.[75]

### California's Physical Infrastructure

With respect to physical infrastructure—highways and airports—in 2000, California voters passed Proposition 35, the Fair Competition and Taxpayer Savings Initiative, to speed restoration of these deteriorating physical assets through competitive bidding and public-private partnerships, not just state agencies planning and performing the work. State employee unions fought the implementation of this measure, with little progress being made.[76]

With respect to energy, California earned a failing grade—having the nation's highest electric energy prices and the highest gasoline prices in 2001–2004. In 2001, during the energy crisis, California signed $43 billion in long-term electric energy contracts at bid prices about ten times the precrisis price. In 2003, after the crisis, the Federal Energy Regulatory Commission (FERC) refused to allow California to abrogate these contracts, even though FERC acknowledged they were at prices that "far exceed market prices for electricity." FERC brought enforcement actions against Enron and is conducting criminal investigations against sixty energy companies for their possible roles in overcharging California billions of dollars as a result of possible unlawful actions.[77]

## CONCLUSION

This chapter summarized information on the nation's largest states, counties, and cities—governmental units that affect the major concentrations of the national economy. State and local governments have a significant impact on the macro environment, largely through their fiscal policies, though not at the federal level of importance. States and municipalities having high taxes and/or serious mismanagement of budgets, necessitating Herculean deficit-reduction efforts, score low marks for their business environment. Another key area having macro impact on the business environment is the condition of the state and local infrastructure, both physical and social.

In the aggregate, California, the state with the largest economy, scored forty-ninth in business friendliness in 2003, having business operating costs 32 percent higher than the national average.[78] The principal causes are its overall high tax rates, its fiscal policymaking procedure, heavy regulatory requirements, and deteriorating physical and public secondary education infrastructure.

As a result, companies and the jobs they provide are leaving California: 289,000 manufacturing jobs alone left between 2001 and 2003, moving to lower-cost states. Small manufacturers like Buck Knives went to Idaho; Coast Converters, which makes bags, left for Nevada; and Taylor-Dunn, a maker of airport carts, moved to Ohio and Missouri. Countrywide Mortgage moved most of its operations to Texas, and Fidelity National, the nation's largest title insurance company, moved from Santa Barbara to Jacksonville. "The jobs that have to stay here are ones that involve direct contact with customers," said Liam McGee, Bank of America's chief in California.[79]

# — PART II —

# Compliance:
# What Government Makes
# Business Do

The purpose of this part is to provide the entrepreneur with assistance in identifying and understanding the myriad rules and regulations that government requires of businesses. Virtually every action an entrepreneur takes has some federal, state, or local government rule or regulation connected with it. Knowing what these are and how to deal with them is a vital task of the business leader. This part is intended to assist you with that task.

Compliance with these rules and regulations is required by law and, depending on the size of the firm and the nature of the violation, noncompliance can result in severe penalties. The next four chapters present federal rules and regulations, and the fifth chapter in this part covers state and local government regulations.

During each phase of a firm's life, there is a set of federal rules that apply. For start-up firms, discussed in chapter 5, regulations are presented that pertain to the nature of the business, type of business entity, workplace selection, preparations for hiring a workforce, protection of company and brand names (if any) and assurance they are not already protected by another, and preparation for becoming a tax collector.

For established firms, discussed in chapter 6, rules and regulations pertaining to ongoing operations are presented: employee issues, product safety, labor health and safety, fair practices, EPA issues, financial reporting, and taxes.

Chapter 7 discusses another set of rules and regulations that apply for businesses seeking to expand: merger and acquisition, antitrust, monopolization, vertical and horizontal market restriction, employee benefits, and environmental law impacts.

For business divestiture, owners looking to sell or liquidate, there is a final set of rules presented in chapter 8 regarding disclosure, employee benefits, EPA cleanup, and antitrust.

The final chapter in this part, chapter 9, addresses the most important state and local rules and regulations affecting each phase of a business' life.

It is the entrepreneur's responsibility to ensure that his/her firm is fully compliant with all government regulations at each stage of a company's life cycle. The checklists provided will help, but they are not exhaustive; rather, they are intended as a representative sample of the most important categories of regulations faced by business owners.

# — CHAPTER 5 —

# Business Start-up Regulations

Nothing is more daunting to the entrepreneur considering start-ing a business than trying to figure out what government rules and regulations he/she will face. "Small business owners often fear," reported a major Small Business Administration (SBA) study, "that they will inadvertently fail to comply with some obscure rule, and that a government inspector will show up, close down the business, and drive them into bankruptcy."[1]

This chapter presents federal rules and regulations applicable to a start-up business and how to avoid noncompliance, with all the penalties that might result. Only federal rules and regulations are included here; state and local requirements are presented in chapter 9.

A logical sequence of questions to consider before you start up is this: does the nature of the business invoke regulations, what legal entity should you choose for the business, is the company name or the product's brand name protected, where will the business be located, who will you hire and what are the consequences of having employees, what kind of records must you plan to keep, how will you comply with worker health and safety rules, and what tax laws will apply to your business?

Depending on the answers to each of these questions, a certain set of rules will be invoked with which you must comply. This chapter is organized as a checklist of the issues you should consider and plan for before you open the doors of your new company.

## THE NATURE OF THE BUSINESS

The type and nature of the business you plan to start will trigger a set of federal rules and regulations requiring compliance. If the business will pro-duce a product, most of the requirements will be invoked. If you intend to provide a service, some but not all of the same rules will apply. If the company will offer a combination of products and services, all regulations will apply, depending on the size and type of business and whether or not the federal government is your customer.

## Products

If your start-up company will produce a physical product, generically called a "good," you must be certain before you begin operations that your good will comply with federal product standards and that the way you will produce it (the production process) will comply with federal process regulations. If either will not, then modify the product or process to comply, or look for a different product before you undertake the expense of leasing/buying machinery and equipment that will produce the noncompliant product. What are these standards and rules? The following is a quick sample.

Child safety has one set of rules. Will the product have sharp edges that might injure a young child, be small enough that an infant could swallow it and choke, will it be flammable, or suffocate an unsupervised child, and so on? If any of these answers is yes, redesign the product to make it safe or abandon it and look for a safe product for the age group you are targeting.

Worker safety has another set of standards. If the production process used to make your product is likely to be risky to the health and safety of your workers, you will need to examine federal Occupational Safety and Health Administration (OSHA) rules and regulations. To comply, you may need to provide your employees with protective devices such as safety glasses, insulated clothing, air filters, shrouds over moving machine parts, and the like. These items can be expensive, and you will need to factor these costs into your financial plan.

Environmental Protection Agency (EPA) rules regarding production operations need to be considered before leasing or buying factory space in which to produce your product. You need to be concerned with the following: will the type of materials that compose the product or the type of operations used to produce it pollute the air or water (rivers and groundwater)? Will production operations generate loud noise or release ozone? Will a by-product of the production process be toxic? How will you dispose of waste? Will the factory release emissions that are legal in the United States, but which might drift into Canadian air space where they may be illegal? These are the kinds of questions you will want to resolve favorably before committing to the business.

Intellectual property is another issue. You may have tentatively chosen a name and logo for your company and a brand name for your product. You need to research these names at your state's office of the secretary of state and at the federal patent and trademark office to be certain they are not already protected by someone else, even though they may not be in use. If you find a conflict, you can choose another name that is not already protected, or offer to buy the protected name from its current holder. The latter is what Toyota Motor Company chose to do when it selected the name Lexus for its new premium car; a similar name was already trademarked by a data research company called LexisNexis. The amount of the settlement was not disclosed, but it was probably less expensive than the cost to redesign the new auto's logo.

## Services

"It may be inconceivable to you," says the SBA, that your home-based business—such as telemarketing and consulting—would have to comply with local, state, and federal regulations, "but it will."[2]

Companies providing services face the same OSHA and patent/trademark issues as goods producers, but they do not face factory operation issues regulated by EPA. Going beyond patent and trademark protection, service companies also face other intellectual property protection issues.

For example, management consulting companies must be careful not to copy the work products of similar companies for their own clients without giving full credit in their deliverables. Banks and insurance companies must take care, when they offer services already provided by a rival, that there is some modicum of difference in their offering and not just a "me, too" copy of another company's invention, especially those that are trademarked.

The rules for all types of companies, whether product producers or service providers, are the same if you adopt a trade name, hire employees, occupy a commercial space, and make money.

Regulatory compliance costs, however, are different. According to a major SBA study, in the mid-1990s, companies engaged in manufacturing carried roughly one-third of all business regulatory costs in the United States. The rest of the costs were borne in approximately equal portions by trade, services, and all other industries. Manufacturers accounted for 70 percent of all EPA-type regulatory costs, and manufacturers' costs were rising, while the others were relatively flat.[3]

## LEGAL ENTITY

The legal entity you choose for your company is a critical decision because of the significant legal and business consequences that result from your choice. The nature of the business will greatly influence the form you choose: some businesses have large capital requirements (arguing for a corporation), others carry high liability risks (arguing for a limited liability partnership, limited liability corporation, or corporation), others are low risk/low capital (arguing for sole proprietorship orpartnership), and some have large marketing requirements (arguing for a franchise).

You have seven options to choose from, only two of which have federal regulatory consequences—franchises and corporations. In addition to the nature of the business, other factors that go into the decision are the speed, cost, and convenience of establishing the company, having partners or not, financing requirements, liability exposure, and tax consequences. The seven options are discussed below.[4]

## Sole Proprietorship

This is the most popular form of business organization for start-ups because it is the quickest, easiest, least expensive to establish, and if requires little government involvement to initiate. Basically, all you need do is this: select a business name (your own, or a fictitious "doing business as" name), file a certificate of trade name or fictitious business name with the appropriate municipal authority and print a notice of it in the newspaper, apply (if necessary) to your city for a business license and pay the license fee, and hang out your shingle.

Other advantages of sole proprietorships are: you own and manage the business, and gain all the profits or bear all the losses—that is, you are responsible to no one but yourself. You can easily sell the business or liquidate it whenever desired. There are no separate business taxes; profits and losses are reported on your individual income tax returns, but you have to file self-employment tax.

There are two major downsides to sole proprietorships: (1) because you are solely responsible for every aspect of the business, you are legally liable for the business' contracts, products, debts, and any illegal acts that you or your employees may commit. All your personal assets, as well as the company's assets, are exposed to the risks of the business, and (2) financing the business is limited to your personal resources , gifts of family and friends, and any borrowings (debt financing) you may be qualified for.

## Partnership

This type of business form is often referred to as a general partnership, in which two or more individuals voluntarily agree to form a business relationship and become co-owners of the enterprise, personally sharing in its management, costs, obligations, liabilities, and profits. Other than obtaining a municipal business license and filing an informational form with a municipal authority, there are no unique regulatory requirements associated with establishing, registering, or announcing partnerships. Their operations are governed by federal regulations presented later in this chapter, such as OSHA, EPA, fair practices, and the like.

The Revised Uniform Partnership Act established a consistent body of law throughout the United States regarding the formation, operation, and dissolution of partnerships. Under this code, partnerships can hold title to property, transact business in the name of the partnership, and perform other business tasks. The partnership can be initiated by formal or informal agreement—oral or written. The formal approach is a written agreement that delineates the responsibilities of the parties and the terms and conditions of their relationship; it can be very brief or quite complex, depending on preference and the nature of the business.

Partners are "jointly liable" for the debts and contracts of the partnership, and they are "jointly and severally liable" for breaches of trust or of fiduciary duty (e.g., fraud or embezzlement) or other illegal acts—meaning that all partners are liable, even if they did not commit the act. The liability is unlimited, including personal assets of the partners.

## Limited Partnerships

There are two types of partners in a limited partnership: general and limited. The Revised Uniform Partnership Act, adopted by states throughout the United States, provides the model governing limited partnerships. The act stipulates the following:

- there must be at least one general and one limited partner, but the number of each is unlimited;
- the general partner(s) invests capital into the business, manages it, and is personally liable for its debts—this liability is unlimited and includes personal assets;
- limited partners invest capital, but do not manage the business and are not liable for its debts beyond the amount of their investment;
- any "person" can be a general or limited partner: individuals, partnerships, trusts, corporations, estates, or associations;
- the formation of a limited partnership is accomplished by signing a Certificate of Limited Partnership that lists the names and addresses of all general and limited partners, the place and nature of the business, and amounts contributed by each partner;
- the Certificate of Limited Partnership is filed with the secretary of state and must be publicly disclosed (usually through newspaper ads); and
- the limited partnership becomes effective upon registration with the state and, if required, the county recorder.

Limited partnerships are often used for one-time business ventures such as real estate developments, oil or natural gas exploration, or motion picture productions. The partnership pays no taxes; profits and losses flow through to the partners, who pay them on their individual tax returns.

## Limited Liability Partnership

A limited liability partnership (LLP) is an entity that is true to its name—the partners' liability is limited to the capital they invest in the partnership;

there is no personal liability. There is no general partner; all partners are of equal stature, and all participate in the management of the firm. This is a particularly popular type of entity for professionals agreeing to work together, such as accountants, physicians, attorneys, and consultants.

LLPs are formed by filing Articles of Partnership with the office of the secretary of state in the state where the partnership is organized. LLPs pay no taxes; profits flow through to the individual partners, who pay them on their individual tax returns.

### Limited Liability Companies

Limited liability companies (LLCs), a recently invented business form, work much like LLPs, except any type of business can be organized under this entity. The owners of the business, those contributing capital, are called members. The members have no personal liability beyond their capital contributions. The LLC pays no taxes, and profits flow through to the members, who pay them on their individual tax returns—provided the LLC meets certain criteria: a limitation on its life span and restrictions on transferring interests.

LLCs are formed when two or more "persons" (individuals, LLPs, corporations, etc.)agree to file Articles of Organization with the secretary of state's office. The company name must include the words "limited liability company," "LLC," or "LC." Forming an LLC is quicker, easier, and far less expensive than forming a corporation and yet has the same liability protection and no separate LLC taxes—hence its growing popularity with small and medium-size businesses.

### Franchises

This popular business form occurs when one party licenses another the right to use its trade name, trademarks, patents, commercial symbols, and other proprietary rights in return for an initial license fee, royalty payments, and other fees for advertising and supplies. The word "franchise" refers both to the name of the business and to the agreement between the franchisor and franchisee, who operate as separate legal entities, usually as corporations or LLCs. There are four types of franchises: distributor (e.g., auto dealerships), processing (e.g., bottling plants), chain (e.g., restaurants), and area franchises (e.g., a geographic region is licensed to one franchisee to subfranchise to others).

Franchisors are required to comply with the Federal Trade Commission's (FTC) Franchise Rule, which is law, requiring franchisors to make presale disclosure nationwide to prospective franchisees. Registration of franchises falls under state law modeled on the FTC's Uniform Franchise Offering Circular, which requires franchisors to make specific presale disclosures to prospective franchisees, including their balance sheets, income statements for the preceding three years, terms and conditions of the franchise agreement, territory restrictions, termination justifications, and so forth. The FTC enforces the disclosure requirements.

## Corporations

A corporation is a legal "person" having the ability to hold and transfer property, raise money, sign contracts, sue and be sued, and conduct business, being liable for its contracts and debts. Corporation law limits the liability of shareholders—the company's owners—to the extent of their investment, permits the transferability of ownership (selling shares to others), centralizes management in its directors and officers, and has perpetual existence unless it is voluntarily dissolved by its shareholders or involuntarily dissolved by its creditors through a bankruptcy proceeding.

The Revised Model Business Corporation Act is used by states as the basis for their corporation codes. A company incorporated in one state can do business in all states. Some states have laws more favorable to the operation of corporations than others (e.g., Delaware and Nevada), but for convenience, most businesses choose to incorporate in the state where they have their principal activities. The name of the corporation must not already be trademarked by another company and must contain the word Corporation, Inc., Co., or Ltd.

The document called the Articles of Incorporation, also known as a corporate charter, is the governing document of the company and must be approved by the state in which the business will be incorporated. Once approved, the charter can be filed with the secretary of state, establishing the corporation. The approving and filing process is complex and must precisely follow procedures required by the state. To ensure compliance, attorneys specializing in this area of practice are usually required, and their fees and registration costs can be considerable.[5]

There are two types of corporations, both of which have limited liability protection for shareholders: C corporations and S corporations. C corporations are the most common type; they file their own corporate tax returns and pay taxes on income. If a C corporation pays dividends, the shareholders receiving the dividends pay tax on them on their own individual tax returns.

An S corporation is a special type. It is established by filing a form with the IRS, not with a state. It can have no more than seventy-five shareholders (who cannot be other corporations or partnerships), and all must be U.S. citizens. It has one class of stock. An S corporation pays no federal income tax; its profits, whether distributed or not, are passed through to the shareholders, who pay tax on them on their individual income tax returns. S corporations are popular when a newly formed corporation is expected to incur major losses or profits that can be offset by other profits or losses by its shareholders on their individual tax returns.

Choose your business form carefully, being especially mindful of the liability and tax consequences.

## INTELLECTUAL PROPERTY PROTECTION

Protecting your business idea and the name you have chosen to brand it is a vital task. It is equally important not to infringe on intellectual property already protected by someone else because that person could sue you for infringement. Your first step is to check if your business or brand name has already been registered. If not, register your company trademark with the Trademark Office, U.S. Department of Commerce, 2021 Jefferson Davis Highway, Arlington, VA 22202, (800) 786-9199.

If your business is based on an invention, you should patent it to protect your ownership, provided no one has already done it. To register a patent, contact the U.S. Department of Commerce, Assistant Commissioner for Trademarks, Patent Applications, Washington, DC 20231, (800) 786-9199.

You will need the assistance of an attorney or agent to properly comply with the Patent Office's requirements of uniqueness and eligibility. Only attorneys and agents registered with the U.S. Patent Office are eligible to present applications and perform patent searches. The office has listings of registered attorneys and agents for you to contact; be prepared to pay a fee for these services.

If you are an author, music composer, or artist you will want to protect your writings, compositions, and art with a copyright, a legal protection for your work. To register a copyright, contact the U.S. Library of Congress, James Madison Memorial Building, Washington, DC 20559, (202) 707-3000. You should always put a notice of copyright on every copy of your work to ensure protection. Notice there is one on the second page of this book.

## BUSINESS LOCATION

Choosing where to locate the business is a critical decision. Marketing success is partially driven by location, as well as operational issues like access to transportation and distribution centers. Rules and regulations also are triggered by location; some cities and states have considerably less onerous requirements than others (discussed later). Federal rules and regulations are the same throughout the United States with a few exceptions, such as Puerto Rico (where there is no federal tax) and Indian Reservations.

### Indian Reservations

If you have a completely free choice as to where to locate your business, your best bet is to locate it on an Indian Reservation. Why? There are 550 federally recognized, sovereign governments run by Native American and Alaskan tribes. These governments have certain rights guaranteed to their people and territories unlike any found elsewhere in the United States. The state of Hawaii has been lobbying for a similar status for Native Hawaiians.[6] Specific federal programs are aimed at improving the life of Native Americans and Alaskans, and businesses take advantage of them by establishing facilities on Indian land, thereby qualifying for training, start-up cost, and tax benefits.

### Enterprise Zones

In almost all states there are "enterprise zones." These locations are specified by state governments as depressed areas needing economic stimuli, especially jobs. Federal funds are provided to states to help pay for businesses to open job-creating activities in these areas. Some enterprise zones are as small as a few city blocks, and others are as large as several square miles. There are tax and other benefits provided to businesses that locate operations in these zones, and start-up and operating costs may well be lower there than would normally be the case. Contact your city or county development office for information on local enterprise zones and the incentives offered.

One concern businesses used to have locating in an enterprise zone was that it might be a brownfield location, one of 600,000 abandoned industrial sites that blight many communities nationwide. Why was this a concern? Before January 2002, the current or any prior owner of a brownfield site could be held liable for the cost of environmental cleanup under the Superfund law. Currently, the Small Business Liability Relief and Brownfields Revitalization Act gives new purchasers of brownfields protection against federal liability if they follow state voluntary cleanup rules, which are usually less rigorous than federal, when they decontaminate the property. If the EPA decides to clean up the site further, the new owners are immune from liability, as are owners of contiguous properties that may have been cross-contaminated.[7]

### Good Locations

Most businesses do not have a completely free choice regarding where to locate. Small businesses typically locate close to the home of the entrepreneur. If you want to open a flower shop, beauty parlor, or day-care center, you probably will locate it near your home for your own convenience and because you know the neighborhood and have a feel for the market for the goods or services the business will offer. If you desire to open a franchise operation—a McDonald's, Ace Hardware, or Dairy Queen store—you may have to locate it where the franchisor says there is an opening, which may or may not be close to home.

If you are looking for a lifestyle change and want to escape the rat race you are currently in, you may desire to move to another state and open a business there. If that is the case, look for a state that is business friendly, meaning low taxes, as few rules and regulations as possible, and a favorable market for your product or service. Some of these state-by-state issues are discussed in chapters 4 and 9. Pick a state and check with its development office and the local chamber of commerce for specific information.

Dun & Bradstreet (D&B) and *Entrepreneur* magazine do an annual ranking of the twenty-five best cities for entrepreneurship. In October 2003, the nation's top ten cities were:

1. Minneapolis/St. Paul
2. Washington, DC/MD/VA area
3. Atlanta
4. Ft. Lauderdale
5. Salt Lake City/Ogden
6. West Palm Beach/Boca Raton
7. Norfolk/Virginia Beach/Newport News
8. Miami, FL
9. Charlotte/Gastonia/Rock Hill, NC
10. Orlando

Four criteria are used: small business growth (number of small businesses with employment growth in preceding year), low risk (bankruptcy rate), economic growth (three-year change in growth), and entrepreneurial activity (number of businesses five years old or younger). The report also ranks the top five cities in each region of the country using the same criteria.[8]

## HIRING EMPLOYEES

If the business you plan to start will require hiring employees, you may be required to comply with federal laws regarding employment. These fall under several categories, as follows:

### Immigration

If your prospective business is going to hire four or more employees, you will need to understand the Federal Immigration Reform and Control Act of 1986,[9] which requires all employers to verify the employment eligibility of all new hires. This law puts the obligation on the employer to process an Employee Eligibility Verification Form I-9, and makes it unlawful for an employer to hire any person who is not legally authorized to work in the United States.

The entrepreneur must see a prospective employee's birth certificate, passport, or naturalization document to verify that the person is a U.S. citizen.

Alternatively, resident aliens may present a "Green Card" to show proof that they are eligible for employment in this country. A photocopy of the document is attached to the verification form. Failure to document eligibility can result in severe penalties for the employer. For employer information, contact the Immigration and Naturalization Service local office or (800) 357-2099.

This act also prohibits discrimination in hiring and discharge based on national origin and on citizenship status—that is, it bars discrimination against foreign-looking or foreign-sounding job applicants who are otherwise eligible for employment. The act's national origin antidiscrimination provisions apply to employers with between four and fourteen employees (fifteen and above are covered by Title VII of the Civil Rights Act), and the act's citizenship discrimination provision applies to all employers with at least four employees.[10] The act is enforced by the Justice Department. For employer information, call the Office of Special Counsel for Immigration-Related Unfair Employment Practices, (800) 255-8155.

### Equal Employment Opportunity

Federal laws, rules, and regulations regarding equal employment opportunity are enforced by the Equal Employment Opportunity Commission (EEOC).[11] There are several categories of EEOC coverage, and prospective employers should be well aware of them as they consider future workforce requirements.

All these laws and regulations are triggered by your having a minimum number of employees. The question is therefore important: who counts as an employee? All full-time, part-time, and temporary workers on a payroll count for the purpose of determining if you have a sufficient number to invoke EEOC and other federal regulations because you have an "employment relationship" with them. Independent contractors are not counted as employees.

Ultimately this is a legal question and has been reviewed by the U.S. Supreme Court. In 1997, in the famous *Walters v. Metropolitan* case, the court sided with the EEOC and ruled "employees should be counted whether or not they are actually performing work for or being paid by the employer on any particular day."[12]

"Failure to hire" someone on the basis of one or more of these laws and regulations can result in a discrimination charge being brought by that person under Title VII of the Civil Rights Act or other acts, if that individual believes his/her employment rights have been violated or because of retaliation. By law, the EEOC must accept the filing of a charge. Charges must be filed with EEOC within three hundred days of the alleged discrimination (or within 180 days in a few circumstances where there is no applicable antidiscrimination state law.)

The following are the equal employment opportunity laws you may face, depending on your employee head count:[13]

- *Equal Pay Act of 1963 (EPA)* prohibits wage discrimination between men and women in substantially equal jobs within the same establishment. It applies to most employers with two or more employees.
- *Civil Rights Act of 1964 (Title VII)* prohibits discrimination in hiring on the basis of race, color, religion, sex, and national origin for employers with fifteen or more employees.
- *The Age Discrimination in Employment Act of 1967 (ADEA)* prohibits age discrimination against individuals who are forty years of age or older, if there are twenty or more employees.
- *Americans with Disabilities Act of 1990 (Title I)* prohibits employment discrimination against qualified individuals with disabilities. The ADA applies to employers with fifteen or more employees. The act's basic rule is this: an employer is not allowed to ask a prospective hire questions about disability or use medical information until after he or she makes a conditional offer of employment.[14]

## Affirmative Action

Employers are required to undertake affirmative action as a condition of entering into a federal contract or subcontract. Affirmative action is not administered by EEOC, but by the U.S. Department of Labor's Office of Federal Contract Compliance Programs (OFCCP).[15] Thus, if your business will be engaged in federal contracting as a prime or subcontractor, you must be prepared to undertake an aggressive affirmative action program with respect to hiring and promoting minorities and women.

## Family and Medical Leave Act

This law requires employers having fifty or more employees to allow workers to take up to twelve weeks of unpaid leave under certain circumstances, such as family illness, pregnancy and childbirth, and other serious family emergency situations. Small businesses must be prepared in their staff assignments and workload planning for this eventuality, especially if a key employee is likely to be absent for as long as three months.

## Fair Labor Standards Act

This law regulates wages and hours, including when you will have to pay overtime. It applies to every enterprise having two or more employees, provided the enterprise is a public agency, hospital, health-care facility, school, or business with gross annual income of $500,000 or more. If your business engages in interstate commerce and fails to meet the other criteria, the law still applies to you.[16]

## RECORD KEEPING

If your business will require even one employee, you must be prepared to keep good records. This is a legal requirement, and it is one of the most costly and burdensome for smaller businesses. In 1992, the SBA estimated that "process regulations" (primarily paperwork) accounted for 40 percent of total business regulatory costs. Most businesspeople, when asked what rules produce the most cost, would likely answer by saying the largest percentage of compliance cost stems from environmental (EPA-type) regulations; yet, environmental cost was only one-quarter of total business regulatory cost.[17]

The following are federal record-keeping requirements:

*EEOC* requires that employers keep all personnel or employment records for one year. If an employee is involuntarily terminated, his/her records must be kept for one year following the termination date.

*ADEA* (Age Discrimination) requires employers to keep all payroll records for three years. Also, they must keep on file any employee benefit plans (pension and insurance ) and any written seniority or merit system program information for the full period the plan or system is in effect and for at least one year after its termination.

*Fair Labor Standards Act* requirements for record keeping apply to Environmental Protection Agency (EPA) contractors. These require employers to keep payroll records for at least three years, plus they must keep for at least two additional years all records (wage rates, job evaluations, seniority and merit systems, and collective bargaining agreements) that explain the basis for paying different wages to employees of opposite sexes in the same establishment.

*Employment Information Report* (EEO-1) is a report filed annually to EEOC by every employer having one hundred or more employees and employers having federal contracts totaling $50,000 or having fifty or more employees. This report provides a breakdown of the employer's workforce by race and gender. For more information on this report, call EEOC at (757) 461-1213.

*OSHA* (Occupational Safety and Health Administration) requires many businesses to keep records and report to OSHA on illnesses and injuries. Every business must report to OSHA any workplace incident that results in a fatality or the hospitalization of three or more employees. Otherwise, if the business employs ten or fewer persons or is listed under certain industry classifications (such as retail stores, barber shops, and insurance offices), it is partially exempt from record keeping. See appendix 5.1 for the list of partially exempt industries cited by Standard Industrial Classification (SIC) codes. If your industry is on the list, it is exempt from OSHA record keeping, unless you are asked to do so by OSHA, the Bureau of Labor Statistics, or your state OSHA.

If at any time during a calendar year the business had peak employment of more than ten persons, it must keep illness and injury records—unless it is exempt under the industry classification. If OSHA, the Bureau of Labor

Statistics, or your state OSHA requests in writing that you keep illness and injury records, you must comply.[18]

All of these regulations apply to all employers covered by federal OSHA regulations and antidiscrimination laws, whether or not an antidiscrimination charge or OSHA claim has been filed. If and when a charge or claim is filed, employers will have additional record-keeping obligations.

## WORKER SAFETY AND HEALTH

The U.S. Labor Department's Occupational Safety and Health Administration (OSHA), established by the Williams-Steiger Act of 1970, has established specific standards that employers must meet for the protection of their employees. Most states have similar standards, which also cover state and municipal employees. You must be prepared to comply with these standards at your workplace by leasing or buying factory or office facilities that comply with these requirements. Record-keeping requirements have already been cited.

OSHA reports that every year more than six thousand people die from workplace injuries, and six million workers suffer nonfatal injuries at work. Injuries alone cost the economy more than $110 billion a year.[19] Worker safety and accident prevention are keys to success for businesses of any size.

If your business will be engaged in any of a large number of industries that are viewed as hazardous, such as construction, nuclear, shipbuilding, or steelmaking, you must be prepared to have your workplace fully conform to OSHA standards. Unless your industry is listed in appendix 5.1, or your company employs less than ten employees, you must comply with OSHA workplace standards. Specific information for each industry is available both from OSHA and your state OSHA office.

Compliance requirements include such commonsense items as posting exit notices above doors and warning notices near hazardous equipment, putting up physical barriers around dangerous conditions, and so forth. Posters and placards can be ordered online from OSHA or from your state OSHA office. Should you or your key employees need training in any of these matters, OSHA offers fee-based training; see www.osha.gov for more information.

## TAXES

One of the roles you will have in your new business is that of tax collector for the federal government, your state, and possibly your city. You will need to prepare yourself for this burden, which is part of running a business.

A word of caution is in order. If this is going to be a real business, the entrepreneur must face these tax issues; if the business is just a hobby, it will likely not be able to claim deductions and other tax advantages. The test of real versus hobby is basically the answer to this question: Is the business' owner making a genuine effort to make a profit by undertaking a significant level of activity in a businesslike way?

The cost of complying with tax regulations is substantial. In the first study of its kind, the Tax Foundation reported that in the early 1990s, the smallest firms (fewer than fifty employees) spent 0.5 percent of their sales on tax compliance activity; the largest firms spent less than 0.1 percent of sales on tax paperwork. A later study by Hopkins and Diversified, in 1995, found that the smallest firms spent closer to 5 percent of revenue on tax compliance costs.[20] Five percent is a realistic rule of thumb to prepare a small business owner with employees for the cost of performing this task.

There are five general types of federal taxes: income, self-employment, employment (employee withholding), capital gains, and excise. Excise taxes are those paid on the sale of commodities like gasoline and cigarettes. If your business will have any employees, you will have to be prepared to withhold and pay federal income tax and FICA tax (Social Security and Medicare) for each employee. (You will also have to withhold and pay for each employee state and local taxes including income, workers' compensation, and unemployment insurance.) If you will be self-employed, you must be prepared to file your own federal income tax and pay your own Social Security and Medicare tax through the federal self-employment tax. Owing to the fact that you will have no employer with whom to split this tax, you will pay the full 15 percent of gross.

The entrepreneur will need to be able to pay at least minimum wage to all employees and make decisions regarding tax year, accounting method, tax ID, and bar coding before initiating the business.

- *Minimum Wage*—Virtually all businesses are subject to federal minimum wage, overtime, and child labor laws. Federal minimum wage went into effect in 1967 at $1.00 per hour and has been raised on numerous occasions since then; in 1997, it was raised to $5.15 per hour, generating an annual salary of $10,712. Some states have higher minimum wage; California's was raised to $6.75 per hour beginning in 2002. The U.S. Department of Labor has information on the current rates and requirements, which often change when a new tax law is enacted; see www.dol.gov/.
- *Tax Year*—You will need to decide what tax year is best for your business—a calendar year or a fiscal year. Most small businesses choose the calendar year (January 1–December 31) for simplicity. If, however, there is a particular reason why a fiscal year is better for you, chose the first day of any month (except December) to begin the year and end with the last day of the preceding month (e.g., July 1–June 30).
- *Accounting Method*—There are two accounting methods—cash and accrual. Cash is the simplest and most widely used method by small businesses, under which the business reports taxable income in the tax year it is received and deducts

expenses in the tax year it pays them. Under the accrual method, the business reports income in the tax year it is earned regardless of when the payment is received, and it deducts expenses in the tax year they are incurred, regardless of when payment is actually made.

- *Tax ID Number*—The business may need a federal tax identification number, the formal name of which is a Federal Employer Identification Number (FEIN). You apply to the IRS for it, and there is no charge. Sole proprietorships and self-employment businesses often use the owner's Social Security number for this purpose, but to keep good records and avoid confusion as to what is personal versus business income and expenses, it is better to begin with a federal tax ID number. For other business forms and/or if you have employees, a FEIN is mandatory.
- *Bar Coding*—If your business will make a tangible product, you will likely need a bar code. While this is not a tax matter *per se*, it is important to have bar coded all merchandise for inventory accuracy—an essential factor when tallying up your assets at tax time. The Uniform Code Council, Inc. (not a government agency) assigns a manufacturer's ID Code for the purpose of bar coding. For information, call the council in Dayton, Ohio at (513) 435-3870.

There are different tax-reporting forms for each type of business: sole proprietor, partnership, partner in a partnership (an individual), C corporation, S corporation, and S corporation shareholder. There are, of course, also employment tax forms for employees. All of these are available from the IRS online at http://www.irs.gov/.

Due to the burden and complexity of tax reporting, many small and medium-sized businesses contract-out payroll and payroll tax matters to a reputable company in their area to avoid spending their time on these administrative matters and, importantly, to avoid errors in withholding and reporting. Your business will certainly need the services of a competent bookkeeper or accountant to prepare and file your quarterly and annual taxes. For more federal tax information, call the IRS at (800) 829-1040.

## CONCLUSION

Before you actually open a business, you have an obligation to yourself to understand that owning and operating a company has more to it than bringing your dream of offering a product or service to reality. There is another side to the business—the rules and regulations. This is not "the fun part."

In this chapter, the most important pre–start-up tasks were identified so that on the day you open the doors of your new business you will be ready to operate with your eyes wide open to that "other" side of doing business. If you follow the checklist presented and meet the federal requirements cited, you will have come a long way toward getting ready for that day. State and local requirement are discussed in chapter 9.

The next chapter deals with issues you will face after the business is open and running—federal operating rules and regulations.

## Appendix 5.1

**Industries Partially Exempt from OSHA Standards[21]**

| SIC Code | Industry Description | SIC Code | Industry Description |
|---|---|---|---|
| 525 | Hardware Stores | 725 | Shoe Repair/Shine Parlors |
| 542 | Meat and Fish Markets | 726 | Funeral Services/Crematories |
| 544 | Candy, Nut, Confectionery Stores | 729 | Misc. Personal Services |
| 545 | Dairy Products Stores | 731 | Advertising Services |
| 546 | Retail Bakeries | 732 | Credit Reporting and Collection Services |
| 549 | Misc. Food Stores | 733 | Mailing, Reproduction, and Stenographic Services |
| 551 | New and Used Car Dealers | 737 | Computer and Data Processing Services |
| 552 | Used Car Dealers | 738 | Misc. Business Services |
| 554 | Gasoline Service Stations | 764 | Reupholster and Furniture Repair |
| 557 | Motorcycle Dealers | 78 | Motion Picture |
| 56 | Apparel and Accessory Stores | 791 | Dance Studios, Schools, and Halls |
| 573 | Radio, TV, and Computer Stores | 792 | Producers, Orchestras, Entertainers |
| 58 | Eating and Drinking Places | 793 | Bowling Centers |
| 591 | Drug Stores and Proprietary Stores | 801 | Offices and Clinics of Medical Doctors |
| 592 | Liquor Stores | 802 | Offices and Clinics of Dentists |
| 594 | Misc. Shopping Goods Stores | 803 | Osteopathic Offices |
| 599 | Retail Stores, Other | 804 | Offices of Other Health Practitioners |
| 60 | Depository Institutions (Banks, etc.) | 807 | Medical and Dental Laboratories |
| 61 | Nondepository Institutions | 809 | Health and Allied Services, Not Elsewhere Classified |
| 62 | Security and Commodity Brokers | 81 | Legal Services |
| 63 | Insurance Carriers | 82 | Educational Services (Schools, Colleges, Universities, Libraries) |
| 64 | Insurance Agents and Brokers | 832 | Individual and Family Services |
| 653 | Real Estate Agents and Managers | 835 | Child Day-Care Services |
| 654 | Title Abstract Offices | 839 | Social Services, Not Elsewhere Classified |
| 67 | Holding and Other Investment Offices | 841 | Museums and Art Galleries |

| SIC Code | Industry Description | SIC Code | Industry Description |
|---|---|---|---|
| 722 | Photographic Studios, Portrait | 86 | Membership Organizations |
| 723 | Beauty Shops | 87 | Engineering, Accounting, Research, Management, and Related Services |
| 724 | Barber Shops | 899 | Services, Not Elsewhere Classified |

# — CHAPTER 6 —

# Business Operations Regulations

Now that the doors to your new company are open and business has begun, your task shifts from planning to actually operating the business. This is the moment you have dreamed of—to be your own boss and to bring to the public something new or better than was available before. Congratulations.

Now is also the time you have to begin to abide by the rules of the road laid down by the federal government for operating your business. This chapter will help you comply with those rules and regulations. In chapter 5, you learned what you must do to prepare to operate the business. Now you must execute—actually perform—those tasks.

Federal operating regulations are essentially the same for brand new companies or for huge corporations that have been in business for decades. There are two key variables: (a) company size, in terms of the number of employees or in some cases dollars of sales, and (b) type of industry. Some industries, those *not* appearing in appendix 5.1, are more hazardous to employees and have stricter OSHA rules, and some industries have more rigorous EPA regulations because they are inherently more polluting. In some cases, these high-impact industries are the same, such as a steel mill, foundry, or trash hauler.

This chapter addresses federal operating rules any enterprise must comply with regarding employee regulations, worker health and safety, environmental protection, product safety, unfair and deceptive practices, product liability, financial disclosure and reporting, and taxes.

## EMPLOYEE REGULATIONS

This category of federal regulations includes fair labor standards, immigration, nondiscrimination, unemployment compensation, workers' compensation, retirement, family and medical leave, unionization, and other employee rights.

### Fair Labor Standards

This set of regulations administered by the U.S. Labor Department sets a level playing field throughout the country for all employers and employees of public institutions, health-care facilities, and businesses having two or more employees and $500,000 or more in annual gross income, or businesses of any size that engage in interstate commerce.

The Fair Labor Standards Act of 1938[1] established two categories of employees: exempt and nonexempt. Exempt employees are not covered by these labor regulations; they are typically defined as managerial, professional, and administrative. In some industries, they would be called salaried, indirect labor. Nonexempt employees are the rest—hourly workers, wage earners—who are covered by these regulations. Some industries refer to these as hourly, direct labor.

An employer must do the following regarding nonexempt employees:

- Pay at least the federal minimum wage. Students and apprentices may be paid less, and employers may deduct from minimum wage the cost of food and lodging, if it is provided.
- Not require employees to work more than forty hours per week without paying overtime, which is one and a half times regular pay for each hour over forty hours for each week worked.
- Not employ persons under the age of eighteen. Child labor is unlawful, except children fourteen and older can work as newspaper deliverers, children fourteen and fifteen may work limited hours in nonhazardous jobs such as restaurants and gasoline stations, and children sixteen and older may work unlimited hours in nonhazardous situations. Children who work in agriculture and child actors and performers are exempt from these regulations.
- Establish hiring, promotion, and retirement standards that conform to federal regulations, such as EEOC and Americans with Disabilities Act.

No employer is required to provide fringe benefits to employees. However, collective bargaining agreements and the labor market may necessitate paying benefits to attract and retain critical-skill employees. Such benefits include length of paid vacations, number of paid sick days, medical/dental benefits, and the like. Depending on the industry and the local labor market, the benefit package for full-time, vested employees can run from approximately 20 to nearly 50 percent of base salary per employee. Cost containment of benefit packages has become a major issue, even in public service union/management negotiations.

## Immigration

It is unlawful for employers to hire illegal immigrants; doing so may result in civil and criminal penalties. The Immigration Reform and Control Act of 1986 established these regulations (addressed in chapter 5), which are enforced by the Immigration and Naturalization Service (INS). The law puts the burden on employers to determine whether the job applicant is qualified to work in the United States. All employers must also post notices in the workplace that cite INS regulations for employment eligibility. These can be obtained from your local INS office or by calling (800) 357-2099.

## Nondiscrimination

The law requires hiring employees by providing equal opportunity to any legally qualified applicant, depending on the size of your workforce. These criteria, along with a definition of "employee," are presented in chapter 5 under Equal Employment Opportunity, where the key regulations regarding hiring are offered.[2]

The Equal Pay Act is invoked with just one employee. The prohibition against discrimination based on national origin and citizenship is operative under the Immigration Act if you have four or more employees; fifteen or more employees triggers the national origin and citizenship antidiscrimination provisions of the Civil Rights Act. The minimum number of employees triggering EEOC issues is fifteen.

Thus, if you have fifteen or more employees, you may not discriminate in hiring, promoting, and firing on the basis of race, color, religion, sex, national origin, citizenship, or disabilities. If you have twenty employees or more, you may not discriminate on the basis of age. If your company is a prime or subcontractor to the federal government, you must also have an affirmative action program in place, regardless of your head count.

Failure to hire or promote someone on the basis of any of these criteria, assuming your company meets the head count requirement, could result in the individual filing a discrimination charge against your company. The EEOC must accept that claim and may undertake an investigation, which could result in penalties if the EEOC finds for the claimant. Nondiscrimination on the basis of national origin is enforced by the Department of Justice.

## Unemployment Compensation

The Federal Unemployment Tax Act of 1935 established the requirement that employers (not employees) pay unemployment taxes to fund a compensation program that assists workers who are temporarily unemployed.[3] Each state administers this program, with its own guidelines and procedures, eligibility requirements, and payment amounts and terms. These must be consistent with federal regulations and guidelines.

The general principle is this: to collect unemployment compensation, an applicant must be able and available for work and be seeking work. Former employees who voluntarily quit or were terminated for "cause" (i.e., violation of a law or company rule, such as drug use or theft) are ineligible for this benefit. You will need to check with your state's employment office to obtain further information regarding the amount of tax you will have to pay and the procedure for doing so.

**Workers' Compensation**

Workers' compensation is a state issue, not federal. Each state has its own rules and regulations, and you will need to learn them from your state's employment department. States typically require employers to pay for workers' compensation insurance or to be self-insured by paying into a contingency fund. Either of these approaches represents a substantial expense for businesses.

For an employee to be eligible to claim workers' comp, he/she must prove an injury was employment related, that is, the injury happened on the job or as a direct result of employment, such as at an employer-sponsored off-site event like a company conference at a hotel or an employee picnic. Unless the employer intentionally injures the employee, the workers' comp payment resolves the issue; in other words, the employee cannot sue the employer for damages.

Workers' comp covers employees in both the private and public sectors, that is, private businesses and government agencies.

**Retirement**

No employer is required under law to establish a pension plan for his/her employees. (A company pension plan is different from Social Security, discussed later under taxes.) If an employer decides to offer a company pension plan, it is subject to the requirements of the Employee Retirement Income Security Act (ERISA).[4] ERISA is administered by the U.S. Labor Department and the IRS, and is designed to prevent fraud and other abuses in connection with private pension plans. Government pension funds (federal, state, and local) are exempt from ERISA.

If you decide to offer your employees a private pension plan, it must conform to a host of ERISA regulations. Some of the most important are the following:

- the pension plan must be in writing;
- a pension fund manager must be named—the manager has a fiduciary duty to act as a "prudent person" in investing and managing the fund's assets;

- no more than 10 percent of the fund's assets may be invested in the securities of the employer's firm;
- specific, complex rules regarding employee vesting are stipulated by ERISA; and
- both employee and employer contributions are made to the fund.

If you do establish a private pension plan, be prepared to undertake the burden of administering the plan and to contribute the employer portion for each covered employee on a regular basis. Outsourcing pension plan management to a professional plan manager is usually recommended for small businesses.

### Family and Medical Leave

The Family and Medical Leave Act of 1993 guarantees workers up to twelve weeks of unpaid time off from work for family and medical emergencies, provided the company has fifty or more employees.[5] Smaller companies are not covered. All levels of government are covered by this act.

To be eligible, the employee must have worked for the employer for at least one year and have performed at least 1,250 hours of service during the twelve months preceding the time off. Employers must provide eligible employees with twelve weeks of unpaid leave over any twelve-month period for the following circumstances: birth of a child, care for a sick child, placement of a child for adoption or foster care, serious health condition of the employee, and care of a spouse, child, or parent with a serious health problem. The employer may require medical proof.

Upon returning to work, the employee must be given the same position or equivalent with the same pay and benefits that he/she had prior to the leave. Seniority does not accrue during the time off. There is one major exception to an employee being restored to work: if he or she was salaried and among the 10 percent highest paid employees, and if the employee's restoration to employment would cause "substantial and grievous economic injury" to the company's operations, then the employer can refuse to restore the employee to work.

### Unionization

Employees have a legal right to form, join, and assist labor organizations, to bargain collectively with employers, and to engage in activities promoting these rights. By law, employers are required to bargain and deal in good faith with unions. These legal rights and obligations were established in 1935 in the Wagner Act, also known as the National Labor Relations Act.[6] This act also established the National Labor Relations Board (NLRB) to oversee union elections, to enforce federal labor laws, and to prevent unions and employers from engaging in unfair or illegal practices. Employees in both the private and public sectors may form or join unions.

Therefore, if your employees seek to form a union of their own to collectively bargain with you regarding wages and hours, or if they seek to join an existing labor union, they have a legal right to do so. If a majority of your employees vote to form or join a union, the union is certified as the "bargaining agent" of all employees, even those who voted not to join. There are specific rules and regulations regarding employees' rights to solicit others to join, and there are specific rules that bear on how and when they may do so. For example, an employer may restrict solicitation activities to nonwork areas (parking lots) and to employees' free time (lunch hour).

If a union is formed or joined, it then becomes the "collective bargaining unit" for all employees within that unit. The union and employer then engage in collective bargaining, which is the official name for negotiations, to determine the terms of employment of union members: wages, hours, fringe benefits, health benefits, retirement plans, work assignments, safety rules, and so forth. Issues not up for collective bargaining are those regarding closed shop and discrimination, both of which are illegal.

The result of this collective bargaining is called a "collective bargaining agreement," which is a contract between the union and the employer for a certain length of time containing the agreed-upon terms and conditions. If the union and employer agree, they may also bargain on such items as plant closures, plant locations, supervisors' duties, and corporate organization.

If a collective bargaining agreement cannot be reached after a reasonable amount of time, the Wagner Act empowers the union's management to recommend a strike. Before a strike is called, a majority of the union members must vote for it. If the employer anticipates that a strike may happen, he or she can legally prevent employees from entering the workplace by instituting an employer lockout. A number of activities and options at that point are available to both employer and union, which go beyond the scope of this discussion.[7]

Suffice it to say, once a number of employees have joined the enterprise, they may elect to attempt unionization, as is their right. This usually happens when employers behave in ways that demonstrate callousness or indifference to workers' needs and rights, which today is unusual. This partially explains why today only approximately 13 percent of the U.S. workforce is unionized, down from one-third of U.S. workers in the 1950s. The founder of a major aerospace company once remarked that he would expect to get a union "only when we deserve it," meaning if his behavior as a nonunion employer were cruel, hostile, or indifferent to his employees, they would retaliate by organizing.[8]

## Other Employee Rights

In addition to the above, federal and state laws also protect employees from discrimination or harassment of certain types: pregnancy discrimination, sexual harassment, and religious discrimination.

The Pregnancy Discrimination Act was added to the Civil Rights Act in 1978 to make it unlawful to discriminate in employment because of pregnancy, childbirth, and related medical conditions. Sexual harassment in employment situations is unlawful under the Civil Rights Act. This means that refusing to have sex with a superior cannot be used as a reason to deny hiring or promotion, and it is illegal to allow a sexually hostile work environment to exist, including verbal remarks, physical acts, or intimidation.[9]

Religious discrimination, while generally illegal, is permitted in certain employment situations. The Civil Rights Act does permit religious organizations to give preference in employment to persons subscribing to a particular religion—usually the same as the organization. Generally, employers have a duty to reasonably accommodate employees' religious practices, holidays, and observances, if undue hardship to the employer does not result.

EEOC has developed guidelines since September 11 to assist employers with issues relating to the employment of Muslims, Arabs, and other ethnic minorities.[10]

## WORKER HEALTH AND SAFETY ISSUES

The Occupational Safety and Health Administration Act of 1970[11] empowered the U.S. Department of Labor to establish rules and regulations to protect the health and safety of virtually everyone employed in the private sector.[12] State and local government employees are exempt from federal regulations, but state OSHA rules apply to them.

OSHA has specific standards for maritime, agriculture, and construction employment.[13] For general industry employment, it has two main standards: general and specific duty. General duty standards are those that impose on employers the general duty to provide their employees with a workplace environment "free from recognized hazards" that may cause or are likely to cause serious physical harm or death.

There are thousands of specific duty standards that OSHA has developed for specific types of industries or workplace situations to prevent physical harm or injury to workers. These include such things as protective clothing for workers in the chemical industry, safety glasses and shoes for metal workers, and adequate lighting in stairways and halls. Other specific standards establish a duty that employers install protective shields around certain types of machinery, safety rails around open pits, warning signs of electric hazard near high voltage electrical equipment, and so forth. Other specific duty standards apply to health as well as safety—are first-aid kits readily available, emergency telephone numbers posted, and fire extinguishers nearby?

OSHA not only establishes the regulations, it also enforces them. By law, OSHA may inspect workplaces to ensure compliance; if a violation is noted, OSHA can issue a citation requiring the employer to correct or abate the situation. If the employer contests the citation, the OSHA Commission will make a determination. If the employer contests the commission's ruling, he/she may appeal to the federal circuit court of appeals, whose ruling is final. Employers who violate OSHA regulations, citations, rulings, or court decisions are liable for civil and criminal penalties.

As an employer, you have the duty to ensure that your workplace is free from hazards, to post OSHA warning signs and placards wherever required, and to abide by all OSHA rules and regulations pertaining to your particular industry and workplace situation. OSHA has developed model policy statements and codes of safe practices for employers' use.[14] Also, you must check with your state OSHA to ensure compliance with state regulations, as well as federal.

## ENVIRONMENTAL PROTECTION

The National Environmental Policy Act of 1969 established the Environmental Protection Agency (EPA) in 1970.[15] The act also established the principle that the federal government will consider the "adverse impact" on the environment of legislation, regulations, rules, and any other federal government action before such action is implemented. This consideration is known as an environmental impact statement. The public has thirty days to submit comments to the EPA once an impact statement has been proposed. After taking public comments into account, the EPA will issue an order announcing whether or not the proposed rule may proceed to implementation. Appeals to EPA rules are made to the circuit court of appeals.[16]

### Proposed Rules

As a business owner, you therefore need to keep abreast of EPA's proposed rules to determine if any are likely to impact your company or industry. If so, you have a right to submit your comments to the EPA during the public review period. This is usually done through trade associations. This is the first and most general impact the EPA can have on your business— tracking proposed rules. There are specific environmental laws and regulations that may impact the business, as follows:[17]

### Air Pollution

The Clean Air Act of 1963 established the principle that the government is concerned about air pollution and is responsible for controlling it. This act has been amended many times, most importantly in 1990, when Congress authorized the EPA to establish comprehensive standards to regulate the air quality throughout the United States. The EPA's air quality standards and regulations are enforced by the states; if states fail to do so, the EPA has the authority to enforce them.

The EPA has subdivided each state into air quality control regions that take into account unique geographic and atmospheric conditions. Following EPA national ozone emission standards, the states and regions develop air quality regulations for each region. Regions not meeting EPA standards are called nonattainment areas. Depending on the level of nonattainment, the EPA requires the region to develop an action plan to mitigate ozone emissions to a safe level. Failure to meet these standards and deadlines can result in states losing federal funds for various activities, such as highway construction money, and losing the right to permit the building of additional factories that pollute.

States develop regulations for meeting emission standards from stationary and mobile sources of air pollution, based on EPA guidelines. For stationary sources, such as factories, refineries, and electric power plants, states usually require the installation of "reasonably available control technology" to abate emissions, taking cost factors into consideration. They may, however, require "best available" control technology, which is more expensive. New construction facilities and some existing stationary sources are required to install this technology. Mobile sources of emissions, cars, trucks, and airplanes, are controlled at the point of manufacture, as well as in making and distributing their fuel and fuel additives. Leaded fuel, for example, was prohibited after 1995.

Toxic pollutants represent a special situation. The EPA has identified more than 180 chemicals that are toxic, such as asbestos and mercury, and can cause serious injury or death to humans. For stationary sources emitting any of these toxic chemicals, the EPA has established the standard that the "maximum achievable control technology" must be used to abate their emission, regardless of cost.

If your business is likely to be a "stationary source" of air pollution, especially if you are likely to emit toxic chemical pollution, you are required to obtain approval from your regional management district or your state EPA before initiating operations. Mobile sources of emission, such as company cars and trucks, are not your concern, having already been approved by the EPA for sale by their manufacturers.

## Water Pollution

The key statute governing water pollution is the Clean Water Act of 1972, as amended several times.[18] The EPA administers this act, setting standards and enforcing them. The key standard deals with "point sources" of water pollution, such as power plants, paper mills, factories, and sewage plants. Point sources must install water pollution control devices meeting one of two standards: best practical control technology (used for existing plants), and best available control technology (required for new construction facilities, regardless of cost). Discharges into rivers, streams, and groundwater supplies must be noted and records kept, using monitoring equipment meeting EPA standards. Samples of discharges must also be kept. Ocean dumping is strictly prohibited, unless an EPA permit is first obtained.

## Noise Pollution

In recognition of the fact that noise can cause physiological and psychological damage to humans, Congress passed the Noise Control Act in 1972,[19] empowering the EPA to establish noise standards for products sold in the United States. Subsequently, the EPA has set noise emission standards for products as diverse as children's toys, gardeners' leaf blowers, and factory whistles. Working with the Federal Aviation Administration (FAA), the EPA sets noise emission standards for aircraft, and working with OSHA it sets standards for workplace noise emissions.

## Hazardous Waste

Beginning in 1976, Congress empowered the EPA to develop national standards for the disposal of hazardous waste. Subsequently, the EPA established "cradle-to-grave" regulations for the proper handling of hazardous substances from their point of origin, use, transportation, and final disposal in approved, regulated sites. Hazardous waste is defined as solid material that can cause or significantly contribute to serious illness or death to humans and pose a hazard to the environment. Nuclear waste is a special category and is controlled by the Nuclear Regulatory Commission.

## Toxic Substances

The EPA has the authority to regulate and control toxic substances. There are two main statutes: the Federal Insecticide, Fungicide, and Rodenticide Act, as amended in 1972, and the Toxic Substances Control Act of 1976.[20] Before pesticides and other toxic chemicals and compounds can be sold, they must be registered with the EPA, which may or may not permit them to be sold and determines under what circumstances they may be used. Most toxic substances have restricted-use requirements.[21] Special EPA and state regulations govern these products.[22]

If your business will engage in activities that will pollute the air or water, emit noise, use toxic substances, or dispose of hazardous waste, you must obtain EPA approval in the form of a license or permit before engaging in that activity. You will also have to be licensed by your state to engage in any business using toxic substances.

## Disclosure

There is one more duty required of the business: you have to disclose environmental liabilities to your shareholders. Since 1992, the SEC has required companies to disclose "material" environmental problems in their financial reports to shareholders because of potential financial liabilities from products and cost of environmental cleanup. The EPA shares company-by-company compliance information with the SEC, enabling the SEC to enforce the disclosure rule.

## PRODUCT SAFETY

Over the years, Congress has enacted a plethora of legislation concerning safety of products of all types—toys, food, drugs, and vehicles. Other laws establish regulations for product testing, labeling, and unfair or deceptive practices. This section will briefly summarize a few of the most important of these federal regulations.

### Consumer Products

The Consumer Product Safety Act of 1972[23] established a new independent agency called the Consumer Product Safety Commission.[24] Its authority is to establish rules and regulations to interpret and enforce the act, perform research on consumer product safety, and collect and interpret data on injuries caused by products. The commission can obtain injunctions to stop the sale of hazardous products, and it can bring civil and criminal charges against their manufactures or retailers.

The commission enforces a number of specific laws on particular topics: Child Protection and Toy Safety, Flammable Fabrics, and Refrigerator Safety Acts. Product safety regarding autos, trucks, aircraft, and boats is administered by other federal agencies.

### Fair Packaging and Labeling

The Federal Trade Commission (FTC) is empowered to regulate packaging and labeling.[25] The Fair Packaging and Labeling Act[26] requires labels to fully disclose information regarding the contents of the package, serving size or dosage, and the name and address of the manufacturer. Other laws FTC enforces are the Wool Products Labeling Act, Textile Products Identification Act, Hobby Protection Act, and Fur Products Labeling Act. The Poison Prevention Packaging Act requires manufactures to use childproof packaging for virtually all household products.

In 2002, Congress added a new labeling requirement in the farm subsidy law requiring country-of-origin information to be included on certain food labels as of 2004. This requirement pertains only to food sold in super-markets and covers beef, pork, lamb, fish, produce, and peanuts. Chicken is exempt because most of America's most popular food is domestically grown. The Agriculture Department reports that 11 percent of America's food is imported, and this amount is growing annually. In 2002, the dollar value of imported food was $45.5 billion, up 11 percent over 2001. The food industry estimates the cost of compliance with the new labeling law will range from $100 million to several billion dollars. Defining the country of origin of fish and shellfish, 68 percent of which was imported in 2001, will be dif-ficult—since much of it is caught in international waters.[27]

Complying with federal labeling regulations is not enough because some states have their own requirements that go beyond federal regulations, and Canadian labeling laws require bilingual (English/French) labeling. Since many packaged products are sold throughout North America, compliance with Canadian law is essential to rationalize distribution.

The state with the strictest labeling rules is California. That state's Office of Environmental Health Hazard Assessment, believing "the consumer should know what is in the products they purchase so they can make in-formed decisions," mandated new labeling requirements, beginning in 2003, for food containing acrylamide, a chemical known to cause cancer in ani-mals. This chemical is found in snack foods, french fries, baked goods, and cereals. The food industry is strongly opposed to this requirement because testing is incomplete and because of distribution problems. Though the re-quirement affects only California, it is the largest single food market in the country, and it is difficult to put warnings on shipments bound for that one state and not others.[28]

### Nutrition Labeling

In 1990, Congress passed the Nutrition Labeling and Education Act, which requires food processors and manufacturers to provide full disclosure of the type and nature of the product contained in the package and prohib-its their making claims that are not scientifically backed. This act covers pack-aged food, raw seafood, vegetables, and fruit. The label must disclose the nutritional content: how many calories per serving, calories from fat, satu-rated fat, cholesterol, and fiber. The law does not regulate meat, poultry, and egg products, which the Agriculture Department regulates. Food sold in restaurants and prepared food sold in retail stores is exempt.

### Warning Labels

If there is even a remote probability that your product could cause accident or injury, you should put a clearly worded warning label on the product. "The duty to warn requires that the consumer receive notice of potential dangers associated with the product. This includes," advises an attorney specializing in insurance defense, "potential consequences associated with foreseeable misuses." The duty to warn extends for the life of the product. For assistance, contact the Consumer Product Safety Commission (www.cpsc.gov).[29]

### Warranties

The Magnuson-Moss Warranty Act[30] of 1975 requires any product priced at $15 or more that has a warranty to display the warranty in a conspicuous manner and to state its terms and conditions in clear and simple language.

### Food and Drug Administration

The Food, Drug, and Cosmetic Act of 1938[31] greatly expanded federal regulation of the food and drug industry.[32] The Food and Drug Administration (FDA) administers the act and has the authority to test products before they are allowed to be sold to ensure their safety and that they do what their manufacturers' claim. FDA can conduct inspections of manufacturers' facilities, order the seizure or recall of products, and seek injunctions to stop prohibited practices or sales of products. Willful violators are subject to criminal penalties.

While the Department of Agriculture regulates most food (meat, poultry, and egg products), the FDA established regulations regarding seafood and shellfish. In 1995, FDA tightened these standards to improve consumer safety. FDA administers quite a number of statutes regulating such diverse items as pesticides, food additives, animal drugs, and radiation.

FDA is probably most well known for its regulatory role concerning drugs and medicines. FDA has broad statutory authority to license new drugs for sale in the United States, following adequate analysis and testing. All prescription and nonprescription drugs sold in the United States must be properly labeled with such information as method of proper use, duration of use, warnings about side effects, and when to discontinue use. FDA establishes and enforces these regulations, which are quite similar to those for cosmetics regarding testing, inspection, and labeling.

### UNFAIR AND DECEPTIVE PRACTICES

The Federal Trade Commission Act of 1914[33] is the statute that authorizes the federal government to establish and enforce acceptable practices in marketing and selling products and prohibits "unfair and deceptive practices."[34] This act and other consumer protection statutes are enforced by the Federal Trade Commission (FTC), established in 1915. The FTC has the authority to order an alleged violator to an administrative hearing and after the hearing to issue cease and desist orders. Appeals to FTC rulings may be made in federal court. The FTC can sue in state courts to gain compensation for aggrieved consumers.

One type of false and deceptive practice is in advertising. There are two tests: (1) the ad contains false information or omits important facts likely to mislead a "reasonable consumer," or (2) the ad makes an unsubstantiated claim. "Bait and switch" is also deceptive advertising. This occurs when a seller advertises an inexpensive item to lure consumers to the store. When the customer arrives, the seller encourages the customer to purchase a more expensive item by saying the store does not have the cheaper item ("those are sold out"), refuses to show the item ("oh, those are in the warehouse and hard to get at"), and/or presses the customer to buy a higher-priced item ("this model is really much better").

The Postal Reorganization Act established the principle that mailing unsolicited products and seeking payment for them is an unfair practice. Anyone receiving unsolicited merchandise may use it, discard it, or otherwise dispose of it without any obligation to pay for it or return it. Unsolicited items received from charitable organizations or by mistake are exempt.[35]

Certain types of telemarketing are also unfair practices. The Telephone Consumer Protection Act of 1991 provides residences (not businesses) with protection against unsolicited, automatically dialed, prerecorded marketing messages, other than by nonprofit groups. The restriction is exempt if a live person initiates the call and gains the permission of the receiver to play the recorded message or if the caller has obtained written permission of the recipient to receive such calls. "Junk faxes" are in the same category, though unsolicited private and political messages are exempt. The Federal Communications Commission enforces this law.

The entrepreneur is responsible for not engaging in unfair or deceptive practices. If you are unsure whether or not a particular activity is legal, seek counsel. Erring on the side of legal and ethical behavior is always good practice.

## PRODUCT LIABILITY

If your business will be engaged in the design, manufacture, distribution, or sale of a product, you will need at least a rudimentary knowledge of product liability.[36] If your product has defects that cause illness or injury to those handling it or using it, you could be liable to recovery by injured parties. This is the law of product liability.

The Uniform Commercial Code has been adopted by all fifty states; it provides for certain types of warranties to be included with the sale of goods. Virtually all products are sold with a warranty, an assurance by the seller that the good meets written, express, or implied quality standards. If the product has defects, has been misrepresented by the seller, or fails to perform according to the written, express, or implied warranty, the seller is liable to a civil action brought by the consumer. This is a warranty of quality, the most common type in consumer products, and is based on contract law.

### Express Warranties

Express warranties are those that conform to a name or description associated with them. A legend reading "state of Washington apples" on a package expresses a warranty that the apples contained in the package are in fact from Washington State. If an aerospace company executive takes a model of an F-35 jet fighter to a congressional hearing and states that the plane will look like the model when built, that is an express warranty affirming or promising that the model is in fact a likeness of the final product.

### Implied Warranties

Implied warranties pertain to merchandise that must meet certain tests:

- the product will perform the purposes intended—a crane will left heavy objects and a boat will float;
- all goods will be of even kind and quality—all batteries in a AAA four-pack are in fact AAA batteries;
- all goods uniformly packaged and labeled will be like kind—all Cheerios in all Cheerios boxes are the same;
- the quality of the goods will meet no objection within the trade—other users of a forklift will find its quality of operation to be normal and acceptable;
- the product will conform to its label's promises if used according to direction—using a lotion topically will ease sunburn pain in minutes;
- all goods of a certain grade or quality will conform to the middle range of that quality or grade—a package of beef labeled "prime" will conform to that grade.

Implied warranties pertain only if the product is sold by a merchant normally engaged in the sale of such products; if you purchase a speedboat from a hardware store, there is no implied warranty that the boat will perform as implied. Food or drink purchased at a restaurant or other retail store and consumed on or off premises has an implied warranty that the food or beverage is fit for human consumption—no foreign objects are contained in your meal. This Uniform Commercial Code concept of consumer expectation has been widely adopted.

Finally, there is an implied warranty that a good is fit to perform the task intended. If a merchant sells a product that is unable to perform the task for which the purchaser states he/she is intending to use the product, there is a breach of implied warranty, and the consumer can sue for recovery. For example, if you purchase a tent for a camping trip and the sporting goods store states it is waterproof and will withstand winds of 20 mph, yet subsequently the tent leaks and collapses in a light rain, the seller has breached the implied warranty.

### Avoid Liability Problems

To minimize future problems with implied warranties, manufacturers and sellers should carefully label merchandise and avoid "puffing" the implied warranty to a level unattainable by the product. For example, putting on the label or in a written warranty that the product is intended only for the use stated is one limitation of implied warranty, a limitation of "fitness." Another useful limiter is a statement on the label that there are "no warranties written or implied beyond those stated here." Another is that the product is sold "as is" or "there are no warranties"—these limit the seller's liability. These limiters must be in writing and highly conspicuous to a "reasonable person."

Dangerous equipment must be so labeled, proper use instructions included, and warnings about improper use of products should always be prominently displayed. Sellers are also liable if they fail to provide adequate information about a product—its proper assembly, storage, and use. If a defect in the product is discovered after it has been sold, the manufacturer has a duty to make a reasonable effort to notify all current users of the problem and to fix or replace it; auto recalls are a good example of this.

Everyone in the distribution chain of a defective product has "strict liability" for injuries resulting from the use of the product. This means manufacturers, wholesalers, distributors, and retail sellers are all liable, and an injured party can sue each person in the chain for recovery and possibly damages.

Product liability is a very important consideration if your business is engaged in producing or selling goods. Taking into account the warranty information provided above will help you minimize future problems. A carefully worded written warranty and well-worded labels on products are a vital first line of defense against liability issues. All well-intended producers and sellers may, however, encounter problems associated with their products, such as someone using them in ways not intended; this is called unforeseen misuse. You will need solid defenses against liability issues and those types of eventualities—as well as solid legal counsel.

## FINANCIAL DISCLOSURE AND REPORTING

All publicly traded companies must comply with a number of statutes and regulations governing financial disclosure and reporting. Privately held companies have no such obligations because they have no shareholders—no one else's money is at risk.

If the entrepreneur desires to issue stock through an initial public offering (IPO), this becomes a federal matter. The company must file a registration statement with the Securities and Exchange Commission (SEC), comply with other SEC regulations, and file periodic financial reports with the SEC. These steps are discussed below:[37]

## Securities Act

The Securities Act of 1933[38] established the requirement that companies wishing to issue securities must follow certain procedures and make proper disclosure. The SEC was established the following year to administer this law—to prevent fraud in securities dealings and to require publicly traded companies to disclose financial information to investors. The SEC has rules pertaining to proper registration of securities, trading in securities by brokers, traders, and financial analysts and advisors, and financial reporting. SEC rules and regulations have the force of law. The SEC investigates suspected violators of these regulations, and the commission's recommendations for criminal prosecution are forwarded to the U.S. Justice Department for prosecution by the U.S. attorney in federal court.

There are three groups of securities:

- *An Instrument:* common stock, preferred stock, bonds, debentures, and warrants;
- *Interests and Instruments Expressly Mentioned:* any investment instrument or financial interest explicitly mentioned in any of the securities acts is a security, such as interest in oil and gas rights, deposit receipts for foreign securities, and a subscription agreement issued prior to organization of a publicly traded company; and
- *An Investment Contract:* any contract through which an investor puts money at risk in a common enterprise that others will largely operate in anticipation of making a profit is a security, such as investments in limited partnerships where a general partner will manage the enterprise.

The most commonly thought of security is common stock traded on a major exchange, such as the New York Stock Exchange or the NASDAQ. IPOs are for common stock.

## Securities Procedures

Firms wishing to issue stock must precisely follow a procedure established by the SEC, as follows:[39]

*Registration.* The company first files a registration statement with the SEC. This statement contains a description of the securities intended to be offered for sale, the business the company is in, the names of the company's management and amounts of stock each person is to receive, any pending litigation, purposes for which money raised by the stock will be used, pertinent government regulations, extent of competition within the industry, and special factors or issues that might have a material effect on the performance of the firm.

In addition to the registration statement, you must also include financial statements certified by a CPA and a copy of your proposed prospectus, which is a summary of the information contained in the registration statement that will be sent to prospective buyers of the stock. There is a twenty-day waiting period before registration statements become effective, unless you request an earlier date, which is usually granted.

There are precise regulations governing what companies may and may not do during the period before filing the registration statement, during the twenty-day waiting period, and after the SEC approves the registration. A firm specializing in the issuance of stock and the underwriting of securities should be consulted regarding these specific activities because violations of regulations are subject to penalties and nonregistration.

*Exemptions.* Certain types of securities are exempt from the registration regulations cited above. Of greatest importance to the entrepreneur are exemptions for short-term notes (not exceeding nine months), insurance and annuity contracts, stock dividends and stock splits, and corporate reorganizations where one security is exchanged for another.

Certain types of transactions are also exempt from SEC registration. Individuals who buy and sell stock are exempt. Intrastate issuances are exempt, provided the buyers and seller of the security all reside in the same state and an overwhelming majority of the business is transacted in that state. Only one state is allowed for this exemption.

Private placements are except, provided an "accredited investor" issues the securities to an unlimited number of other accredited investors and to no more than thirty-five "nonaccredited investors" to raise capital for legitimate business purposes. These terms are carefully defined as to the net worth and income of the individuals and institutions participating in a private placement. There is no limit on the amount of capital that can be raised. Solicitations to the public are not permitted. Finally, small offerings to accredited and nonaccredited investors are exempt, provided these do not exceed $1 million in a twelve-month period.

*Reporting.* The Securities Act of 1933 governs the initial offering of securities. The Securities and Exchange Act of 1934 governs subsequent trading in securities, which the SEC regulates. SEC regulations require that financial reports be issued by companies having registered securities, assets of $5 million or more, five hundred shareholders or more, or whose securities are traded on a national exchange.

These "reporting companies" must file the following with the SEC: Form 10-K, an annual report; Form 10Q, a quarterly report; Form 8K, a monthly report when a material event occurs, for example, a merger. The SEC stipulates the form and content requirements for each of these reports.

## Stock Trading

Once your IPO is complete and your stock is being traded, you must now abide by a number of SEC regulations, in addition to the reporting requirements mentioned above.[40]

SEC regulations strictly prohibit insider trading. Insiders are the company's officers, directors, and employees; in-house or outside lawyers, accountants, and other professionals; and anyone having a fiduciary duty to the company. Persons falling into any of these categories who trade in the company's stock using nonpublic material information to make a profit are liable for prosecution for insider trading—because they are taking advantage of the public to make personal gain. Only certain days of the year are reserved for trading company stock by insiders.

*HealthSouth case.* Richard Scrushy, former CEO of HealthSouth, was indicted on eighty-five criminal counts involving $2.7 billion in fraud, including insider trading. He was the first CEO of a major company indicted under the Sarbanes-Oxley law.[41]

Persons providing material nonpublic information to others are in the act of making a stock tip, which is illegal. Tippers are usually insiders. The person so tipped is the tipee. If the person who accepts a tip makes personal gain based on the information provided by the tipper, the tipper is liable for tipee the amount of that gain because it was based on nonpublic material information. Both the tipper and the person accepting the tip are liable for criminal and civil prosecution.

*ImClone case.* The famous ImClone Systems case illustrates this. Samuel Waksal, ImClone's CEO, tipped his daughter (and others—including Martha Stewart) that the stock's price would drop because the FDA was not going to issue its approval for the firm's major new drug. The daughter and Martha Stewart sold their stock immediately, before it dropped the next day. Waksal was prosecuted, pled guilty, and was sentenced to over seven years in federal prison and required to pay a multimillion-dollar penalty, plus recovery of the amount his daughter made by her sale of the stock. Martha Stewart's conviction was based on giving false evidence, not insider trading.

One aspect of the ImClone case was that employees of the company and of Waksal's stock brokerage "blew the whistle" on Waksal's illegal actions. Under the Sarbanes-Oxley Act of 2002, employees and agents of publicly traded companies who report suspected illegal acts in financial reporting or financial transactions cannot be retaliated against by their employers. This law has a broad scope; it applies to publicly traded companies and to those who advise them, such as brokers, attorneys, bankers, and the like. Anyone who retaliates or advises retaliation against a whistle-blowing employee is liable for prosecution and, if convicted, criminal penalties.[42]

The SEC can be very helpful both to small and large businesses. It has five regional centers throughout the United States that are further divided into twelve local offices. It regularly conducts government/business forums on specific topics; there is an annual forum, for example, on Small Business Capital Formation.[43] For more information call the SEC at (202) 942-8088.

## TAXES

In chapter 5, a checklist is provided of the things you need to do in preparing to operate a business. A key item concerns taxes.

By now you have your federal tax ID number, have established your tax year and accounting method, and are ready to bar code every item you produce. You have also set up a salary and wage policy for your employees, paying at least minimum wage. You must now obtain the appropriate tax reporting and paying forms and rates, both federal and state, depending on the legal structure of your business (sole proprietor, partnership, etc.).

For companies with employees, the most valuable publication is the annual IRS Publication 15, "Circular E, Employer's Tax Guide."[44] See appendix 6.1 for an employer's calendar guide to paying federal taxes based on Circular E.

### Employee Taxes

Now you are ready to execute your tax obligations, beginning with citizenship verification of each employee. It is strongly recommended that you contract out your payroll preparation to a local company specializing in that work, provided you have more than a handful of employees.

Every employee must fill out and sign an IRS form W-4 for income tax withholding, and then you must calculate the amount of withholding for each employee based on his/her disclosure on that form. Similarly, you will have to calculate and withhold the appropriate amount for each employee's FICA (Social Security and Medicare tax). For each employee, all states require workers' compensation taxes and unemployment insurance, and five states require disability insurance taxes.

### Self-Employment Taxes

If you are a sole proprietor with no employees, you will have the task of paying your own taxes; this is done quarterly. The federal self-employment tax covers your Social Security and Medicare, which you will need to estimate on the basis of projected quarterly revenue of the firm. Since you have no employer/employee split, you will pay 100 percent of your Social Security and Medicare tax. Typically, as a rule of thumb, for the average self-employed professional paying federal self-employment and income tax, the total federal/state tax rate is approximately 50 percent of gross income, but this of course depends on your individual income tax bracket.

### Excise Taxes

If your business makes or sells a product that has federal excise tax, such as alcohol and cigarettes, you must be prepared to calculate and pay these per-unit taxes to the IRS. Usually, your cash register's program can be set up to segregate these items to provide periodic reports on your excise tax obligations.

### Corporation Taxes

If you incorporate your business, you will have to pay corporation taxes to the IRS and your state, unless you incorporate as an S corporation. These entities pay no corporate taxes; individual shareholders pay individual income taxes. You will likely need a professional's assistance to calculate your particular tax obligations. IRS's tax information number is (800) 829-1040.

A bookkeeper or accountant should prepare your quarterly and annual tax returns and payments to the IRS and your state and city. If you have employees, you will pay withholding tax either biweekly or monthly, depending on your prior tax payments.

### CONCLUSION

This chapter has provided you with a brief summary of eight of the most important areas governed by federal laws and regulations, and, if you have followed the checklists provided, it is operating in compliance with them. This is by no means intended in such a short space to be a complete list of every federal regulation, but it is a summary of some of the most important areas governed by federal law. A great deal of attention has been paid to employee issues because of the large number of regulations pertaining to them. If your firm has no employees, these items can be ignored.

Assuming that your business is now off and running and is a thriving success, it is time to review rules and regulations governing business expansion. This is the topic of chapter 7.

## APPENDIX 6.1

Annual Federal Tax Calendar for Employers[45]

By January 31: Furnish each employee a completed form W-2 and each independent contractor a completed form 1099. As appropriate, furnish form 1099-R for distributions from pensions, annuities, retirement or profit-sharing plans, IRAs, insurance contracts, and the like, and form 1099-Misc. for miscellaneous income.

By February 15: Request new form W-4 from exempt employees and from each employee who claimed exemptions from withholding last year.

On February 16: Any form W-4 previously given to you claiming exemptions from withholding has expired. Begin withholding on the basis of new form W-4 for the current year. If an employee has not provided a new form W-4, begin withholding as if he/she were single with zero withholding.

By February 28: File forms 1099 and 1096 with the IRS.

By February 29 or March 1: File forms W-2 and W-3 with the Social Security Administration. If tip income is involved, file form 8027 with the IRS.

By March 31: File electronic forms 1099 and W-2 with the IRS and the Social Security Administration if you are required to file electronically.

By April 30, July 31, October 31, and January 31: Deposit Federal Unemployment Taxes (FUTA) with a Federal Reserve Bank or other depository if the tax due is more than $100. File form 941, Employer's Quarterly Federal Tax Return, and deposit any undeposited income, Social Security, and Medicare taxes. You may pay these taxes with form 941 if your total tax liability for the quarter is less than $1,000. If you deposited all taxes when due, you have ten additional days from the due dates above to file the return.

On December 31: Form W-5, Earned Income Credit Advance Payment Certificate, expires. Eligible employees who want to receive advance payments of the earned income credit next year must give you a new form W-5.

Throughout the Year: Every Two Weeks or Monthly: Pay by check, money order, or cash to a Federal Reserve Bank or other authorized financial institution the following taxes: income tax withheld and employer and employee Social Security and Medicare taxes. The deposit schedule must be determined before the calendar year begins and is determined from the total taxes reported on your forms 941 (line 11) in a four-quarter look-back period. Generally, if your look-back period begins July 1 and ends June 30 and you reported $50,000 or less of taxes, you are a monthly schedule depositor. If you reported more than $50,000, you are a biweekly (every two weeks) schedule depositor.

# — CHAPTER 7 —

# Business Expansion Regulations

Now that your business is maturing and performing well, it is time to consider expansion. Businesses can grow from within or they can grow by adopting one of four fundamental growth strategies that utilize external expansion: Market-share building, vertical or horizontal integration, and mergers and acquisitions.[1] These external strategies have significant federal regulatory oversight associated with them.

This chapter summarizes federal laws and regulations pertaining to all types of external expansion: mergers and acquisitions, purchases of assets, consolidations, subsidiary operations, joint ventures, and other types of business combinations.

Front and center in this discussion is antitrust law, which makes it illegal to engage in any of these expansion activities if the result will substantially lessen competition or tend to create a monopoly. State antitrust regulations are discussed in chapter 9. The U.S. government also regulates two other areas that can be affected by an acquisition-produced expansion: employee benefits and environmental impacts.

## MERGERS AND ACQUISITIONS

A classic strategy for business expansion is to merge with another company or acquire it. Using either approach, the firm grows by adding the business of another firm to expand its product offerings, add new markets, gain physical or financial assets, acquire new talent to fuel future growth, and of course to gain new customers—all with the intention of increasing revenue and profits.[2]

## Preconditions for M&A Activities

Beyond the desire to achieve the strategic outcomes just listed, what fuels mergers and acquisitions (M&A)? Successful privately held companies' M&A activities are stoked by their having generated and saved cash to go shopping for acquisition candidates. If they have insufficient cash, their solid performance can make them credit-worthy to debt-finance their acquisitions. For publicly held companies, the "currency" fueling their M&A transactions is their stock, plus their cash and credit worthiness for supplemental payments if needed.

For either type of firm, the state of the macroeconomic environment is crucial to undertaking M&A activities. For privately held firms, if business conditions are good, the firm is generating cash, and interest rates are low, the time is ripe to go shopping. If you are a publicly held company and interest rates are low and your stock price is high, go on the hunt; if your stock price is low and rivals' are high, expect to be hunted.

The late 1990s was a period that met these conditions. M&A activities reached an all-time high in 2000, when more than 11,100 deals were made with an approximate value of $1.7 trillion. Conditions changed dramatically during 2001–2003, when the sluggish economy and the relentless bear stock market depressed stock prices, slowing M&A activity to a crawl, even though the cost of capital reached half-century lows.[3]

## General Rules

Mergers and acquisitions of publicly traded companies must be conducted according to strict guidelines provided by law and regulation. There are two types of regulations: general and industry-specific. General regulations are applicable to M&A activities of all publicly held companies that meet certain dollar thresholds. These include filing a premerger notification with federal regulators, consideration of anticompetitive consequences resulting from the merger, possible price fixing and price discrimination, and the historical experience and level of aggressiveness of the acquiring party.

Industry-specific antitrust regulations add an overlay to these general provisions for certain industries that have their own set of M&A rules: airlines, banking, communications and broadcasting, defense contacting, insurance, and public utilities.

## ANTITRUST

As companies grow and gain market share, they must be ever mindful of antitrust considerations. Why? Capitalist economies vitally depend on competition. One dominant player can stifle competition by gaining a monopolistic or even a near-monopoly position in an industry. How? A dominant player may be in a position to control major portions of the entire value chain of an industry—from sources of supply, to manufacturing, distribution, and the prices of products.

## Oil

That was the situation in the U.S. oil industry at the time the Sherman Antitrust Act was passed by Congress in 1890. The Standard Oil Trust, headed by John D. Rockefeller, held a virtual monopoly of the oil industry in the United States—from wells, to refineries, to distribution systems, to retail outlets. It controlled supply, and it controlled prices.[4] Theodore Roosevelt, using the power of the Sherman Act for the first time in a major case, prosecuted the oil trust. In 1911, the Supreme Court found in favor of the government and broke up Standard Oil into thirty separate companies that then competed with each other.

Nearly ninety years later, in the context of a now-global oil industry, the industry began reconsolidation. Two of these former Standard Oil companies were permitted to merge to create ExxonMobil (formerly the Standard Oil Co. of New Jersey and Standard Oil Co. of New York). To gain this permission, the two companies were required to make the largest divestiture in Federal Trade Commission history—2,400 gas stations and one refinery.[5] Other former Standard Oil entities merged with different companies: Chevron (former Standard Oil of California) acquired Texaco (and earlier Gulf Oil), and BP (British Petroleum), which had previously acquired Sohio (former Standard Oil of Ohio), acquired Amoco (former Standard Oil of Indiana).

## Telephones

Another famous use of the Sherman Act's antitrust power was the decision in 1983 by a federal judge to break up AT&T on the grounds that the company had exercised "restraint of trade" through its near-monopoly of local and long-distance telephone service. The judge's order was to create seven regional telephone companies ("baby bells") providing local service in their areas, and AT&T was to provide only long-distance service throughout the United States.

With the Telecommunications Act of 1996, this carving-up of turf was eroded, with baby bells acquiring each other and later gaining rights to offer customers long-distance service. AT&T also tried to gain local service rights in selected areas. As of 2000, there were three survivors of the seven baby bells: Verizon (the merged company of Bell Atlantic and NYNEX, plus GTE), SBC Communications (Southwest Bell having acquired Pacific Bell and Ameritech), and Bell South. U.S. West had been acquired by Sprint. The year of the Telecommunications Act, 1996, was the then-largest merger year on record, much of it because of telecom mergers: 10,000 mergers with $660 billion changing hands.[6]

## Antitrust Law

Four statutes form the foundation of American antitrust law and make anticompetitive behavior illegal:[7]

*The Sherman Antitrust Act of 1890*[8] made "restraint of trade or commerce" illegal. "Unreasonable" restraints include written, oral, or inferred agreements among two or more parties to fix prices, boycott a third party, limit quantities of production, divide markets geographically, require tie-in sales (to buy one product you must also buy another), and to require reciprocal deals (I'll buy from you, but you must buy from me).

The Sherman Act also made it unlawful for a company to "monopolize, or attempt to monopolize" trade through "unreasonable methods." This is the only act that provides for criminal penalties for violators, as well as civil damages. Only the government is allowed to bring charges under the Sherman Act; private parties cannot participate in government-initiated antitrust enforcement. Courts have the authority to order a host of civil remedies: contract cancellations, asset divestiture, business liquidation, patent licenses, breakups, and the like.

*The Clayton Act of 1914*[9] made it unlawful to undertake certain business practices that are conducive to restraining competition. These illegal business policies include mergers, acquisitions, price discrimination, exclusive contracts, tie-in contracts, and interlocking boards of directors—provided the effect of these practices "may be to substantially lessen competition, or tend to create a monopoly."

*The Federal Trade Commission Act of 1914*[10] and as amended in 1938 made it illegal to engage in "unfair methods of competition" or deceptive business practices such as deceptive advertising, bait and switch, harassment of or untruths about competitors' products, coercive marketing, breach of contract, intimidation, and commercial bribery. This act established the Federal Trade Commission (FTC), one of the government's regulatory and enforcement agencies.

*The Robinson-Pattman Act of 1930*[11] made it illegal to engage in price discrimination in the sale of goods because it is an anticompetitive practice. Price discrimination must involve goods of "like grade and quality" being sold to at least two different buyers at roughly the same time for different prices. Actual injury must be proven by a plaintiff to recover damages. Indirect price discrimination, also illegal, is more difficult to prove than direct discrimination because sellers have clever techniques to provide preferred customers with lower prices through favorable credit terms, lower freight charges, and so forth.

The Robinson-Pattman Act exempts the sale of services, such as real estate, securities, or leases. The statute also exempts price variations justified by cost differences, changing market conditions, and meeting a competitor's price (not beating it).

## Enforcement

These four laws, plus thousands of orders and regulations handed down by the courts and the FTC, are the essence of American anticompetition law. This body of law is enforced by the FTC's Bureau of Competition[12] and by the Justice Department's Antitrust Division.[13] Every president's administration has had its own approach to enforcement, some being more vigorous than others.

The least vigorous were the Harding-Coolidge-Hoover administrations, from 1921 to 1933. These Republican administrations held the philosophy that "associated activities" of businesses was legitimate and appropriate. As a result, they did not prosecute and actually encouraged business combinations, producing during the decade of the 1920s the high watermark of concentration of American industry and finance. In manufacturing and mining during that decade, there were 1,268 business combinations involving the merger of four thousand firms and the disappearance of six thousand firms. Some 3,744 public utility companies disappeared through merger, and almost half the banks disappeared through merger or failures—from 30,139 to 16,053 by 1935.

By 1933 when Herbert Hoover left office, 594 corporations owned 53 percent of all corporate wealth in the United States; the other 387,970 corporations owned 47 percent. The J.P. Morgan Bank alone controlled directly or indirectly about one-fourth of the nation's total corporate assets, according to the Senate Banking Committee. These same concentrations were present in virtually every important field: railroads, electric power, banking, and natural resources—copper (four companies owned over half), iron ore (U.S. Steel owned up to 66 percent), nickel (International Nickel Co. owned 90 percent), bauxite (Alcoa held a monopoly), coal (eight companies owned 75 percent), oil (five companies produced 33 percent), and hydroelectric power (six companies controlled 100 percent).

Even though antitrust and anticompetitive statutes are on the books, they have to be enforced. The 1920s are a stunning example of a governmental philosophy unwilling to do so, with the net effect that the nation during the "roaring '20s" largely returned to the pre-Sherman Act era of the 1880s. The Roosevelt administration reversed this *laissez-faire* philosophy with breathtaking speed immediately upon FDR's inauguration in 1933.[14]

## Restraint of Trade

The Sherman Act states any contract, combination, or conspiracy in restraint of trade shall be illegal, and any person who makes such a contract or engages in a conspiracy or combination shall be guilty of a felony.[15] What are restraints of trade? There are two types of restraints of trade: horizontal and vertical.

*Horizontal.* Horizontal restraints of trade involve two or more competitors at the same level of distribution engaging in a contract, conspiracy, or combination to restrain trade. Horizontal restraints could include boycotting, price fixing, or market splitting.

A boycott example is this: the three wholesalers of a commodity in a city agree not to supply a particular retailer with goods or agree not to make purchases from a particular manufacturer.

Price fixing occurs among competitors engaged in the same line of business. This is the situation where they agree to set prices for the goods or services they sell or buy. "Price fixing" means raising, depressing, fixing, pegging, or stabilizing the price of a commodity or service. Sellers or buyers of goods or services can be charged with this practice, but it is usually sellers.

Market splitting or market sharing involves an agreement among competitors in the same line of business to carve up a market so that each competitor will exclusively serve only designated portions of it, usually based on geography.

*Vertical.* Vertical restraints of trade involve two or more parties at different levels of distribution agreeing to restrain trade. Such restraints could include vertical price fixing and non–price-restraint agreements.

Vertical price fixing involves an agreement among two or more companies at two levels of the distribution chain to set prices for their products. An example is the situation where a manufacturer will supply its product only to retailers who agree to sell the product at prices set by the manufacturer. Exclusive territories is an example of non–price restraints; this is the situation where a manufacturer assigns exclusive sales territories to retailers or limits the number of dealers in a particular geographic area.

## Monopolies

The Sherman Act makes it a felony to monopolize or attempt to monopolize trade by engaging in a combination or conspiracy with others. A company gains monopoly power when it has the ability to control prices or exclude competition within a particular market. Markets can be defined broadly to include the territory where the firm and its competitors sell their product or service. This could be a local area, a state, a region of the country, or the entire nation.

Courts have followed a general guideline for defining monopoly power. If a firm has 70 percent or more of market share, it has monopoly. If the firm has 20 percent or less of market share, it does not have monopoly power. Market shares ranging from 20 to 70 percent are open for judicial determination depending on all the relevant circumstances.

Another feature of monopoly behavior is predatory pricing. This is the situation where a firm prices its product or service below average cost with the intent to drive out competition.

## MERGER AND ACQUISITION LAW

The Clayton Act governs mergers, and the Celler-Kefauver Act of 1950,[16] which amended the Clayton Act, governs acquisitions. These two acts enable the federal government to prevent or prosecute anticompetitive mergers or acquisitions. Between them, they apply to all types of external expansion: mergers, purchases of assets, consolidations, subsidiary operations, joint ventures, and other types of combinations. It is unlawful for a company in any line of business to acquire the stock or assets of another firm if the effect of that acquisition may be "substantially to lessen competition, or to tend to create a monopoly."[17]

To determine if a merger or acquisition is unlawful, the Justice Department and courts review several factors: line of commerce, section of the country, and likelihood of lessening competition or creating a monopoly.

### Line of Commerce

To determine if the merger or acquisition will be unlawful, the relevant market served and the product serving it must be defined. To determine this, the principle of functional interchangeability of products is used. This means if consumers use two or more products interchangeably, that is, as substitutes for each other, the products fall into the same line of commerce. An example would be a Chevrolet and a Honda; consumers could use either car as a substitute for the other, putting them into the same line of commerce.

### Section of the Country

This is geographically determined as the market served by the product. The market is the section of the country that will feel the effect of the merger or acquisition. The territory could be the entire nation, for nationally sold brands, or particular regions of the country. If a small, regional supermarket chain were purchased by a large, national supermarket company, the effects of the acquisition in the regional area are the ones that would be considered.

### Probability of Substantial Lessening of Competition

The Justice Department tries to prevent anticompetitive mergers and acquisitions. Sometimes its warnings go unheeded. If the Justice Department brings suit against a merger or acquisition, it has to convince a court that the probable likely effect of the new combination would be a substantial reduction of competition or the creation of a monopoly in the affected section of the country for that line of commerce. Courts base their decisions on probabilities; potential lessening of competition or creation of a monopoly does not have to be proven.

An example of this procedure having been used to prevent an acquisition occurred in 1998, when Lockheed Martin began the process of acquiring Northrop Grumman, both major aerospace/defense contractors. The Justice Department and the Defense Department both objected to the $10.5 billion acquisition on antitrust grounds, saying the combination would probably result in noncompetitive pricing to the Defense Department for particular types of military airborne electronic equipment, a business line these two companies largely dominated on a national basis. Lockheed dropped the acquisition attempt.[18]

### Types of Mergers

There are four types of mergers governed by federal regulations: horizontal, vertical, market extension, and conglomerate.[19] There are exceptions from federal regulations, including one for small businesses.

Generally speaking, at least two conditions are necessary for a merger to have a likely anticompetitive effect: (1) the market must be substantially concentrated after the merger, meaning that there are only a few firms, making it easier for them to collude, particularly regarding prices; and (2) it must be difficult for new firms to enter the market in the near term and provide effective competition to keep prices down, that is, high entry barriers.

*Horizontal mergers.* A horizontal merger is the situation where two or more companies that compete in the same lines of business in the same geographic market area combine, that is, two head-to-head competitors merge. If all McDonald's and Burger King restaurants in the greater New York City area merged, this would be a horizontal merger. The Justice Department, the FTC, and courts look at a number of factors to determine if the merger will restrain trade. These factors include the following tests: (1) is there a trend toward concentration in that market, (2) how economically efficient will the merged company be, (3) what is the past history of the firms involved, (4) what is the level of aggressiveness of the companies being merged, and (5) will the merger harm the welfare of consumers?

The merger is generally viewed as illegal if the merged company will have 30 percent or more of market share of the business line in the affected market and the merger would cause an increase in concentration of 33 percent or more in the affected marketplace. These criteria can be rebutted in court if the merging firms believe they have evidence that will overcome them in their particular circumstance.

*Vertical mergers.* A vertical merger is a situation that results in the integration of the operations of a supplier and a customer, that is, a seller and a buyer. If Hewlett Packard (H-P), a major PC manufacturer, were to acquire Best Buy, a major retailer of PCs and a customer of H-P, that would be a forward vertical merger—H-P moving forward in the distribution chain. If Best Buy were to acquire H-P, that would be a backward vertical merger—Best Buy moving rearward in the distribution chain to control a source of supply.

Vertical mergers do not result in expansion of market share because the companies involved serve different markets. Nevertheless, such mergers may be anticompetitive because they could result in preventing competitors from buying goods from or selling goods to the merged firm. Regulators and courts look at several factors to assess legality or illegality of such mergers: (1) what are the past histories of the firms, (2) what is the trend toward concentration in the industry in question, (3) how high are the barriers to entry in that industry, (4) how economically efficient will the resultant company be, and (5) will the merged company eliminate competition?

*Market extension.* A merger that results in market extension is one of two types. The first type is a geographical market extension. This is a merger between two companies that engage in similar lines of business but do not compete because they service different sales territories; these firms merge to extend each firm's market reach. An example is a law firm based in New York City that merges with a Chicago law firm—to extend each firm's reach into another geographic market.

The second type is a product market extension. This is a merger of two firms that have a similar type of business line, but whose sales do not overlap. For example, a major brewery acquires a winery, enabling the beer company to extend its beverage offering into the wine market.

*Conglomerate.* These types of mergers are between companies in completely unrelated businesses. The legality of such mergers is reviewed under a number of theories that are largely inapplicable to small businesses.

General Electric (GE) is a conglomerate, having acquired over the years companies engaged in manufacturing diverse products such as household appliances, jet engines, medical instruments, and plastics. GE's proposed acquisition of Honeywell International was barred by European Union regulators on antitrust grounds because they believed overlapping business lines between the two companies might harm European firms' competitive standing.[20]

### Exemptions from Antitrust Law

There is precedent for an antitrust exception for small businesses. Regulators and courts have developed a principle, called the small business doctrine, that permits two or more small companies to merge without liability under the Clayton Act, provided the merger allows them to compete with a large company more effectively.

Another exception-by-precedent is the "failing company doctrine." This is a defense that can be used against prosecution for antitrust. A company is permitted to merge with a competitor that is failing provided no other reasonable alternatives are available for the failing firm, no other purchaser is available, and the assets of the failing company would disappear from the marketplace if the merger were denied.

Selected industries, businesses, and activities have been exempted from federal antitrust laws. These include agricultural cooperatives, export activities of U.S. companies, insurance businesses regulated by states, labor unions, railroads, shipping, and the securities industry. Utilities are exempt from federal law because they are regulated by states.

Certain industries are exempt by implication, that is, federal courts have interpreted statutes in such a way as to imply that other, like activities are exempt. Airlines are an implied exempt industry because railroads are expressly exempt by statute—both being in the transportation industry.

Court decisions have exempted specific industries. For example, Major League Baseball is exempt as a result of a Supreme Court ruling in 1922.[21] Surprisingly, other professional sport leagues are not exempt from antitrust regulations. See appendix 7.1 for a list of exemptions to federal antitrust enforcement.[22]

### Reporting and Notification Procedure

Mergers and acquisitions involving publicly traded companies (even if only one of the companies is publicly traded) must carefully follow a set of procedures prescribed by law and regulations.[23] The Hart-Scott-Rodino Antitrust Improvement Act of 1976[24] established the requirement that certain companies must file premerger notifications with the FTC and the Justice Department of any proposed merger or acquisition. The Williams Act, an amendment to the Securities Act, added precise reporting requirements by the acquiring company to the government and to the target company and its shareholders.[25]

*Waiting period.* If the merger requires reporting, the parties must file a notification form and wait fifteen days for cash offers and thirty days for securities transactions to enable the government to study the merger's implications and challenge it if anticompetitive results are anticipated. Notification reporting requirements are extensive and may include providing the government with highly confidential information from company records.

During the waiting period, the government may initiate an action to prevent the merger. The FTC currently reviews only about 4 percent of all mergers and acquisitions and challenges approximately 2 percent. If the Justice Department challenges the merger, it is in the form of a lawsuit filed in federal court on an expedited basis; companies rarely contest such lawsuits because of the time and expense involved. FTC challenges are heard by administrative law judges, a process that can take months or years to be resolved. Voluntary settlement of differences between the FTC and the companies is encouraged, and, if they are agreed upon, the FTC then files this result, called a consent decree, with a federal court, which routinely approves.

Filing a premerger notification is required if two qualifications are met: (1) one party in the transaction has sales or assets of at least $100 million and the other party has at least $10 million in sales or assets; and (2) the acquiring company will own $15 million or more in stock and assets of the acquired firm or 50 percent or more of the voting stock of a company having sales or assets greater than $15 million. If the parties do not meet both criteria, they are exempt from filing the premerger notification.

*Divestiture.* To permit a proposed merger or acquisition to go forward, regulators may require a portion of one or both of the acquiring or acquired company's businesses to be divested to prevent overlapping businesses or an anticompetitive situation from resulting by the postmerger firm. These divestiture arrangements are usually negotiated in the consent decree process. The ExxonMobil divestiture has been discussed.

*Nestlé example.* Another example occurred in 2003, when the FTC granted approval of Nestlé's $2.8 billion acquisition of Oakland-based Dreyer's Grand Ice Cream, Inc., the nation's largest ice cream maker with annual sales of $1.4 billion. Before the acquisition, Swiss-based Nestlé had a smaller share of the U.S. ice cream market than the 17 percent held by its archrival, Unilever, the Anglo-Dutch giant. Nestlé's acquisition of Dreyer's would have raised its market share beyond Unilever's to 20 percent of the $21 billion U.S. ice cream market. To gain its approval, the FTC required Nestlé to sell three of Dreyer's superpremium brands to Canada's Cool-Brands International. These brands included Godiva, Whole Fruit, and Dreamery. With this divestiture, Nestlé rose to market share parity with Unilever following its acquisition of Dreyer's.[26]

## INDUSTRY-SPECIFIC REGULATIONS

Publicly traded companies engaging in M&A activities that meet the dollar thresholds must follow the general rules cited above. Other companies in certain industries must abide by industry-specific rules pertaining to them. Independent regulatory agencies or executive branch departments that have oversight for these industries review their M&A plans. For example, telephone company mergers must receive approval from the Federal Communications Commission, and defense contractors need Defense Department approval.

The following is a checklist of the industries that are required to have industry-specific merger reviews, regardless of other federal criteria (publicly traded and dollar level of the transaction):[27]

### Accounting Firms

In the post-Enron era of increased scrutiny of the entire financial industry, the SEC has ruled that accounting firms that audit U.S. public companies must now register with the Public Company Accounting Oversight Board to be permitted to conduct such audits. Registration requirements pertain to all American accounting firms, as well as those that are foreign-held, provided the foreign firms "play a substantial role in the preparation or issuance of audit reports" on U.S. public companies.[28]

### Airlines

The Federal Aviation Administration (FAA) regulates the airline industry. The acquisition of more than 10 percent of the outstanding shares of a domestic airline requires FAA approval.

### Banking

The Bank Merger Act of 1966 provides that a bank merger not challenged by the Justice Department within thirty days of approval by the pertinent regulatory authority cannot be challenged under the Clayton Act. The act also provides that anticompetitive effects could be offset if the merger improves the "convenience and needs" of communities served by the bank.

The pertinent regulatory authority could be one of three agencies depending on the circumstances: (1) if the acquirer is a national bank, the Treasury Department's Comptroller of the Currency has authority; (2) if the acquirer or the resulting bank is a federally insured state-chartered bank outside the Federal Reserve System, the FDIC has authority; and (3) if the acquirer or the resulting bank is a state-chartered bank and a member of the Federal Reserve System, the Board of Governors of the Federal Reserve System has authority. These three authorities take into account the Justice Department's own review of the transaction.

## Communications and Broadcasting

The Federal Communications Commission (FCC) has authority to provide regulatory oversight of the entire communications and broadcasting industry in the United States: telephone, radio, television, wire, wireless, satellite, and cable. It grants and approves license transfers, and revokes licenses to use the public airwaves and other interstate or international means of communication or broadcasting. It also administers and enforces the Telecommunications Act of 1996, which partially deregulated the telephone industry. For antitrust enforcement, however, the FCC largely defers to the Justice Department and the FTC.

## Defense Contracting

With the end of the cold war, the Defense Department adopted policies that encouraged the consolidation of the defense industry so that a few strong companies would survive defense budget cuts to be viable competitors, rather than having numerous weak players. Over the next decade, a merger and acquisition wave ensued, resulting in five large companies: Lockheed Martin, Boeing (having acquired McDonnell Douglas and the defense/space businesses of Rockwell International and Hughes Aircraft), Northrop Grumman (having acquired a dozen companies including Westinghouse's radar division, Litton Industries, Newport News Shipbuilding, and TRW), Raytheon, and General Dynamics.

The Department of Defense plays the primary role in reviewing proposed mergers from an anticompetitive standpoint, looking at impacts on the nation's industrial base and on future contract/price competition. The department then coordinates its findings through a formal procedure with the Justice Department and the FTC, who handle enforcement. Only one large proposed merger was denied by Defense/Justice on anticompetitive grounds: Lockheed Martin's proposed acquisition of Northrop Grumman in 1998.[29]

## Insurance

The insurance industry is regulated by the states. Firms acquiring insurance companies are normally required to gain state approval and make substantial financial disclosures to state regulators.

### Public Utilities

Public utilities are regulated at the state level, usually by an agency called the Public Utilities Commission (PUC). The PUC typically sets rates, approves mergers and acquisitions, and makes decisions regarding deregulation procedures. On matters regarding supply and distribution, there is close coordination with the Federal Energy Regulatory Commission (FERC), and on matters regarding nuclear power, the PUCs coordinate with the federal Nuclear Regulatory Commission (NRC).

### Securities Industry

Companies in the securities industry that underwrite stock issuances; trade in stocks, bonds, and other debt securities; issue or manage mutual funds; and advise investors are regulated by a number of laws: the Securities Act of 1933, Securities Exchange Act of 1934, Trust Indenture Act of 1939, Investment Company Act of 1940, Investment Advisers Act of 1940, and the Sarbanes-Oxley Act of 2002.[30] All these laws and subsequent amendments and rulings affecting this industry are regulated and enforced by the SEC, which must approve their mergers and acquisitions.

### EMPLOYEE BENEFIT IMPACTS

One of the most important aspects of the due diligence procedure an acquiring company should undertake is a thorough investigation into the target company's compliance with labor and employee benefit laws.[31] If the target company has an underfunded employee retirement program, has a history of employee discriminatory practices, or is engaged in litigation arising from unfair employee practices, the risk to the acquiring firm's future balance sheet may be too great to go forward with the acquisition.

### Labor Law

The target company's compliance with a host of labor laws is a key precondition to acquiring it. Laws pertaining to employees include the following: discrimination (of all types, including age, sex, race, etc.), sexual harassment, immigration, wage and hour, drug testing, Medical Leave Act, and so forth. As a result of the acquisition, the acquirer may wish to reduce the workforce of the target company; to do so, it will need to comply with the Worker Adjustment and Retraining Notification Act (WARN), which requires notification prior to plant closings and layoffs and requires job retraining under certain conditions.

## Benefit Laws

This area represents one of the most significant potential liabilities to the acquiring firm. The acquirer must conduct careful due diligence regarding the target firm's defined pension benefit plans, postretirement medical and life insurance plans, and deferred compensation plans to avoid buying a company that carries substantial financial liabilities and future litigation baggage.

A major issue today for many target companies is their underfunded employee pension plans. Underfunding resulted from legal corporate strategies that tapped these once overfunded pension plans in the late 1990s to achieve other corporate purposes: pumping up earnings, reducing costs, paying retiree health costs, and paying layoff and severance charges. Today, an acquiring company would likely have to pour cash into these underfunded pension plans to bring them up to ERISA-required standards, making companies in this situation less attractive acquisition candidates.[32] Plans affected by these laws include defined pension plans, 401(k) plans, Keogh, and ESOP.

The following is a checklist of current major laws governing employee benefits:

- Employee Retirement Income and Security Act of 1974 (ERISA)
- Multi-Employer Pension Plan Amendments Act of 1980 (MEPPAA)
- Retirement Equity Act of 1984 (REA)
- Single Employer Pension Plan Amendments Act of 1986 (SEPPAA)
- Tax Reform Act of 1986 (TRA 1986)
- Omnibus Budget Reconciliation Acts (OBRA) of 1987, 1989, 1990, and 1993
- Unemployment Compensation Act of 1992 (UCA)
- Retirement Protection Act of 1994 (RPA)
- Statements 87, 88, and 106 of the Financial Accounting Standards Board,1998.

Nothing less than full compliance with these and other laws and regulations regarding employee benefits is the responsibility of the target company or the acquiring company—after the acquisition. Go into an acquisition with your eyes wide open as to future liabilities, along with future business expansion opportunities. This area of federal regulations—labor law and employee benefits—can sink an acquiring firm after it takes on the load of carrying a target company's prior noncompliance.

## ENVIRONMENTAL LAW

Environmental laws impose a host of compliance and reporting requirements on acquiring and target companies.[33] Noncompliance can result in large liabilities for both parties. Full disclosure is required of hazardous conditions, presence of toxic substances, and other factors affecting the environment, such as emissions, spills, contamination, cleanup, and so forth.

The following is a brief checklist of pertinent environmental laws, enforced by the Environmental Protection Agency (EPA):

- Clean Air Act and Clean Air Act Amendments of 1990
- Federal Water Pollution Control Act and Clean Water Act
- Toxic Substances Control Act
- Federal Insecticide, Fungicide, and Rodenticide Act
- Resource Conservation and Recovery Act
- Emergency Planning and Community Right to Know Act
- Comprehensive Environmental Response, Compensation, and Liability Act (Superfund)

The "Superfund" law empowered the EPA to deal with hazardous wastes that have been spilled, stored, or abandoned.[34] This law could present an acquiring company with enormous, unseen future liability. If the target company, or a predecessor company on the same site, spilled or stored hazardous waste, the acquiring company may be liable for the cost of cleanup.

The EPA can order cleanup. If the party fails to do so, the EPA can perform cleanup and recover the cost from one of four parties: the party that generated and deposited the waste, the transporter of the waste to the site, the owner of the site at the time of disposal, or the current owner or operator of the site. The liability is such that a party responsible for only a portion of the waste may be liable for all the cost of cleanup. Parties can then apply to the Superfund for reimbursement.

Environmental liabilities must be disclosed to shareholders in companies' financial reports. An SEC regulation in 1992 established this requirement because of the potentially large financial impact environmental exposure may cause for a company's balance sheet. The SEC and EPA share information to ensure corporate compliance with environmental regulations.

## CONCLUSION

Expanding a successful business is a delightful management challenge—the type of "problem" most leaders hope to have. Of all the techniques available to achieve growth, external expansion strategies may require compliance with federal regulations: mergers, acquisitions, consolidations, and joint ventures. Federal review and approval of these is designed to guard against anticompetitive results of the expansion to protect consumers. Some administrations are more vigorous in their enforcement than others. The small business doctrine may exempt federal review, depending on your company's exact size and other criteria.

A body of federal laws and regulations comes into play if you are a publicly traded company, you acquire a publicly traded company, or if you or the resulting company is a federal contractor. If you meet any of these criteria, you must then look at additional criteria, such as the dollar level of the companies involved in the merger, to determine if your transaction is governed by federal regulations. A final criterion is the type of industry you are in; some, such as airlines and communications, require federal approval regardless of the other criteria. Even if the government approves your merger or acquisition, there are other federal regulations you will want to review because of their potential future impacts on the company, especially those in the area the legalities in the areas of labor, employee benefits , and the environment.

Whether or not you have gained federal regulatory approval to expand your company, at some point you may wish to sell or liquidate the business. Chapter 8 discusses the federal regulations that govern divestiture.

## APPENDIX 7.1

**Exemptions to Antitrust Enforcement**

| Exemption | Source and Scope of Exemption |
| --- | --- |
| Agricultural Co-ops | Clayton Act, 1914, and Capper-Volstead Act, 1922, permit agricultural cooperatives to set prices. |
| Business' Joint Efforts | Supreme Court, 1961; businesspeople cooperating to obtain legislative, executive, or judicial action are exempt, unless "objectively" a guise to make anticompetitive use of governmental processes. |
| Defense Industry Activities | Defense Production Act, 1950, allows the president to approve and exempt certain activities to further the national defense. |
| Exporters | Webb-Pomerene Act, 1918, allows cooperative activity; Export Trading Company Act, 1982, permits Justice Dept. to exempt certain exporters. |
| Fisheries | Fisheries Cooperative Marketing Act, 1945, exempts insurance companies in states where fishing industry is regulated. |
| Insurance Companies | McCarran-Ferguson Act, 1945, exempts insurance companies in states were the industry is regulated. |
| Joint Ventures' Research | National Cooperative Research Act, 1984, and |
| Production | National Cooperative Production Amendments, 1993, permit research or production of a product, process, or service by joint ventures consisting of competitors. |

| Exemption | Source and Scope of Exemption |
|---|---|
| Labor | Clayton Act, 1914, permits unions to organize and bargain without violating antitrust laws and specifies that strikes and other labor activities do not normally violate federal law. |
| Oil Marketing | Interstate Oil Compact, 1935, permits states to set quotas on oil to be marketed in interstate commerce. |
| Professional Baseball | U.S. Supreme Court, 1922, ruled that professional baseball is exempt because it is not "interstate commerce." |
| Regulated Industries | Industries governed by a federal regulatory agency are exempt because the agency has primary authority, such as airlines under the FAA. |
| Small Businesses' Cooperative Research | Small Business Administration Act, 1958, permits small firms to undertake cooperative research. |
| State Actions | U.S. Supreme Court, 1943, ruled that actions by a state are exempt if the state clearly articulates and actively supervises the policy behind its action. |

# — CHAPTER 8 —

# Divestiture Regulations

The day has arrived when you want out of the business. The reasons for this decision are your own. Perhaps you have lost enthusiasm for the product or industry, your energy has been sapped by years of long hours, you want to do something different with your life, retirement beckons, or you have been made an offer you can't refuse. Your preferred exit strategy is to sell the business. If a buyer at the right price cannot be found, you will liquidate the company.

What are the regulatory impacts of divestiture?[1] These depend on the type of company, whether it is a liquidation or sale, type of buyer, and impacts of the transaction. This chapter summarizes the regulations a company faces when it decides to sell out or liquidate and shut down. These regulations fall under the following headings: disclosures, workers' benefits, environmental cleanup, and antitrust.

## DISCLOSURES

The types of disclosures required vary with the nature of your business entity, of which there are three major types: privately held companies, partnerships, and corporations. Dissolutions of all types of businesses require that legal notices be published.

### Privately Held Companies

Any type of privately held company being sold to another privately held company requires disclosure to the state or municipal authority that issued to the company being sold its business license or recorded its certificate of partnership, certificate of limited partnership, or its limited liability company (LLC) articles of organization. Both buyer and seller will want to record the transaction with a state or county agency. There may also be a state or county sales tax associated with the sale. Property ownership regulations require recording the transfer of any real property involved to assign tax liability to the new owner. There are no federal requirements for disclosure.

If this is the liquidation of a privately held company, the municipal business license or other business documents should be terminated to avoid future billing, and the tax assessor should be notified of the liquidation to terminate property tax billing, if any business property is involved. A clean liquidation is done by donating any remaining tangible assets—land, buildings—to a 501(c)(3)-qualified charitable organization or public institution to clear your name of future property tax, possibly reduce environmental impact liability, and to claim a tax deduction for the donation. This discussion pertains to all privately held business entities: sole proprietorships, general partnerships, limited liability partnerships (LLPs), LLCs, and franchises.[2]

## Partnerships

In addition to the above, the dissolution of a partnership of any type also requires that a notice of dissolution be given to all partners and directly to involved third parties (e.g., those having contracts with the partnership). Such notice must be published in newspapers for all non–directly involved parties to be informed. Dissolutions of partnerships occur if all partners agree to sell or terminate the business, the partnership was for a limited term and that time is up, or if one or more partners ceases to be a party to the partnership. In the latter case a new partnership agreement, called a continuation agreement, can be formed among the surviving partners and any new partners.

## Corporations

If a publicly traded company is acquired or liquidated, or if a privately held company is acquired by one that is publicly traded, a more significant set of rules comes into play, both federal and state. The first of these requires financial reporting and disclosure. The transaction must be reported to the Securities and Exchange Commission (SEC) and to state regulators, including the secretary of state's office, to report the change in ownership and probably the liquidation of the securities and the corporate name of the acquired company. Under American corporation law, a corporation is a legal entity that exists in perpetuity unless a specific period of duration is stipulated in its articles of incorporation, or it is terminated using one of five procedures provided in the Revised Model Business Corporation Act, which provides uniform law throughout the United States for establishing, operating, and liquidating corporations. The five procedures are:

1. *Voluntary Termination*—the shareholders agree to dissolve the company;
2. *Involuntary Bankruptcy*—creditors sue for recovery, causing the corporation to declare bankruptcy;
3. *Merger*—one corporation agrees to be absorbed by another and ceases to exist;
4. *Consolidation*—two or more corporations agree to combine, forming a new corporation, and the prior corporations cease to exist; and
5. *Tender Offer*—one corporation makes an offer to acquire another corporation directly to the second corporation's shareholders; this is a hostile offer that the target corporation usually fights, having rejected a previous offer of merger.

Federal laws and regulations apply to all categories of corporate dissolution or consolidation, whether friendly or hostile. There are reporting requirements to the SEC, protection procedures for dissenting shareholders, and the Williams Act established the procedure for tender offers, including disclosure to the management and shareholders of target companies. Antitakeover regulations at both the federal and state levels are precise and must be followed scrupulously to avoid prosecution.

## WORKERS' BENEFITS

A company that has a qualified employee pension or contribution program or other retiree benefit programs, such as health insurance and deferred compensation, must face the following responsibilities with the liquidation or sale of the company:

### Pension Plans

The Employee Retirement Income Security Act (ERISA)[3] regulates private pension plans and protects the rights of employees and retirees throughout the life of a private pension program. The U.S. Labor Department enforces this law with respect to fiduciary standards and disclosure, and the IRS enforces ERISA's vesting, funding, and participation provisions. Employers pay 100 percent of contributions to private pension plans. For these payments to be tax deductible, the IRS must approve the plan under seven categories of requirements, including plan termination insurance.

To terminate a private pension plan, the company must file a notice of voluntary plan termination with the Labor Department and the IRS. The pension plan must be fully funded at the time of termination or have sufficient assets to pay pension liabilities. Otherwise, the U.S. Pension Benefit Guaranty Corporation (PBGC) will step in. PBGC guarantees pension payments if a plan is terminated with insufficient assets to meet its pension liabilities (called "unfunded" plans), but the amount of PBGC's payment is often below the amount the employer promised. Companies are liable for up to 30 percent of their assets if they terminate an unfunded plan.

US Airways terminated its pilots' pension plan in early 2003 as part of its effort to exit Chapter 11.

PBGC's own assets come from annual assessments on companies covered by ERISA. In 2000, PBGC had a $9.7 billion surplus that moved to a deficit in 2003 of $11.2 billion, largely because unfunded plans of big steel and retailers filed massive claims. PBGC's insurance program was at "high risk" and needed "urgent attention," stated a 2003 General Accounting Office report, with an even larger threat to PBGC's solvency looming on the horizon from auto manufacturers, steel companies, and airlines, whose claims were not yet filed. In early 2004, Congress enacted a bailout for PBGC of at least $16 billion.

*United Airlines example.* United Airlines' is potentially the largest. Forced into bankruptcy in December 2002, when the federal Air Transportation Stabilization Board rejected its application for $1.8 billion in loan guarantees, citing "deficiencies" including unfunded pensions of $6.4 billion, United sought to cut all types of costs as part of its plan to exit from Chapter 11. The CEO stated that United's pensions "are among the cash liabilities that our business plan has to face" to exit from bankruptcy.[4]

While private "defined benefit" pension plans were once popular with employers (because their contributions to the plan represented a tax deduction) and employees (because they made no contribution), today the majority of companies (52 percent) have elected not to offer pension plans or to terminate existing "defined benefit" retirement plans. Indeed, in 2000, only 12 percent of private companies had "defined benefit" pension plans and an additional 7 percent had both "defined benefit" plans and "defined contribution" plans.

Why so few? ERISA's onerous paperwork, reporting, and other compliance requirements make defined benefit pension plans very costly and difficult to operate. These plans require the employer to pay a given level of benefits upon retirement, funded out of revenues. Unfortunately, because many companies made pension promises to employees (estimated at $1.5 trillion) and funded their pension plans short of that commitment ($1.2 trillion), the number of "unfunded" plans and their deficits are growing. In 2002, claims filed at the Pension Benefit Guaranty Corporation exceeded all previous years combined. Congress is facing this growing crisis.

## Contribution Plans

Instead of pension plans, many businesses have elected to offer a "defined contribution" plan, typically a 401(k) plan, where the employee decides what percent of his/her salary to contribute (usually up to 10 percent) and the employer makes a matching contribution. In 2000, 29 percent of private employers had "defined contribution" plans only, and another 7 percent offered them in combination with "defined benefit" pension plans. Younger employees prefer 401(k) plans because they are portable, and the employee selects where to invest the funds. Older employees like them because they can be rolled over into an IRA, whereas pension plans cannot.[5]

### Health Plans

Another law, the Consolidated Omnibus Budget Reconciliation Act (COBRA) of 1985,[6] guarantees employees or their beneficiaries the right to be offered the opportunity to continue their group health insurance coverage after dismissal or death of the employee, or the loss of coverage resulting from certain events delineated in the law. COBRA requires employers to inform their employees and beneficiaries of their rights, and covered employees or beneficiaries may be required to pay a group rate premium after termination of employment or death to continue beneficiaries' health benefits. The Labor Department enforces these regulations.

### Deferred Compensation Plans

Another area of future liability that would not likely show up on a company's balance sheet is deferred employee compensation obligations. Some employees, especially senior executives, may have deferred compensation agreements covering salary, bonus, or stock that require payment at a future date or when the company's stock reaches a certain price. These obligations need to be taken into account at the time of liquidation or sale.

### ENVIRONMENTAL CLEANUP

Under the Superfund Act,[7] liability for cleanup of hazardous waste continues even after a company sells or abandons property where hazardous materials have been spilled, stored, or abandoned. The Environmental Protection Agency (EPA) enforces the Superfund law.

The EPA can order a party to clean up a hazardous site, or, if they refuse, the EPA itself can clean up the site and recover the cost from any and all parties who were responsible for generating the waste, transported it, owned the site when the material was dumped, or the present site owner. Even if your firm was only one of the above and therefore responsible for only a portion of the waste disposal, the EPA could determine that you have full responsibility for the cleanup cost. Your liability does not end with the sale of the property. If you are charged with the cost of cleanup, you can seek reimbursement from the Superfund.

Nuclear waste is a special category, governed by the Nuclear Waste Policy Act of 1982. The Nuclear Regulatory Commission (NRC) regulates nuclear power plants and monitors their performance. The EPA sets standards for radioactivity and regulates storage and disposal of radioactive waste.

At the time of liquidation of a publicly held company having environmental liability, such as hazardous or radioactive waste, SEC regulations require disclosure of these facts to the SEC, the EPA, and to shareholders through the company's financial reports, provided the company's environmental liability may have a material impact on its financial condition.

## ANTITRUST

There are no antitrust regulatory consequences associated with the liquidation of a privately held company. Publicly held companies' liquidations must be reported to the SEC and the company's industry-specific regulators, if any.

In the case of the sale of one company to another, the buyer and the seller will want to evaluate in advance the possibility of antitrust consequences of their transaction. Typically, smaller businesses are not affected by antitrust because they represent a small fraction of an entire industry, even after they are combined into one company. The combination of two larger companies that would, after being combined, represent 20 percent or more of their industry's market share may well be reviewed by the Justice Department and/or the Federal Trade Commission on antitrust grounds.

If either company in a merger or acquisition is a member of a specific industry regulated by a particular regulatory agency (for example, a radio station regulated by the FCC), the appropriate federal or state regulatory agency will review the proposed merger and must approve it before the transaction can go forward. Companies in this industry-specific category include airlines, banking, broadcasting, defense contracting, insurance, public utilities, railroads, securities, and telecommunications.

## CONCLUSION

This chapter summarized federal and some municipal regulations regarding divestiture through the sale or liquidation of privately held and publicly traded companies. If the divestiture is in the form of a sale, and if your company and your buyer are both privately held, there are few regulatory consequences to the sale. Depending on your business' legal entity, appropriate reporting and recording with municipal authorities will be required, along with any changes of title to property.

If either the buyer or seller is publicly traded or engaged in certain activities that have industry-specific regulatory requirements, you have one remaining set of federal regulatory hurdles to jump—divestiture regulations with the appropriate federal and state regulatory authorities. If either party to a sale is publicly held and the resulting company exceeds 20 percent of industry market share, there may be an antitrust investigation by the SEC or FTC.

If the divestiture is in the form of liquidation of the business, there are no regulatory requirements if you are privately held, except for notifications to municipal licensing or recording authorities. You may also have a notification and compliance requirement to the Labor Department and IRS for employee benefit plans and to the EPA for environmental hazard cleanup. If you are publicly held and liquidate, you have the same regulatory reporting and compliance requirements as though you were purchased, plus those of privately held companies regarding employee benefits and environmental hazards. All sales and liquidations require posting a legal notice in a newspaper.

# — CHAPTER 9 —

# State and Local Rules and Regulations

F or most businesses, state and local rules and regulations are the ones they face and deal with every day without realizing that many of these are, in fact, mandated by federal law. States and municipalities have the right to enact regulations that exceed federal standards, but they may not have local regulations that fail to meet federal requirements. The effect is that all fifty states have a basic set of business regulations that are quite similar, being based on federal requirements, with variations and additions on particular items of local importance going beyond federal minimum regulations.

In previous chapters, federal laws and regulations are summarized that deal with each phase in the life of a business, from start-up to divestiture. In this chapter, state and municipal regulations affecting all phases of the life of a business are summarized. Federal regulations will not be repeated here, except occasionally to show linkage or conformity with rules across the fifty states.

This chapter presents a checklist of the steps a company will follow to start up, operate, expand, and divest a business, whether privately owned or publicly traded, based on state and local laws and regulations. California's regulations are used as the principal example, being a worst-case situation.

## START-UP REGULATIONS

After you have decided on your product or service, targeted your market, determined that your chosen business name is not being used by others, and decided on a location, you are well along in the start-up process. The first regulatory issue you face is registering your business with a municipal authority to obtain a license or other documentation, depending on your business entity. The municipal authority in your jurisdiction might be a county, city, town, township, village, borough, or some other governmental unit authorized by your state to register businesses.

### Choose a Business Name Not Already Taken

There are two reasons why it is important to validate that your chosen business name is not already in use: (1) using the same name as another is a poor marketing devise, creating confusion in the mind of customers, and (2) using a name already trademarked could result in your being sued by that trademark holder for "willful infringement." There are civil and possibly criminal penalties for infringement. Trademarks and service marks may be registered in a state for a term of ten years. Thus, it is vital that you perform due diligence to be certain your chosen name is not already protected.

There is no one place to look to validate the uniqueness of your chosen business name because there is no national database for names. You should start locally, in your town or city, expand the search statewide, and then nationwide.

Even if the business is not intended to go nationally and you select and advertise a business name already trademarked by another company doing business in another part of the country (or even if that business is no longer in operation but the name is still protected), that company can still sue you for infringement.

To determine that your chosen name is not already protected, start by looking in your area's telephone directories for the same name you have selected, or names that are very similar. Finding none, go to your county clerk's office and search their database of fictitious business names (FBNs) and other registered business names that are not FBNs.

The secretary of state's office in every state maintains a roster of trademarked names in their database. In some states, this can be searched through the Internet; in others, you have to file an application, pay a fee, and the clerks will perform the search. Some states require that you hire a search firm to do the investigating. Some secretary of state offices also maintain a roster of FBNs you can search.

There is a federal government trademark database that can be accessed through the Internet; go to www.uspto.gov/web/menu/tmebc/index.html. For more careful searches, you will need to hire an agent who is registered with the U.S. Patent and Trademark Office.

Finally, if your business will have a Web site, you must determine that your chosen name is not already registered. Checking domain names is easy by going to www.internic.com for a list of registrars.

## Trade Name

After determining that your chosen business name is not already taken, you are ready to register it. If it is your own name, nothing more is required than to obtain a business license under your name. If you use a trade name, that is, John Doe doing business as ("dba") John's Plumbing Service, you are required by the Trade Name Registration Act to register this fictitious business name with your municipal authority (usually the county), pay the registration fee, obtain a license to do business under that name, and place an ad or legal notice in a local newspaper to announce your business under this name.

Counties typically permit up to three FBNs to be registered on one form. A fee is required for each name. Not only can individuals and husbands and wives register fictitious business names, but also partnerships, general partnerships, limited partnerships, joint ventures, corporations, and business trusts. The benefit to you is that by registration, you protect this trade name against its use by others.

For further registration information, go to the Small Business Administration's (SBA) Web site, then click on "states," and go to your state's home page for county information.[1]

## Registration and Licenses

The type of registration required by your municipal authority will depend on your business entity—whether a sole proprietorship, partnership, limited liability partnership (LLP), limited liability company (LLC), or corporation.[2]

*Sole proprietorship.* If your business is a sole proprietorship, you need a business license to operate legally; sometimes this is called a local tax registration certificate. These can be obtained from your city hall or other municipal office. You will fill out a form, declaring your trade or business name (this can be your name or a fictitious business name). Often there is no fee below a specified threshold level of revenue, and thereafter the annual renewal fee varies with your reported revenue. Most importantly, from the municipality's standpoint, your business has been registered, so that the local government can keep track of it and tax it appropriately if you become a success. For more information, go to your state's home page on the Internet and search for "business license" or "county information." Also, the SBA home page (www.sba.gov) has a link to all states' home pages.

*Partnership.* If your business is a partnership or a general partnership, you must register your Partnership Agreement with your county government. There is a registration fee.

*Limited liability partnership.* If your business is an LLP, you must file your Certificate of Limited Partnership with the secretary of state's office. The current fee in California is $70. The state taxing authority usually requires an annual minimum tax for LLPs; in California, the Franchise Tax Board charges $800 per year.

*Limited liability company.* If your business is an LLC, you must file your Articles of Organization with the secretary of state's office. There is a one-time filing fee.

*Corporation.* If your business is either a C or S corporation, you must file your Articles of Incorporation with the secretary of state's office. There is a filing fee. California recently reduced this fee to encourage business formations.

Be advised, when you file your business documentation with your state, you will also be registering your business name. If you are registering an LLP, LLC, or corporation, you will need a federal tax ID number (FEIN), and your business name must be approved by the secretary of state; if it is discovered that your chosen name has already been registered, you will have to refile and pay another fee. A typical practice is that secretary of state offices will accept a $10 temporary registration fee to protect your business name for sixty days while you finalize your due diligence to determine that your name is clear.

*Seller's Permit.* If you are engaged in wholesale or retail selling or leasing of merchandise, you will also need to obtain a Seller's Permit. This will allow your business to collect sales taxes on the articles you sell or lease. Tangible goods must be involved to require a Seller's Permit, not pure services. For example, an auto dealership or car rental agency needs a Seller's Permit, but a consulting company does not.

To be certain whether or not you need a Seller's Permit, ask your taxing authority for clarification because they issue Seller's Permits. In California, the taxing authority is the Board of Equalization. A Seller's Permit is needed for each location where goods are sold, but all addresses can be included on one application. No fee is charged in California, but a security deposit is often held against failure to pay sales taxes when the business is closed. If there is any change of ownership in the business (it is sold or new partners are added), you must inform the issuing office promptly.

*Specialized licenses.* Many businesses are engaged in activities and industries that require specialized licenses or permits. Depending on the nature of the activity, the issuing agency might be federal or state. Federal examples include the following: a company working in the securities industry (financial advisor, stockbroker) must register with the Securities and Exchange Commission (SEC), a company working in medicines or pharmaceuticals must register with the Food and Drug Administration (FDA), and companies working in radio or television require a Federal Communications Commission (FCC) license. Any company working with toxics or other environmental hazards will need both federal—Environmental Protection Agency (EPA)—and state permits.

Certain vocations are regulated only by states: insurance, public utilities, and a host of others. For example, in California, locksmiths must be licensed by the Bureau of Security and Investigative Services, furniture makers are licensed by the Bureau of Home Furnishings, and guide dog trainers are licensed by the Board of Guide Dogs.

Knowing were to go for the right type of license can be tricky. For example, if your retail store sells alcoholic beverages or handguns, you will need a liquor license or a retail firearms license from your county. If your business makes alcoholic beverages or handguns, you will need a license from the federal Bureau of Alcohol, Tobacco, and Firearms. Some professions, like plumbers, need multiple city licenses to do business in several municipalities.

See your state's home page for specialty licensing requirements or go to your state's office of small business for help. In California, the number of professions and activities that require specialty licenses is so considerable the state has an Office of Permit Assistance and publishes a guide: *California Permit Handbook*.

### Business Location

Choosing a good business location is a vital decision. The right location is a function of several factors: market attractiveness, physical requirements, distance from home, cost, and zoning regulations. All the factors that make certain locations attractive for particular types of business—pedestrian traffic, ample customer parking, proximity to other major businesses, proper physical features and size—also make such property expensive to purchase or lease. Think carefully about your business' true marketing and cost requirements before selecting your location.

If your business does not require an "A" location because, for example, you are a specialty manufacturer making a product sold through resellers, you can select a "B" or, better still, a "C" location to keep overhead costs low. Leasing space in a second-tier industrial park is an example of a "C" location—it's not pretty, but its price per square foot is attractive. Some retail businesses have high margins because they locate exclusively in low rent "B" locations—enough customers are attracted to the brand name, even though the store is in a secondary location. Outback Steakhouses are only in "B" locations, and their margins are fatter than competitor restaurants in "A" locations, such as major shopping malls.

*Zoning.* Of critical importance in your location selection process is zoning, sometimes called land use regulations. All municipalities have zoning regulations and restrictions. These include preserving certain areas strictly for residential, retail, commercial, mixed-use retail/commercial, and light industrial or industrial. Other zoning restrictions govern the number of same-type establishments permitted in the same general area; a major political fight at Los Angeles City Hall was over the number of liquor licenses that could be issued in South Central. Still other restrictions deal with environmental impacts: certain zones are preserved for nonemitting establishments.

*Certificate of Occupancy.* You may be required to obtain a Certificate of Occupancy from your city or county Zoning Department if you plan to occupy a new or used building for a new business.

In California, there is also the state's Coastal Zone regulation. If a business is established within a certain distance from the Pacific Ocean shoreline or any of its inlets (like San Francisco Bay), it requires a state Coastal Zone variance before obtaining a Certificate of Occupancy or a construction permit. Other zoning restrictions include protection of historic areas, nature preserves, scenic areas, and endangered species' habitats. Individual buildings may be protected as historic landmarks or heritage sites. The Planning Commission or Zoning Board of your municipality will have information on zoning issues.

*Home-based businesses.* These are in a special category. Zoning regulations for residential areas where home-based businesses may be conducted are such that if the business has no impact on the community, such as a typing service, it generally is permitted, unless and until a neighbor files a complaint. If, however, customers would come to the home, retail sales would be conducted there, or physical work would be performed (e.g., auto repair work in your garage), zoning regulations would prohibit these activities as too impacting on a residential area. If you live in an apartment or condominium, there may be restrictions in your lease or Covenants, Conditions, and Restrictions (CC&Rs) forbidding any home-based business activity.

## OPERATING REGULATIONS

Now that the planning process for your business is completed, you are ready to go into operation. There are four regulatory areas that require your attention from an operating standpoint: employee issues, health and safety, compliance with county codes for operating an establishment, and tax.

Many start-up companies are simply not prepared for the extent of government rules and regulations that they face as they go into operation. As a result, approximately half of all start-ups quit out of frustration before the end of their first year.[3]

**Employee Issues**

Employee regulations are invoked only if you actually have employees. Only one employee may be enough to trigger this category of regulations, unless he or she is your spouse, who actually volunteers his/her time to the business, that is, without pay. In some states, having one employee triggers several state employee regulations, and, generally speaking, having four or more paid employees (full- or part-time) triggers many federal employee regulations. See chapter 5 for details on federal employee/compliance thresholds. Independent contractors are not counted as employees.

State employee issues include hiring, antidiscrimination, salary, unemployment insurance, workers' compensation, disability insurance, and family and medical leave. State and local regulations must, of course, comply with federal standards, but in some states they go above and beyond federal standards. For example, the federal minimum wage is $5.75, but California's minimum wage, as of January 1, 2002, is one dollar higher. San Francisco is considering raising its minimum wage to $8.75.

*Hiring employees.* When hiring employees, you must be mindful of both federal and state antidiscrimination laws with respect to race, sex, religion, national origin, age, disabilities, and, in California, sexual preference of employees. No one can be turned away as a potential hire on any of these grounds. Regarding antidiscrimination on the basis of sexual preference, in California it is now illegal to discriminate against a gay or lesbian person, a transgender person, or even a person who appears to be transgender, regardless of the image you wish your business to project.

*Antidiscrimination enforcement.* The federal Equal Employment Opportunity Commission (EEOC) has an opposite number in every state and in many counties and cities; these are called Fair Employment Practices Agencies (FEPA). There are more than one hundred state and local FEPAs today throughout the United States. The federal EEOC and the state and local FEPAs have Work-Sharing Agreements that divide up their workload on charges of discrimination to avoid duplication in the processing of these charges. All such charges are dual-filed under both federal and local law, regardless of which jurisdiction the complainant files in originally. Only one agency investigates the charge, but the charging party's rights are preserved under both federal and state laws.

Some state and local FEPA laws have longer filing periods in which to make a charge, cover more employers (such as very small businesses not covered by federal rules), or provide greater protections than federal law (such as laws prohibiting marital status discrimination). In these cases, FEPA may be the one to investigate the charge, but both federal and local agencies will file a final determination.[4]

*Salary.* All employers must pay at least minimum wage. Federal minimum wage currently is $5.75 per hour, but many states have set a higher minimum wage. California's is $6.75, for example. Other than paying at least minimum wage, there are no other requirements for paying compensation to employees.

For example, if you choose to offer employees bonuses or profit sharing, that is entirely your decision. Other employee benefits, such as 401(k) programs, private pension programs, deferred compensation (to gain a tax advantage), and the like are all discretionary. If they are offered, these programs must comply with federal and state regulations governing them, as discussed above. Paying Social Security, Medicare, and unemployment tax is nondiscretionary.

Paying for overtime is not an issue; federal law requires it. How to calculate it is an issue. Only California, Alaska, and Wyoming require employers to pay overtime after an eight-hour workday, not after a forty-hour week. This opens employers to lawsuits because of this far less flexible requirement. This rule hits companies hard that depend on flexible schedules, such as call centers, where people usually work ten- or twelve-hour days, four days per week; these firms are leaving California because call centers can be anywhere.[5]

*Unemployment insurance.* All states require businesses to pay unemployment insurance if the company employs one or more employees for twenty weeks in a calendar year or pays gross wages of $1,500 or more in a calendar year. The taxes are payable at the rate of 2.7 percent on the first $8,500 in annual wages of each employee. Thus, if your business has only one employee, or you employ a domestic helper on a regular basis receiving compensation above a certain dollar amount, you are required to pay 100 percent of the state-mandated insurance premium. See your state employment department for unemployment insurance criteria and payment requirements.

How is "employer" defined? In California, for example, an employer is any "employing unit" having one or more persons employed "for some portion of a day" and pays wages in excess of $100 during any calendar quarter, or a person performing domestic service in a private home, private club, fraternity, or sorority and pays wages in cash of $1,000 or more during a calendar quarter or during the preceding calendar year. Unemployment benefits can be claimed for up to thirteen weeks, longer with renewal, capped in 2002 at a weekly rate of $450.[6] A 2003 law raised maximum benefits to $840 per week beginning in 2005.[7]

*Workers' compensation insurance.* As an employer, you are required by federal and state law to provide workers' comp insurance for your employees. This is paid 100 percent by the employer. Employers have the obligation to inform employees of their rights to workers' comp benefits, usually by providing a pamphlet prepared by the state employment department and by posting a notice in the workplace that summarizes employee rights and benefits. Premiums on workers' comp insurance have grown dramatically in recent years and are now a significant element of a business' overhead cost. According to the Workers' Compensation Research Institute, California's workers' comp claims average 33 percent above the median of twelve large states surveyed, making these premiums the highest in the nation.[8] See chapter 4 for a discussion of these costs.

*Disability insurance.* If your business is located in one of the five states that mandates disability insurance (DI), your business is required to collect through payroll withholding employee-paid premiums and forward them to your state's administrator. The five states having DI are California, Hawaii, New Jersey, New York, and Rhode Island; Puerto Rico also has a DI requirement. DI is a partial wage-replacement insurance plan for eligible workers who suffer loss of wages when they are unable to work due to non–work-related injury or illness, or a medically disabling condition resulting from pregnancy or childbirth. Under California's DI plan, eligible employees can collect up to fifty-two weeks of DI after a seven-day waiting period. The Employment Development Department (EDD) administers the state plan, and state authorities must approve private, voluntary plans.[9]

In California, the employee contribution to disability insurance is 0.9 percent of gross wages with wage limit of $56,916 per employee, effective in 2003. The cost to employers is the collection and payment of these premiums to state authorities.[10]

*Family Temporary Disability Insurance.* This is a program currently available only in California. In 2004, California began a major new program to extend disability compensation to cover individuals who take time off from work to care for a seriously ill child, spouse, parent, or domestic partner, or to bond with a new child. This is a state-mandated program that covers all employees, with no exceptions. This is an employee-paid program that employers collect through employees' payroll withholding. The contribution rate is 0.08 percent of taxable wages with a taxable wage limit in 2004 of $68,829, rising to $79,418 in 2005. After a seven-day waiting period, eligible employees can file claims for up to six weeks during a twelve-month period. This program is administered through the state disability insurance program.[11]

### Example: California Employment Regulations

Owing to the fact that state laws vary with numbers of employees and extent of regulations, a "worst case" situation—California—is examined from an employer's viewpoint. In general, if a California-based company hires one employee or more, the employer must comply with the following state regulations:

- *New-Employee Registration Program.* Within twenty days of date of hire, report to the Employment Development Department (EDD) the name, address, and other information regarding the new employee. This procedure is part of a state-wide effort to find parents who owe child support.

- *Workers' Compensation.* Purchase workers' compensation insurance from the State Compensation Insurance Fund[12] or from a private insurance carrier. Notify employees of their rights and benefits under this program.
- *Job Safety and Health.* Fully comply with federal Occupational Safety and Health Administration (OSHA) and state regulations (California Department of Industrial Relations, Division of Occupational Safety and Health). These regulations require the employer to file an illness and injury prevention plan, report work-related injuries and illnesses causing lost work time, and keep records of work-related injuries and illnesses.[13]
- *Tax.* This is discussed below.
- *Posting of Required Notices.* There are twelve notices that require posting in English or Spanish in a prominent location in all workplaces under federal and California law.[14] The titles of these notices are:

  1. "Emergency"—telephone numbers of emergency services (police, fire);
  2. "Pay Day Notice"—dates when pay will be given: weekly, biweekly, or monthly;
  3. "California Minimum Wage"—$6.75 per hour, plus meals and lodging provisions;
  4. "Federal Minimum Wage"—$5.75 per hour, overtime pay at one and a half times regular pay, no child labor, and federal enforcement provisions;
  5. "Equal Employment Opportunity Is The Law"—prohibition against discrimination based on race, color, sex, religion, national origin, age, disability, sexual preference, and so forth;
  6. "Safety and Health Protection on the Job"—summarizes federal and state OSHA rules and regulations;
  7. "Time Off for Voting"—rules giving two hours off, if needed, to vote;
  8. "Employee Polygraph Protection Act"—federal requirement to post showing rights, prohibitions, exemptions, and enforcement;
  9. "Family & Medical Leave"—summary of California Family Rights Act, providing (in firms having five or more employees) time off without pay for family emergencies, childbirth, and pregnancy;
  10. "Injuries On The Job"— summary of workers' compensation benefits resulting from job-related injuries;
  11. "Notice To Employees: This Employer Is Registered under the California Unemployment Insurance Code"—summarizes unemployment and state disability insurance;
  12. "Harassment or Discrimination in Employment"—summarizes antidiscrimination regulations based on race, color, religion, sex, sexual orientation, ancestry, medical condition, age (forty and above), and so on.

- *Posting of Specialized Notices.* In addition to these required notices, there may be other notices that need posting, depending on your industry and types of equipment used, such as construction, forklifts, lasers, chemical hazards, asbestos, low-income employees with dependent children, government contracts, agricultural labor, medical records, and citations.[15]

- *Pamphlets.* All California employers must provide employees with three pamphlets:[16]

  1. "Sexual Harassment Compliance"—summarizes federal and state regulations;
  2. "UI/SDI"—summarizes information regarding unemployment insurance and state disability insurance;
  3. "Workers' Comp"—summarizes state workers' compensation insurance, which must be carried for all employees of companies having three or more employees for on-the-job injuries.[17]

## Health and Safety

Federal OSHA standards are mirrored at the state level by all states. Some states go beyond the federal requirements for worker safety and health, especially for certain industries that are particularly hazardous. As just mentioned, workers in these industries must be provided notification of hazards and risks of accident and injury, and specialized hazard notices must be posted prominently at the workplace.

Each state's office or division of Occupational Safety and Health also requires record keeping of work-related injuries and illnesses, if time off from work results.[18]

## Compliance with Codes

State and county codes for operating business establishments are numerous and sometimes complex. Businesses of every imaginable type have a county code with respect to its operations. For specific information on your business' codes for your county, the National Association of Counties (NACO) has gathered a register.

At their Web site, there is an alphabetical listing of types of businesses and activities for which they have county code information;[19] some of the topics are: animals, firearms, food safety, home-based businesses, media, personnel management, telecommunications, and zoning and planning. See appendix 9.1 for the current list of county codes and ordinances by subject.

State and county codes govern virtually every aspect of business activity, from establishing and operating it, to its divestiture. Of particular importance are codes that directly affect your operations, such as zoning codes or environmental codes regarding air pollution emissions, waste or contamination discharges, use of pesticides or other toxic chemicals, and disposal of scrap. Many states' regulations go well beyond federal rules on certain of these operating issues, and you will need to consult your state and county codes for precise regulations. An example is limits on greenhouse gas emissions; California's EPA was the first in the nation to set these standards, raising prices on cars.[20] Your state or county Chamber of Commerce or other business associations can be particularly helpful in threading your way through this regulatory labyrinth.

## Tax—Federal and State

Next is an overview of taxes that companies are required to collect and pay to the federal government (IRS) and to state government. Tax responsibilities vary with type of business entity and whether or not your business has employees or is required to collect sales and excise taxes.[21]

You will need to obtain from the IRS and use a Federal Employer Identification Number (FEIN), also known as a tax ID number, on all your tax filings. There is no charge. Sole proprietors may use the owner's Social Security number, but all other business entities, whether or not they have employees, are required to use their FEIN on returns.

*Sales tax.* If your business sells tangible goods, you will collect sales taxes at the combined rate required by your state, county, and city and send those amounts monthly to the state tax collecting authority using your state sales tax number. Sales taxes are based on gross receipts, not business earnings, which means you must pay sales taxes on transactions, even if the business does not make a profit.

There is a state statutory sales tax rate (in California, it is 7.25 percent, the highest in the nation) and additional local-option sales taxes that cities and counties add to the statutory rate (bringing the total in Los Angeles County and City to 8.25 percent).

Sales tax and use tax applies to retail purchases, retail sites, rental, storage, use, or consumption of tangible personal property and certain services associated with tangible goods (e.g., dry cleaning). In some states, certain commodities are exempt from sales tax, such as food and prescription medicine. For retail businesses having operations in several states, sales taxes collected in each state must be paid to the state where the sale is transacted.

*Sole proprietors.* If your business entity is a sole proprietorship, you are the business owner, and you will pay taxes on business income through the usual federal and state individual income tax process. The business pays no separate taxes, except possibly sales taxes. For tax filing purposes, business income is treated as your personal income.

There are three additional steps for sole proprietorships: (1) you will fill out Schedule C of IRS Form 1040, where you report annual business income, loss, and expenses; (2) you will file a quarterly return and pay quarterly estimated income taxes to the IRS and your state (there are penalties for failure to file quarterly); and (3) you will also pay federal self-employment tax.

Self-employment tax is paid annually based on business earnings. It is your contribution to Social Security and Medicare, and it is currently made at the full rate of 15.3 percent of earnings up to $84,900 and 2.9 percent above that amount. Half of this tax is deductible on your individual income tax return. If a sole proprietorship makes less than $400 in profits in its business year, no federal self-employment tax is required and you do not have to file Schedule C with your individual tax return. In some states, like California, you have to file an individual income tax return even if your business earned less than $400.

*Partnerships.* If your business entity is a partnership of any type, the partnership does not pay taxes, the partners do. Partnerships are called "pass-through tax entities," which means that business earnings of the partnership are passed through to the individual partners who report and pay these earnings on their individual income tax returns to the IRS and the state.

There are four special requirements: (1) the partnership must report (not pay) profits and losses by filing an annual "informational return" to the IRS and state; (2) the partnership must file an IRS Schedule K-1 and a similar state return, reporting each partner's share of profits and losses; (3) partners must file quarterly estimated returns to the IRS and state; and (4) partners must pay annual federal self-employment tax on the same basis as a sole proprietorship, discussed above, if earnings exceed $400.

*Limited liability companies.* If your business entity is an LLC, the typical tax reporting and paying procedure is much like a partnership. In rare exceptions, LLC members can choose to have their LLC treated like a corporation for tax purposes; these regulations are so unique they are beyond the scope of this discussion. Almost all LLCs are "pass-through tax entities," and so LLC members' income is reported on their individual income tax returns. If the LLC has only one member, it is treated as a sole proprietorship for tax purposes. If it has two or more members, it is treated like a partnership for tax purposes, requiring the four features of partnership taxing and reporting.

In addition, some states, like California, require LLCs to pay two additional taxes: an annual LLC tax ($800 in California) to be licensed for business in the state as an LLC, and an annual LLC income tax based on a percentage of total income.

*Corporations.* In addition to sales and employee taxes (discussed below), C Corporations pay taxes on corporate earnings at the current federal and state mandated rates. These payments are made quarterly to the IRS and state and are filed with IRS Form 10-Q and a similar state form. Generally speaking, S Corporations are treated like LLCs for tax purposes. Corporate tax structures and requirements are too complex for an overview discussion.

*Employees.* If your business has one or more employees (full- or part-time), you will have to do the following for each employee for every type of business entity:

- Withhold federal income taxes and FICA (Social Security and Medicare) taxes from employees' wages and send these amounts with reports periodically to the IRS.
- Pay the employer's half of Social Security and Medicare tax for each employee, based on his or her gross wages. Employers and employees each currently pay 7.65 percent of the employee's wages up to $84,900 and 1.45 percent of wages above that amount. Employers withhold the employee portion of FICA from paychecks and pay it periodically.
- Annually fill out IRS Form W-2 for each employee, reporting wages and withholding to the employee and to the IRS and state tax authority.
- For independent contractors (not employees), annually fill out IRS Form 1099 to report wages for each independent contractor and provide copies to him/her, as well as to the IRS and state tax authority.
- Pay 100 percent of the federal Unemployment Insurance tax for each employee. The federal tax rate is currently 2.7 percent on the first $8,500 in annual wages paid to an employee. (If you also pay state unemployment tax on the same wages, you are allowed a maximum tax credit of 5.4 percent.) A business is required to pay this tax only if it paid gross wages of $1,500 or more in a calendar year or if it had one or more employees for at least twenty or more weeks (nonconsecutive) in a calendar year.
- Register and pay 100 percent of state Unemployment Insurance tax for each employee. In California, the tax rate for new employers is 3.4 percent of each employee's first $7,000 in wages. After three years, the rate changes depending on the number of claims former employees have filed. The more claims filed, the higher the rate. In recent years, the rate has ranged from 0.7 to 5.4 percent on the first $7,000 of wages paid to employees in a given year.
- Withhold state income taxes from employees' paychecks and file quarterly a wage and withholding report to your state's employment development or tax collecting agency.

## Taxes—City

In addition to these federal and state taxes, businesses must also pay city taxes in the municipality in which they are located or in which they do business. Once again, a typical worst-case situation is examined: the city of Los Angeles. The true worst case is the city of New York, which has more taxes and higher rates than any large city and for that reason is not typical.

There are twenty-four major types of taxes and charges businesses must pay if they are located in or do business in the city of Los Angeles. These major tax types are found in various sections of the city's Business Tax Ordinance and the city's Municipal Code.[22] See appendix 9.2 for a summary of these taxes and charges.

In addition to these two dozen taxes, the city of Los Angeles also has separate tax rates for other types of businesses: amusement parks, auctioneers, baseball and other sporting events, billiards, bowling allies, coin-operated amusement machines, coin-operated phonographs and music machines, Christmas tree stands, circuses, collection agencies, dance halls, money-lenders, motion picture (and TV, radio) producers, sideshows, storage facilities, theaters, transporting persons for hire, and vending machines.[23] For these tax rates, contact the city's Office of Finance.

There are tax exemptions. The Small Business tax exemption in Los Angeles provides that if a business has $5,000 or less in taxable and nontaxable gross receipts in a calendar year, it will qualify for the exemption. The New Business exemption covers the first two years of operation of a new firm; the company will not be required to pay the applicable minimum tax or additional taxes if its gross receipts are less than $500,000 per year. Construction, film production, and certain other businesses are not exempt.

While he was mayor of Los Angeles, Richard Riordan, a wealthy man who owns a number of businesses, moved a couple of them from Los Angeles to the neighboring city of Glendale. He was much criticized for this action by members of the L.A. City Council. His retort was straightforward: his companies could not compete being based in Los Angeles, with its high taxes and heavy regulatory requirements. In his own self-interest he did what he had to do, he stated, until his tax and regulatory reform proposals passed. They did not.

## BUSINESS EXPANSION REGULATIONS

When a business expands through merger, acquisition, joint venture, or other collaborative means, there are state and federal antitrust considerations that need to be taken into account.[24] Even though states have enacted their own anticompetitive laws, most of which are similar to federal law, federal law prevails. Under the Constitution, no state can enact laws that regulate interstate commerce.[25]

Since 1982, when the U.S. Supreme Court struck down antitrust laws in thirty-seven states as violating the interstate commerce clause, state laws have tended to apply only to corporations incorporated in that state, or which have a substantial portion of their business in that state. These recent state laws differ, making compliance challenging.

As a common denominator, current state statutes impose three requirements, all of which are favorable to a corporation's management in the event of a hostile takeover (often by out-of-state companies):

1. *Fair price provisions.* During takeover attempts, these laws require that all shareholders of targeted companies receive the same price, not just those who tendered their shares.
2. *Waiting period provisions.* State laws restrict the sale of acquired companies' assets for a period of time after the merger, making leveraged takeovers less attractive to potential buyers.
3. *Cash-out and control share provisions.* These provisions require a bidder to buy 100 percent of a company's stock at the same price it purchased earlier portions of the company's stock, when the transaction exceeds certain dollar thresholds.

Also, once a bidder purchases a stipulated percent of a company's outstanding stock, the bidder must obtain prior approval from shareholders who hold large blocks of the company's stock before buying more.

Under federal law, states have the authority to sue to block mergers they believe are anticompetitive, even if federal regulators take no action. It is imperative that you obtain specific corporate anti-takeover information in the state where the target company is located.

### Enforcement

During periods of time when federal antitrust regulators are reluctant to undertake aggressive enforcement, states often fill this role. This was the case during much of the 1980s, when states became active, filing antitrust suits under state and federal law. For example, nineteen states joined the Justice Department in the Microsoft antitrust case, and nine declined to accept the settlement. In 1998, twenty-five states threatened to file an antitrust lawsuit against major airlines for predation against small carriers, with the intent of forcing them out of airports in their states.[26]

In 2003, thirty states agreed to coordinate their antitrust investigations of Oracle Corporation's $7.3 billion hostile takeover bid for PeopleSoft, Inc., under the lead of the Texas attorney general and in cooperation with the Justice Department's investigation. These states, under a formal joint prosecution agreement, share information and costs and divide responsibilities in a coordinated manner. What prompted this move is not a lack of federal enforcement, but concern among the states about potentially costly technology transitions for state agencies and universities that may result from the merger, especially considering state budget shortfalls.[27]

By mid-2003 at least twenty states had passed or had pending legislation to establish laws similar to Sarbanes-Oxley. This is creating a potential jumble of contradictory policies for national companies. New state regulations will at the least trigger extra paperwork for companies doing business in places like Kansas, Connecticut, Nevada, and California. Some of these states' rules are tougher than those imposed by the SEC. Oklahoma, for example, filed criminal charges against MCI executives because their attorney general said, "I don't think this company has been punished. I intend to prosecute them criminally."[28]

Enforcement of states' anticompetitive laws is directed by their attorneys general. These individuals have made national headlines in recent years for their prosecution of tobacco companies, for prosecutions of racketeers and organized crime syndicates, and for investigations, prosecutions, and settlements in the securities industry for fraud and other alleged crimes.

Among the most prominent is Eliot Spitzer, attorney general of New York State, who used that state's regulatory authority and federal law to prosecute

STATE AND LOCAL RULES AND REGULATIONS

some of the largest investment banking houses and stockbrokerage firms on Wall Street. Spitzer's success in aggressively prosecuting the likes of Merrill Lynch and Citigroup's Salomon Smith Barney, and the success, among others, of prosecution by the state of Massachusetts of Morgan Stanley for making "false and misleading" statements, have sparked the drafting of new legislation in Congress to reassert federal primacy in securities regulatory enforcement, concentrating these activities in the SEC versus state prosecutors and regulators.[29]

## BUSINESS DIVESTITURE REGULATIONS

The sale or liquidation of a business requires certain actions on the part of its owner(s). These fall into four categories: disclosure, workers' benefits, environmental cleanup, and antitrust. If your company has no employees, has no environmental hazards to clean up, and has only a small market share of your industry, you need not be concerned with anything but disclosure. On the other hand, if the opposite is the case, these regulatory issues must be faced at the time of divestiture. See chapter 8 for a discussion.

Disclosure of the sale or liquidation of privately held companies of all types of business entities is to the state or county agency that issued your firm's business license, Certificate of Partnership, or LLC Articles of Organization. This disclosure ensures the proper termination of these licenses or their transfer and recording to the name of the buyer. There are no federal disclosure requirements for the divestiture of privately held businesses, unless there are unfunded workers' benefits, environmental hazard cleanup, or antitrust impacts from having 20 percent or more of your industry's market share.

Other disclosures vary from county to county and city to city. You or your buyer will likely be required to pay a tax on real property being transferred, and you will likely have to certify that you have no outstanding employee benefit requirements and no hazardous waste contamination to clean up.

Any real property being transferred will require recording by the county recorder, for which the buyer pays the fee. If a business is sold or dissolved before the end of a tax year, any outstanding taxes or other county or municipal charges accrued or owning are due and must be paid on the date of the sale of a business or its termination. Most cities provide a thirty- to sixty-day grace period for payment before taxes are delinquent.

If the liquidation or sale is that of a corporation, there are special rules governing this. See chapter 8 for a brief discussion.

## CONCLUSION

This chapter reviewed state and local rules and regulations governing privately held and publicly traded companies through their life cycle: from start-up, through operations, expansion, and divestiture. Most small and medium-sized businesses primarily face state and local regulatory issues, and so this discussion is critical to their success. Federal regulations normalize state requirements and provide a minimum level of regulations for all states and municipalities.

Many states and municipalities have chosen to go well beyond federal minimums for certain areas of regulation governing particular business activities—such as workers' benefits, health and safety, and environmental emissions. You will need to consult your county's codes to be certain of compliance with your particular situation. All states and municipalities have their own tax and fee requirements.

This concludes part II, which deals with regulatory compliance—federal, state, and local. You are now ready for part III, which discusses how government can assist business.

## APPENDIX 9.1

### County Codes and Ordinances[30]

---

**Subject Headings**

| | |
|---|---|
| Adult Entertainment | Media |
| Affirmative Action | Miscellaneous |
| Agricultural Lands | Noise |
| Animal Wastes | Open Space Preservation |
| Animals | Outdoor Advertising & Signs |
| Bank Shares Tax Replacement | Partnership Agreements |
| Benchmarks and Indications | Partnerships |
| Brownfields Redevelopment | Personnel Management |
| Building Code | Pest Management |
| Campaign Lobbying & Finance | Planning |
| Communities | Public Health & Safety |
| Comprehensive Watershed Planning | Public Participation |
| Coroner Elections | Recycling |
| Curfews & Loitering | Residency Requirements |
| Drug & Alcohol Testing | Restoration |
| Education and Outreach | Sewage/Sewers |
| Elected Officials | Sexual Harassment |
| Environmental Protection | Smoking in Public Places |
| Ethics | Solid Waste |
| Exotic Animals | Storm Water Management |
| Firearms | Sustainability Values |
| Firearms (Shooting Range) | Sustainable Building Practices |
| Fireworks | Sustainable Development |
| Food Safety | Telecommunications |
| Forest & Open Space Preservation | Tobacco Sales to Minors |
| Forest Buffers, Open Space Conserv. | Trespass |
| GIS Mapping/Inventory/Data | Utilities |

| | |
|---|---|
| Graffiti | Wastewater |
| Hazardous Wastes | Water |
| Home-Based Businesses | Water Quality & Source Protection |
| Impact Fees | Wetlands |
| Investment Policies | Wetlands, Watersheds & Drinking |
| Junk & Litter Control | Water Protection |
| Lake Protection & Management | Workplace Violence |
| Lobbying | Zoning & Planning |

## APPENDIX 9.2

**Business Taxes and Charges in the City of Los Angeles[31]**

The following are twenty-four major types of taxes and charges imposed by the city of Los Angeles on businesses based within the city limits or on businesses based outside the city but which do business within the city limits, according to various sections of the Business Tax Ordinance and articles and chapters in the Municipal Code. Some businesses must pay multiple types of taxes and charges.

- *Retail Sales Tax*—selling any goods, wares, or merchandise for any purpose other than resale, for example, drug stores, grocery stores, hardware stores, restaurants, and the like. Tax rate: $110.86 for the first $75,000 or less of gross receipts, plus $1.48 per $1,000 or fraction part thereof in excess of $75,000. [Sec. 21.167]
- *Wholesale Sales Tax*—selling of goods, wares, or merchandise for the purpose of resale, for example, a wholesale grocer selling goods to a grocery store. Tax rate: $118.25 for the first $100,000 or less of gross receipts plus $1.18 per $1,000 or fraction part thereof in excess of $100,000. [Sec. 21.166]
- *Wholesale and Retail Seller's Tax*—businesses that sell both wholesale and retail pay at the rates shown above and must segregate their sales by type. A tax apportionment applies if the seller is located outside the city and sells within it or is located within the city and sells both within and outside it; out-of-state sales are exempt.
- *Miscellaneous Services Tax*—businesses engaged in advertising, aircraft support, apparel subcontracting, bookbinding, check cashing, drapery subcontracting, mailing services, metal plating, music teaching, public relations, shoe shining, temporary help, travel agency, typesetting, and so forth. Tax rate: $49.67 for the first $12,000 or less of gross receipts plus $4.14 per $1,000 or fractional part thereof in excess of $12,000. [Sec. 21.189.1]
- *Professions and Occupations Tax*—service activities that are not classified as "miscellaneous services" are taxed as professions and occupations, for example, attorneys, dentists, barbers, auto mechanics, and so on. Tax rate: $106.43 for the first $18,000 or less of gross receipts plus $5.91 for each additional $1,000 or fractional part thereof in excess of $18,000. A tax apportionment is permitted for gross receipts derived from sales within and outside the city limits. [Sec. 21.190]

- *Health Maintenance Organization Tax*—businesses that undertake to arrange for the provision of health-care services to subscribers or enrollees or pay for or reimburse any part of the cost for those services are taxed as HMOs, for example, Kaiser Permanente, PacifiCare, Blue Cross, and others. Tax rate: $106.43 for the first $18,000 or less of gross receipts plus $5.91 per $1,000 or fractional part thereof in excess of $18,000. [Sec. 21.191]
- *Independent Telemarketing Agency Tax*—persons engaged in the business of marketing services or goods, wares, or merchandise using telecommunications devices at a call center having twenty-five or more persons on behalf of three or more clients continuously, none of which has ownership interest in that person's business. Tax rate: $91.64 for the first $25,000 or less of gross receipts plus $3.67 per year or fractional part thereof in excess of $25,000. [Sec. 21.80]
- *Multimedia Business Tax*—businesses that (1) produce films, disks, tapes, software, or other recording devices whether visual or audio through the integration of two or more media, including computer-generated graphics and video, film, slides, videotapes, audiotapes, and photographs; (2) provide computer programming services related to the above; (3) develop online and Internet services including Web sites. Exemptions: motion picture, television, and radio producers; radio and television broadcasting; and adult entertainment. Tax rate: $118.25 for the first $100,000 or less of gross receipts plus $1.18 per $1,000 or fractional part thereof in excess of $100,000. [Sec. 21.189.4]
- *Child Care Providers Tax*—businesses providing nonmedical care for children under eighteen years of age in need of personal services or supervision on less than a twenty-four-hour basis. Tax rate: $23.65 for the first $20,000 or less of gross receipts plus $1.18 for each additional $1,000 or fractional part thereof in excess of $20,000. [Sec. 21.189.3]
- *Rental of Dwelling Units Tax*—persons engaged in the business of conducting or operating a hotel, rooming house, apartment house, or other dwelling units. Exemption: If gross receipts for all in-city locations are less than $20,000 per calendar year, no tax is due and no Tax Registration Certificate is required. Tax rate: $110.86 for the first $75,000 or less of gross receipts plus $1.48 per $1,000 or fractional part thereof in excess of $75,000. [Sec. 21.99]
- *Rental of Commercial Property Tax*—persons engaged in the business of renting or letting a building to tenants for purposes other than a dwelling. Tax rate: $110.86 for the first $75,000 or less of gross receipts plus $1.48 per $1,000 or fractional part thereof in excess of $75,000. [Sec. 21.98]
- *Contractor Tax*—persons engaged in the business of constructing, altering, repairing, or demolishing any building, highway, road, or other structure. Tax rate: $177.38 for the first $60,000 or less of gross receipts plus $1.18 per $1,000 or fractional part thereof in excess of $60,000. In-city contractors pay an additional $2.96 per $1,000 or fraction of all salaries and fees paid for services rendered in the city in connection with out-of-the-city projects. [Sec. 21.188]
- *Commission Merchant or Broker Tax*—persons who bring buyers and sellers of goods, wares, or merchandise together while serving in the capacity of an independent contractor and not as an employee of another. Example: independent

auction agents. Tax rate: $91.64 for the first $25,000 or less of gross receipts plus $3.67 per $1,000 or fractional part thereof in excess of $25,000. An apportionment rule applies for brokers located outside the city who do business within the city and vice-versa. [Sec. 21.79]

- *Laundry, Cleaning and Dyeing Agent, Collector, Linen Supply, and Shoe Repair Tax*—persons engaged in the business of washing, drying, cleaning, dyeing, or pressing any clothing or similar article of property; letting use of towels, lines, bedding, and so forth, or collecting or delivering such articles; repairing or rebuilding shoes for fee or charge for such services. Tax rate: $110.86 for the first $75,000 or less of gross receipts plus $1.48 per $1,000 or fractional part thereof in excess of $75,000. [Sec. 21.102]
- *Personal Property Rental Tax*—persons engaged in the business of leasing or renting any tangible personal property not taxed elsewhere. An apportionment rule applies for activities within and without the city limits. Examples: autos, trucks, vans, and trailers. Tax rate: $177.38 for the first $60,000 or less of gross receipts plus $2.96 per $1,000 or fractional part thereof in excess of $60,000. [Sec. 21.192]
- *Auto Parks Tax*—businesses that conduct any automobile parking place, storage lot, or storage place where motor vehicles are parked or stored for a fee. Tax rate: $177.38 for the first $30,000 or less of gross receipts plus $5.91 per $1,000 or fractional part thereof in excess of $30,000. [Sec. 21.56]
- *Commercial Tenant's Occupancy Tax*—every tenant renting a building or structure of any kind on land in the city for purposes other than dwelling, sleeping or lodging, or renting space. Tax rate: $1.48 per $1,000 or less of charges attributable to each calendar quarter. [Art. 1.3, Chap. 2 of Municipal Code]
- *Transient Occupancy Tax*—each transient shall pay a tax for the privilege of occupancy in any hotel in the city. Tax rate: a percentage of the rent charged by the hotel. [Art. 1.7, Chap. 2 of Municipal Code]
- *Utility Users' Tax*—all users of telephone, electricity, and gas utilities will pay a tax. Tax rate: a percentage rate on the charges made for such services. Exception: a household where at least one person is sixty-two or older and has total household income of below a minimum determined by Housing and Urban Development (HUD). [Art. 1.1, Chap. 2 of Municipal Code]
- *Sewer Service Charge*—a sewer service charge is imposed for receiving, transporting, pumping, treating, and/or disposing of sewage through the city's sewer system. Charge: a percentage rate for each 100 cubic feet of water supplied to the premises. [Art. 4.1, Chap. 6 of Municipal Code]
- *Sanitation Equipment Charge*—a charge is imposed for the collection and disposal of household refuse for single-family dwelling units and multiple dwelling units for the replacement of sanitation equipment. Charge: made through the electric billing process. [Art. 6.1, Chap. 6 of Municipal Code]
- *Dwelling Unit Construction Tax*—every person who constructs a new dwelling unit, modifies an existing one, converts an apartment to condominium, or develops mobile home park sites shall pay a tax. Tax rate: $200 per dwelling unit. [Art. 1.10, Chap. 2 of Municipal Code]

- *Residential Development Tax*—every person who constructs or causes to be constructed any new dwelling unit in the city in which that person has an equity or title. Tax rate: $300 per dwelling unit. [Art. 1.13, Chap. 2 of Municipal Code]
- *Parking Occupancy Tax*—every person who exercises the privilege of occupying space in any parking facility in the city shall pay a tax. Tax rate: a percentage of the parking fee paid to the parking facility owner. [Art. 1.15, Chap. 2 of Municipal Code]

# — PART III —

# Assistance:
# What Government Can Do
# to Help Business

Part II deals with compliance, the rules government lays down with which business must comply. In this part, we address the other side of the coin: what government can do to assist business. There is a rather long list of the ways government can provide companies with help. A critical point, however, is that while the help is there, waiting for you, you must ask for it. No one from the federal or state government will knock on your door insisting that you accept help. The initiative must come from you.

Therefore, this part identifies the types of assistance the federal and state governments have to offer and coaches you on how to ask for it. One form of help, the federal government's role in protecting intellectual property, has already been discussed in chapter 5.

There are essentially two kinds of federal assistance: financial and marketing. Chapter 10 summarizes financial assistance of various types offered by the federal government through business loans, loan guarantees, insurance, research and development funding, and other financial vehicles.

Chapter 11 discusses the federal government as a market—how to sell directly to it and through prime contractors. Specific Small Business Administration (SBA) programs for selected types of businesses are discussed: preferences for woman- and minority-owned business, small businesses, set-asides, guaranteed bond programs for contractors, and the like. The chapter also covers SBA counseling, and technical and management training programs.

Chapter 12 covers governmental assistance at the state and local levels, addressing such items as enterprise zones, stimulus packages to attract businesses to their areas, and state help in export promotion and lobbying in Washington, D.C., to gain federal business or favorable treatment.

# — CHAPTER 10 —

# Federal Financial Assistance

"Even though I'm from the government, I'm here to help you," is an old joke, satirizing the regulatory side of government. The truth of the matter is that government can be a tremendous help to an entrepreneur or a mature business in any number of ways. In this chapter, federal financial assistance to business is discussed. In chapter 11, marketing and contracting assistance is discussed.

The U.S. government can help business in many ways: grants, loans, loan guarantees, R&D funding, subsidies, equity financing, insurance, counseling and training, and tax deductions. The defense contracting industry enjoys special benefits. These are the topics of this chapter. Some of these federal financial programs were addressed in chapter 3, where they were presented as levers of power of the federal government. Here they will be summarized from a business's perspective as a form of assistance.

## Eligibility as a Small Business

Quite a number of federal financial programs are targeted at small businesses. To determine your eligibility as a "small" business, go to the Small Business Administration's (SBA) Web site and see the Office of Size Standards.[1] Generally speaking, if the business is independently owned and operated, is organized to make a profit, and meets the following criteria, it is eligible for SBA loans or other assistance:[2]

- *Wholesale Industry*—not more than one hundred employees;
- *Manufacturing*—not more than five hundred employees, but in some cases 1,500 employees;
- *Construction*—three years' average annual sales of not less than $16 million and not more than $28.5 million, depending on the specific business type;

- *Special Trade Construction*—average annual receipts not to exceed $115 million;
- *Retail*—three years' average annual sales of not less than $6 million and not more than $24.5 million, depending on business type;
- *Service*—from $4 million to $29 million in annual receipts;
- *Agriculture*—average sales over previous three years from $5 million to $10.5 million.

## FEDERAL GRANTS

The largest type of federal grants is to individuals through Social Security and Medicare payments, the government's largest grant programs by far. There are also federal grants in the form of transfer payments to states and municipalities to underwrite the cost of certain public activities, such as road building, public housing, and operating transit systems. In 2001, these totaled $305 billion.[3] Finally, there are federal grants to nonprofit organizations like universities and policy research institutions (known as think tanks) to undertake research.

Grants to universities and research institutions are provided in return for some service, such as performing research to cure diseases (e.g., National Institutes of Health grants to university medical schools) or undertaking policy analysis of national security issues (e.g., Defense Department grants to RAND Corporation or the Center for Naval Analysis). The deliverable required of the grant's recipient is typically a research report.

In FY-2002, total federal government research funds, including those paid to defense contractors and government laboratories, were $96.9 billion. Of this total, according to a RAND study, federal spending for scientific research at U.S. universities amounted to $21.4 billion, the largest single source, funding projects that improve health, understanding of the natural world, education, national defense, and other areas. Almost half of that amount ($9.6 billion) went to medical schools.[4] Another recent RAND study summarized all federally funded R&D activities related to the fields of construction, building, and housing in fiscal year 1999.[5]

The General Services Administration (GSA) produces a semiannual "Catalog of Federal Domestic Assistance."[6] This is the single, authoritative, government-wide comprehensive source document of federal assistance program (nonforeign) information provided by the executive branch. It is available in hard copy, CD-ROM, diskette, or online at www.grants.gov/. Table 10.1 summarizes the twenty grant categories available.

For additional information on "Business and Commerce," see www.grants.gov/business.

The SBA does not offer grants to start businesses, but it does offer grants for technology development and to expand and enhance organizations that provide small businesses with management, technical, or financial assistance. These grants generally support nonprofit organizations, intermediary lending

Table 10.1
**Federal Government Grant Topics**

| | |
|---|---|
| Agriculture | Health |
| Arts | Housing |
| Business & Commerce | Humanities |
| Consumer Protection | Information & Statistics |
| Disaster Prevention & Relief | Law, Justice & Legal Services |
| Education | Natural Resources |
| Employment, Labor & Training | Regional Development |
| Energy | Science & Technology |
| Environmental Quality | Social Services & Income Security |
| Food & Nutrition | Transportation |

institutions, and state and local governments that in turn assist small businesses.

### Small Business R&D Grants

The SBA has three federal research and development programs that make grants to small businesses specifically for technology development, all of which require that the company meet the following qualifications to be eligible for funding: have five hundred or fewer employees, be at least 51 percent U.S.-owned, and be organized for profit.[7] The three types of grants are:

1. *Federal Small Business Innovation Research (SBIR)*—this program grants approximately $1 billion a year to companies in early stage R&D development activities that show future commercial potential. In 2000, this program was reauthorized for eight years with several enhancements—more small business data rights protection and more balance between small business and the federal government. The enhancements also included the establishment of the FAST Program (described below).[8]
2. *Federal and State Technology Partnership Program (FAST)*—this program encourages research and development by small businesses, technology transfer from universities to small businesses, and the commercialization of technology developed through SBIR funding. All fifty states are eligible to participate in FAST, allowing them to receive grant funding to support the SBIR program in their state. Any individual, organization, or other entity in a state is eligible to participate. FAST permits only one proposal from each state to be submitted to the SBA for funding. Proposals are reviewed against six criteria by a panel drawn from the SBA, the Defense Department, and the National Science Foundation. The cost of the awarded activity is shared between federal and state governments on a sliding scale favoring states that have not received prior SBIR awards.[9]
3. *Federal Small Business Technology Transfer Outreach Program (STTR)*—this program grants $60 million for cooperative R&D projects involving small businesses,

universities, and federally funded research laboratories. The key to winning one
of these grants is having a "cooperative" R&D project, meaning your small business' R&D project is linked to a university's research program or a federally supported lab's program.

Though funding for these programs comes from a variety of federal agencies, the SBA administers them. Under the SBIR program, ten federal agencies with annual external research and development work of more than $100
million must set aside 2.5 percent of their funds for award to small businesses.
Under the STTR program, five agencies with annual external R&D work
exceeding $1 billion must set aside 0.15 percent for collaborative efforts
between small businesses and nonprofit research centers. A state's eligibility
under SBIR/STTR is determined by the total value of contracts awarded to
small business by the state under the SBIR and STTR programs in FY-1995.
The total value of contracts must be less than $5 million for the state to be
eligible.

## FEDERAL LOANS

The federal government offers forty-four different direct loan programs.
These are highly specialized programs targeted at specific industries and
circumstances. They are listed by the federal agency providing them in
appendix 10.1.[10]
Direct loans to business are a declining portion of federal financial assistance because these loans show up on the federal budget as a direct cost,
making indirect loans (such as credits and loan guarantees) and subsidies
more attractive to the government because they are hidden and do not require annual appropriations.

### SBA Loan Programs

Of central importance to the entrepreneur are the Small Business
Administration's three separate financing programs: loans, investment , and
bonding.[11] Investment and bonding programs are discussed in chapter 11
because they relate to federal contracting.
The SBA loan program is structured in such a way that the government
does not compete with private and other lenders, but guarantees loans made
by them to qualifying small businesses.[12] SBA sets the guidelines for the loans,
while others actually make the loans: private or commercial lenders, community development organizations, and microlending institutions. The SBA
backs these loans—all or a portion—with a guarantee that will eliminate some
of the risk to the lender by using federal appropriations received by the administration, provided the loans are structured under SBA requirements. The

SBA loan guarantee transfers the risk of nonpayment up to the amount of the guarantee from the lender to the administration.

Therefore, when a business applies for an SBA loan, it actually applies for a commercial or community development loan structured according to SBA requirements and administration approval. Community development agencies, unlike commercial lenders, can get the government's backing for their loans to finance a portion of the small business' needs. All these loans require collateral, to the extent available, to secure the loan. Personal guarantees of repayment from the principal owners of the business are required, and liens on their personal assets, such as residences, may be required.

There are several SBA loan programs for small businesses, including the Contract Loan Program, Seasonal Line of Credit Program, Builders Line Program, Small Asset-Based Line, and the Standard Asset-Based Line. The three most popular and most often used programs are: the Basic 7(a), the Microloan 7(m), and the CDC 504.[13]

*Basic 7(a) Loan Guaranty Program.* This is the SBA's primary business loan program. It helps qualified small businesses obtain financing when they might not be eligible for business loans directly from commercial lending sources.

This is also the SBA's most flexible loan program because financing is guaranteed for a variety of general business purposes, such as working capital, equipment rental, furniture and fixtures, land and building (purchase, renovation, or construction), leasehold improvements, and debt refinancing. Under special conditions, the term of the loan is up to ten years for working capital and generally up to twenty-five years for fixed assets. The Basic 7(a) loan is available to start-ups and existing small businesses and is delivered through commercial lending institutions. Approximately sixty thousand of these loans are made per year, totaling $12 billion.[14]

The SBA can guarantee as much as 85 percent on loans up to $150,000 and 75 percent on loans more than $150,000. In most cases, the maximum guarantee is $1 million. Both fixed and variable rates are available, pegged at no more than 2.25 percent over the lowest prime rate for loans with maturities less than seven years and up to 2.75 percent for seven years or longer. For loans less than $50,000, rates may be higher. The SBA's fee to the lender, which is passed on to the borrower, to guarantee the loan is based on the loan amount and the maturity, ranging from 0.25 percent of the guaranteed portion of the loan for maturities of less than one year to as much as 3.5 percent on loans over $700,000. The SBA's Office of Field Operations and its district offices administer the program.[15]

*Microloan 7(m) Loan Program.* With this program, the SBA provides short-term loans through nonprofit intermediaries from $500 to $35,000 to small business start-ups or existing businesses. These loans are for businesses needing working capital for the purchase of inventory, supplies, furniture and fixtures, and machinery and equipment for start-up or expansion. Loans can also be used for management or technical assistance. These funds cannot be used to pay existing debts or to purchase real estate. The loans are made by specially designated intermediary lenders (nonprofit organizations with experience in lending and in technology assistance), and the SBA guarantees them. Interest rates are negotiated between the intermediary and the small business. Microloans are available in selected locations in most states.[16] For a list of Microloan lenders by state, see www.sba.gov/sbir/Info/Microloan-Lender-Preferred-Lenders/.

Each year, the SBA provides approximately $100 million in microloans. The default rate is about 15 percent on average (meaning the borrower missed two payments). In the event of default, the SBA pays 75 percent of the outstanding loan amount. The average net loss is approximately 4 percent on these loans, compared with 7 to 8 percent on commercial bank loans.[17]

*Certified Development Company (CDC) 504 Loan Program.* This program provides long-term, fixed-rate financing to existing small businesses requiring fixed asset financing, such as brick and mortar, acquisition of machinery and equipment, and for expansion or modernization. These loans cannot be used for working capital, inventory, consolidating debt, or refinancing.

Attractive features of CDC 504 loans are low down payment (10 percent of total project cost), fixed interest rate for a maximum of twenty years, and below-market interest rates. These are complex loan packages requiring at least 10 percent equity from the borrower, senior- and junior-lien from a CDC, and a maximum SBA debenture of $1 million (up to $1.3 million in some cases). CDCs are private, nonprofit corporations that contribute to the economic development of their communities or regions.[18]

Eligibility requirements for the CDC 504 Program are as follows: business' net worth is under $6 million, net profit after taxes is under $2 million, meets SBA size standards, and is organized for profit. Any type of business qualifies—retail, service, wholesale, or manufacturing.

To summarize these programs, if you are planning to start a company, need a low-interest loan of between $35,000 and $1 million, and have little collateral, the Basic 7(a) Loan Guaranty Program is the one for you. If you have an existing business that needs a significant amount of long-term capital to expand, you need the CDC 504 Loan Program. Microloans are highly specialized loans of very small amounts that are targeted for small business start-ups or existing firms participating in community development programs.

## Small Disadvantaged Businesses

The SBA administers two business assistance programs for small disadvantaged businesses (SDBs): the Small Disadvantaged Business Certification

Program and the 8(a) Business Development Program. The primary focus of these programs is to assist small disadvantaged businesses in winning federal contracts. These programs are discussed in chapter 11.

The SBA offers direct and guaranteed loans for SDBs. "This program," states the Office of Small Disadvantaged Business, "is a procurement tool designed to assist the government in finding firms capable of providing needed services, while at the same time, helping to address the traditional exclusion of minority owned firms from contracting opportunities." The SDB Program's track record is outstanding: there were more than three million minority-owned businesses in the United States in 1997, representing nearly 15 percent of all U.S. businesses.[19]

Only companies that have been certified by the SBA as SDBs are eligible to participate in this program. To be eligible, the applicant must be a small business as defined in SBA rules and be at least 51 percent unconditionally owned and controlled by one or more U.S. citizens who are socially and economically disadvantaged as defined by law. The company must have been in business for at least two years and show clear signs of future potential for success. Once certified as an SDB, the firm is eligible for a three-year period, after which they must reapply for certification.

The SBA appropriation has approximately $9 to $10 million per year set aside for the SDB Program. In 2001, approximately 2,500 certifications were issued. This program provides loans and loan guarantees as well as contracts for certified small disadvantaged businesses.[20]

## Special Assistance Loan Programs

In addition to the loan and loan guarantee programs already mentioned, SBA offers three special assistance loan programs: for disabled veterans, disaster situations, and defense-dependent small firms.[21] The SBA has conducted special studies to understand the particular needs of disabled veterans to enable them to succeed in business. Such individuals are eligible for special consideration under all SBA loan guarantee programs. This includes liaison personnel in each field office, in-depth management counseling and training, and prompt/priority processing of loan applications. The SBA does not provide any special direct loan programs for disabled vets, only loan guarantee programs.

The SBA's Disaster Loan Program offers financial assistance for rebuilding homes and businesses in the aftermath of a disaster. The SBA offers low-interest loans with long-term repayment for such situations, declaring that it "will do everything possible to meet the needs of those otherwise unable to put their lives back together."

Defense Loan and Technical Assistance (DELTA) is a joint SBA-Defense Department program for defense-dependent small businesses adversely affected by defense reductions such as budget cuts, base closures, or contract terminations. The program offers financial and technical assistance to help such companies diversify into commercial product businesses or commercial markets while remaining part of the defense industrial base. The SBA may guarantee 75 percent of a loan up to $1.25 million under the Basic 7(a) Program or up to $1 million under the CDC 504 Program.

### Agricultural Loans

The U.S. Department of Agriculture provides through its Rural Business-Cooperative Service Program (known as the RBS Program) direct loans and guaranteed loans for agricultural purposes.[22] This program assists public, private, or cooperative organizations (for profit or nonprofit), Indian tribes, and individuals in rural areas obtain loans to improve, develop, or finance business in rural communities.

Loans may be used for purchases, modernization, or development of land, buildings, facilities, leasehold improvements, machinery, and supplies. Maximum loan amount is $10 million with a thirty-year repayment term for buildings and land, fifteen years for machinery and equipment, and seven years for working capital. Interest is paid quarterly at the prevailing prime rate. Direct loans may not be used to pay off creditors in excess of the value of the collateral.

The government has obligated $30 million in 2001 and $50 million in 2002 for this program's direct loans; for guaranteed loans, $948 million was obligated in 2001 and $2.9 billion was estimated for 2002. In 2001, a total of forty-six direct loans were made, ranging from $35,000 to $10 million; 559 guaranteed loans were made, ranging in size from $35,000 to $25 million.

## FEDERAL CREDIT SUBSIDIES

In addition to direct and guaranteed loans, the government also subsidizes certain activities by providing credit that has to be repaid, making this a type of loan. Today, the dollar value of these credit subsidies far exceeds the amount of federal loans. Federal credit subsidies are provided for education, agriculture, housing, small business, transportation, and the export-import bank. They are designed to stimulate business activities in certain economic sectors that otherwise would not happen if free market forces alone were at work.

Subsidies are payments from a federal agency to a business that is engaged in the activities for which that agency has oversight. No goods are provided to the government in return. Congress has authorized more than two hundred separate loan subsidy programs,[23] many of which began during the Great Depression, such as the Wagner-Steagall Act that created the Federal

Housing Authority to finance and supervise slum clearance and the construction of low-cost housing.

Today, Fannie Mae, Freddie Mac, and the Department of Veterans Affairs all provide subsidized housing loans. Other credit subsidies are provided by the SBA through their loan programs, by the Export-Import Bank through their subsidized loans to stimulate exports, and by the Interior Department through their rural electrification loans to rural-based businesses.

One of the largest categories of loan subsidies is for agriculture.[24] These subsidies began with the Agricultural Adjustment Act of 1933, which was declared unconstitutional by the Supreme Court in 1936, but was subsequently reenacted by Congress in 1938. Under this act, whose basic feature is federal intervention in domestic agriculture to adjust supply and prices, the U.S. Department of Agriculture pays farmers to limit their crops and provides commodity loans on surplus crops.

This is a type of subsidy to farm businesses in the form of price supports, that is, an amount of money that represents the difference between the cost of producing the crop and the crop's current market price. American farms produce a number of crops (e.g., cane sugar) at costs far higher than foreign competitors; to sell these products at the prevailing U.S. market price requires a subsidy to offset those higher domestic costs.

These federal loan subsidies have to be repaid, but this cost is also subsidized: the interest rate is below prevailing commercial rates, collateral requirements are lower than commercial requirements, maturities are longer, the government pays the administrative expenses, and if the loan defaults, the government absorbs the cost.

Another "subsidy" benefits the shipbuilding industry by prohibiting U.S. Navy vessels from being built overseas and by barring the navy from using foreign-owned ships. Similarly, the "Buy-American Act" confers preferences to domestic producers in government procurements. The Small Business Act provides an indirect subsidy to small businesses by requiring that a "fair" portion of government contracts be set aside for small business.

## EQUITY FINANCING

Venture capitalists may offer small and growing businesses equity financing. This is different from debt financing, where the business borrows money from a lender and must repay it, with the lender taking no ownership in the business. In equity financing, the business receives an investment of capital from an outsider who takes a percent of ownership of the business in return for the investment. This is not a loan but an investment and does not have to be repaid, but the investor will share the profits.

Venture capitalists (known as VCs) are the individuals or firms that make these investments, usually in return for approximately 25–30 percent ownership (equity) of the company. They rarely take more than a minority interest in the firm because they want the entrepreneur owner/operator to have the largest stake in the company as an incentive to perform well. Investments by "angels" are different; these are wealthy individuals who make smaller equity investments than VCs for shorter periods of time.

If your firm is ineligible for a commercial loan or an SBA loan of any type, equity financing may be your only avenue to raising the capital needed to launch or expand the business. To approve a commercial loan, commercial banks typically want to see three years of profitable performance of the business, which means that the company will have been in business for at least four or five years. They also want collateral for their loan, and if the business has few fixed assets, it may not be creditworthy.

SBA loan or guaranteed loan requirements are less demanding, but they still require an outstanding business plan and projected earnings within the first couple of years. Barring your meeting these criteria, you may have no choice but to sell a piece of the business to a VC to obtain the needed capital.[25]

The SBA can be very helpful in finding equity financing.[26] The administration has rosters of Small Business Investment Companies (SBICs); these are venture capital companies that make most of their equity investments through the SBIC program.[27] The SBA also has a New Markets Venture Capital Program that provides equity financing.[28] Such companies as Apple Computer and Federal Express had SBIC financing at critical stages of their growth.

Two success stories cited by the SBA are Staples and Outback Steakhouse.[29] Staples, the office supply retail giant, started with one store in Brighton, Massachusetts. In 1987, the company obtained $500,000 in equity financing through the SBA's SBIC Program, and its growth took off. By 2001, Staples had more than 1,500 stores with sales of $11.6 billion and 58,000 employees. Similarly, Outback Steakhouse started in 1990 with $2 million in sales. Soon after, it obtained equity financing through the SBIC Program to expand its upscale casual dining operations, and it has continued to grow at an exponential rate. A decade later, Outback had $1.6 billion in sales and 38,000 employees.

## INTERNATIONAL FINANCING AND INSURANCE

The SBA and the Overseas Private Investment Corporation (OPIC) both offer a variety of financing and, in OPIC's case, insurance programs for American companies doing business abroad.

### SBA Programs

The SBA has four programs that provide financing to small companies engaged in international business or that are adversely affected by competition from imports.[30] First is the International Trade Loan Program that guarantees up to $1.25 million for facility and equipment financing, upgrades, or working capital for business development and foreign market expansion.

Second is the Export Working Capital Program that provides pre- and postexport working capital for export sales. This could be a line of credit or structured loan, depending on the individual transaction. Loans have twelve-month or shorter maturities, 90 percent SBA guarantee, and a maximum amount of $1 million.

Third, the SBA has Export Express, an expedited loan program where the administration guarantees 85 percent of the loan up to $150,000 for use in a single export transaction to secure a letter of credit, a revolving line of credit, or for working capital to finance export development activities such as attending a foreign trade show.

Finally, the SBA also offers the Pre-Qualification Loan Program, which is a special version of the Basic 7(a) Loan Guaranty Program, specifically designed to promote exports. This "pre-qual" program uses intermediaries to assist prospective borrowers in developing viable loan application packages to secure a 7(a) loan. This program is open to veteran-, women-, and minority-owned businesses. The maximum loan is $250,000.

## OPIC Programs

If you are thinking of expanding your business internationally or your business already has international activities, you will want to look into an independent agency of the U.S. government called the Overseas Private Investment Corporation (OPIC). OPIC provides both insurance and financing for U.S. firms engaged in international business.

This agency was established in 1971, to promote U.S. exports and thereby to expand U.S. employment. Since that time, it has generated more than 280,000 U.S. jobs by stimulating $65 billion in exports. OPIC's operations are on a self-sustaining basis because it charges market-based fees for its services. In 2003, it had over $4 billion in reserves.

In 2003, OPIC added a Small Business Department. This unit, which focuses on small and medium-size businesses, administers the agency's direct loan program. The department includes the Small Business Center, which provides direct loans for businesses with less than $35 million in annual revenue, and the Small and Medium Enterprise Department, which provides direct loans for businesses with annual revenue up to $250 million. OPIC also has established a partnership with Worldbusiness Capital, a private company that financially supports small businesses as they expand overseas.[31]

OPIC's financing program includes both direct loans and loan guarantees. Loan terms are typically from three to fifteen years. OPIC's staff analyzes the applicant's business plan to assure acceptability under the agency's lending guidelines. If the financing is for a particular foreign project, the criteria to be met include the following: the project must be consistent with U.S. foreign policy objectives of helping to economically develop the country where the project is located, the local government must have a good human rights record, there must be no loss of U.S. jobs resulting from the project, and the project must conform to U.S. standards of worker health and safety.

OPIC's insurance programs are of vital importance to companies that have foreign-based assets that could be vulnerable to political, social, and economic risk—and to terrorism. Specifically, OPIC will insure a U.S.-based company's foreign operations against the risk of expropriation, civil war and other civil unrest, terrorism, local currency becoming nonconvertible, and "business income" loss, an indemnification against loss of cash flow or repatriation of profits or dividends. OPIC does not normally insure against devaluation of local currency, but has done so on occasion. Over the years, OPIC has paid more than 90 percent of insurance claims filed.[32]

## FINANCIAL COUNSELING AND TRAINING

The SBA offers numerous financial counseling and training services to small business. There are programs available at local SBA offices, Small Business Development Centers, and Web sites that help you apply for a loan, explain credit, and discuss factors that will help you obtain a loan.

### Loan Application Procedure

Applying for an SBA loan is quite similar to applying to a bank for credit, and the SBA has a coaching program to assist you with the process.[33] Your loan application should always have a short cover letter briefly explaining who you are, what your business is about, the amount and purpose of the loan, and your plans for repayment.

The application should provide a detailed description of your business:

- Date of information and application
- Type of organization or business form
- Location of the business
- Product or service
- Brief history of the business
- Proposed future operations
- Competition
- Customers
- Suppliers

The SBA will also want to review your management team. You should provide a resume for yourself and any other key executives showing your experience and track record in this industry. Include a personal financial statement for each executive/owner. Clearly show where your 20 percent equity will come from (savings, selling stock, etc.). Enclose your and other owners' federal income tax returns for the past year or two.

Provide a business plan that shows how the loan will be repaid, including repayment sources, amounts, schedules, budgets, and other appropriate information. Provide a pro forma (a projected income statement) showing sources of all funds to be used in the business and the proposed uses of both equity and borrowed funds. A projection of future revenue and expenses must be included, including cash flow. You must show that the business can achieve positive cash flow within a reasonable period of time. Explain the assumptions you are using and support your projected figures with data.

## Loans for Existing Businesses

For existing businesses seeking funds to expand, provide a current financial statement showing profit, loss, assets, and cash flow. Provide information on accounts payable and accounts receivable and a schedule of term debt. Include a current balance sheet.

Other items should be included if they apply, such as a copy of a lease, franchise agreement, purchase agreement, Articles of Incorporation, product plans and specifications, copies of licenses, letters of reference, letters of intent, contracts, and partnership agreement. Identify your collateral clearly—real property, equipment, or other tangible assets. Some lenders may require securing the loan with a pledge of the collateral, in the event of default. The lender will assess your ability and capacity to repay the loan using every source of information you provide.

The lender will also assess your creditworthiness using information you do not provide.[34] This includes looking at your personal credit rating from one of the major credit-reporting companies: Equifax, TransUnion, Experian, and the like. The lender may also separately appraise your collateral. For example, if you have listed your personal home as collateral, the lender may have an appraiser assess its current market value, less your current mortgage balance.

Other types of collateral are discounted by lenders; for example, trucks and heavy equipment values are assessed at current depreciated value × .50. The same is true of furniture and fixtures. Cars, office equipment, perishable inventory, jewelry, mutual funds, and IRAs are valued at zero—so do not include these. On the other hand, Certificates of Deposit are valued at 100 percent. Choose your collateral wisely.

## DEFENSE CONTRACTING

The defense contracting industry is in a special category and is unlike any other industry because it receives a host of benefits from the federal government for doing its work. Not only does the government pay on time, its checks never bounce. Being a prime contractor or a subcontractor to the Defense Department has very substantial benefits to a business of any size.[35]

To facilitate financing, defense contractors receive progress payments from the government. These periodic payments, usually quarterly, fund the bulk of the work in process that the company is performing under contract for the Defense Department. This minimizes or eliminates the need for the company to undertake borrowing at commercial rates, with the added costs that would represent.

Defense contractors selling equipment to allied or friendly nations through the Pentagon's Foreign Military Sales (FMS) Program not only receive progress payments, but also their customer countries can receive FMS credits to help finance their purchase of the company's products. FMS contracts reduce risk to the manufacturer because the company sells to the U.S. government, which then sells to the foreign government.

In the area of research and development, defense contractors bid for and, if successful, win R&D contracts to develop new technologies and new products, putting them on the leading edge of technology. Often, these R&D activities produce crossover products or dual-use products that have both military and civilian use. The Boeing 707, the first American commercial jet airliner, is the classic example; the basic R&D for that aircraft was funded by the U.S. Air Force to develop the KC-135 airborne tanker. Boeing modified that military design to produce the 707. Even R&D directly paid for by defense contractors can be deducted. Independently funded R&D (known as IRAD) is allowable as a tax deduction.

Once a contractor's equipment is purchased by the military, the government has an incentive to help sell that same equipment (minus some classified items that may be on board) to allied nations, thus further benefiting the contractor. There are two reasons for promoting export sales: (1) having the same equipment in allied hands facilitates interoperability of the equipment on the battlefield, eases logistical and supply problems, and makes it easier to coordinate tactics; and (2) sale of the same equipment reduces the per-unit cost of the item to our government because the contractor benefits from economies of scale of larger and longer production runs. Approximately half of all military jet fighters produced in the United States since the mid-1970s have been sold to allied nations.

## TAXES

Through its fiscal policy, the federal government powerfully influences business decisions. This is especially true with respect to tax policy. Very often business leaders give decisive weight to the "tax consequences" of a business decision—either positive or negative.

Positive tax impacts on business can occur in many ways: by promoting the purchase of machinery and equipment to take advantage of accelerated depreciation schedules, by establishing defined pension programs to take a "before tax" deduction on employer contributions, by investing in research and development activities to claim an R&D tax credit, and so forth.[36]

Tax incentives impact three important business activities:

1. *Research and Development*—expensing investments in new technologies;
2. *Pollution Control Equipment*—issuing tax-exempt bonds to install equipment; and
3. *Investments*—highly favorable depreciation schedules.

Tax incentives favorably impact several specific industries:

- *Pharmaceuticals*—tax credit for orphan drug research;
- *Mining*—accelerated write-off of costs;
- *Shipping*—income tax deferral;
- *Energy*—tax incentives for new energy sources;
- *Export*—income tax deferral; and
- *Small Business*—lower tax rates on corporate income.

Table 10.2 summarizes various types of tax benefits to business arising from a variety of federal tax incentive programs for fiscal year 2003. These "savings" to business also represent "costs" to the U.S. Treasury of lost (or deferred) tax revenue.[37]

These federal tax benefits to business of nearly $49 billion were developed for important policy reasons, such as building hospitals, stimulating exports, developing new technologies, starting housing developments, employing low-skill workers, and the like. These tax breaks were also developed as a result of hard bargaining and lobbying by special interests to achieve their own ends. The latter reason and how they did it are discussed in chapter 13.

## CONCLUSION

The federal government has numerous ways and means to stimulate economic activity and growth within the country by helping entrepreneurs achieve their dreams and by helping established businesses grow and prosper.

The most powerful incentives the government has are financial: federal grants, low-interest loans, guaranteed loans, credits, and other forms of financial aid to American business. Some of these programs are highly specialized, such as those to Small Disadvantaged Business and to exporters, and others are more widely focused, such as those to small businesses of any kind and type.

**Table 10.2**
**Benefits to Business of Federal Tax Incentives, Fiscal Year 2003, $ in Billions**

| Type of Tax Benefit | Amount ($) |
| --- | --- |
| Science and Technology | |
| Expensing of research and experimentation | 2.0 |
| Credit for increasing research | 2.9 |
| Energy | |
| Various incentive programs | 0.9 |
| Natural Resources and Environment | |
| Special treatment of mining and timber | 0.6 |
| Special treatment of other natural resources | 0.3 |
| Commerce and Housing | |
| Financial and insurance institution benefits | 3.0 |
| Housing investment incentives | 3.9 |
| Machinery and equipment investment incentives | 2.8 |
| Lower tax rate on smaller companies | 6.5 |
| Credit for low-skill-level jobs | 0.2 |
| Special ESOP rules | 1.0 |
| Tax credit for business conducted in U.S. overseas possessions | 2.5 |
| Miscellaneous investment incentives | 0.8 |
| Overseas Operations | |
| Deferral of overseas income | 7.4 |
| Exclusion of foreign sales income | 4.8 |
| Special treatment of inventories | 1.4 |
| Exclusion of interest | |
| On industrial development bonds | 7.2 |
| On bonds for education | 0.3 |
| On bonds for hospitals | 0.3 |
| **Total** | **48.8** |

The track record of the Small Business Administration has been one of great success. The SBA's mentoring, counseling, and training programs—are also reviewed. Nationally, the SBA has helped stimulate small business start-ups (574,000 in 2001) and employment (55.7 million), with small business being responsible for at least two-thirds of all net new jobs in 2002. Small business is the nation's largest employer with 50.2 percent of all people employed and paying taxes. Small business proprietors' income in 2001 was $745 billion.[38]

As this chapter shows, Uncle Sam is a wonderful lender, offering cut-rate financing through direct and guaranteed loans to small businesses of all types, hoping these—like Staples, Outback Steakhouse, Federal Express, Apple

Computer, and a host of others that once had SBA financing—will become big businesses one day, paying even more taxes and employing even more taxpayers.

Chapter 11 discusses the federal government as a market: how to sell to it, contract with it, and how it can help the entrepreneur grow his/her business.

## APPENDIX 10.1

Types of Federal Direct Loans by Agency and by Catalog of Federal Domestic Assistance (CFDA)[39]

| CFDA No. | Agency | Loan Program Title |
|---|---|---|
| 11.415 | NOAA | Fisheries Finance Program |
| 59.046 | SBA | Microloan Demonstration Program |
| 59.049 | SBA | Office of Small Disadvantaged Business Certification and Eligibility |
| 20.905 | DOT | Disadvantaged Business Enterprises—Short Term Lending Program |
| 44.002 | NCUA | Community Development Revolving Loan Program for Credit Unions |
| 59.002 | SBA | Economic Injury Disaster Loans |
| 59.008 | SBA | Physical Disaster Loans |
| 59.011 | SBA | Small Business Investment Companies |
| 64.103 | VBA | Life Insurance for Veterans |
| 64.116 | VBA | Vocational Rehabilitation for Disabled Veterans |
| 64.118 | VBA | Veterans Housing—Direct Loans for Certain Disabled Veterans |
| 64.126 | VBA | Native American Veteran Direct Loan Program |
| 10.051 | FSA | Commodity Loans and Loan Deficiency Payments |
| 10.056 | FSA | Farm Storage Facility Loans |
| 10.075 | FSA | Special Apple Program |
| 10.076 | FSA | Emergency Loan for Seed Producers |
| 10.404 | FSA | Emergency Loans |
| 10.406 | FSA | Farm Operating Loans |
| 10.407 | FSA | Farm Ownership Loans |
| 10.410 | RHS | Very Low- to Moderate-Income Housing Loans |
| 10.411 | RHS | Rural Housing Site Loans and Self-Help Housing Land Development Loans |
| 10.415 | RHS | Rural Rental Housing Loans |
| 10.417 | RHS | Very Low-Income Housing Repair Loans and Grants |
| 10.421 | FSA | Indian Tribes and Tribal Corporation Loans |
| 10.444 | RHS | Direct Housing—Natural Disaster Loans and Grants |
| 10.445 | RHS | Direct Housing—Natural Disaster |
| 10.449 | FSA | Boll Weevil Eradication Loan Program |

| CFDA No. | Agency | Loan Program Title |
|---|---|---|
| 10.760 | RUS | Water and Waste Disposal Systems for Rural Communities |
| 10.766 | RHS | Community Facilities Loans and Grants |
| 10.767 | RBS | Intermediary Relending Program |
| 10.768 | RBS | Business and Industry Loans |
| 10.770 | RUS | Water and Waste Disposal Loans and Grants (Sec. 306C) |
| 10.774 | NSIIC | National Sheep Industry Improvement Center |
| 10.850 | RUS | Rural Electrification Loans and Loan Guarantees |
| 10.851 | RUS | Rural Telephone Loans and Loan Guarantees |
| 10.852 | RUS | Rural Telephone Loan Bank |
| 10.854 | RBS | Rural Economic Development Loans and Grants |
| 10.855 | RUS | Distance Learning and Telemedicine Loans and Grants |
| 10.858 | RUS | RUS Denali Commission Grants and Loans |
| 10.859 | RUS | Assistance to High Energy Cost—Rural Communities |
| 83.537 | FEMA | Community Disaster Loans |
| 93.342 | HRSA | Health Professions Student Loans |
| 93.364 | HRSA | Nursing Student Loans |
| 84.268 | ED | Federal Direct Student Loans |

**Glossary of Agency Names**

| | |
|---|---|
| DOT | Department of Transportation |
| ED | Department of Education |
| HRSA | Health Resources & Services Administration, HHS Department |
| FEMA | Federal Emergency Management Administration |
| FSA | Farm Service Agency, Agriculture Department |
| NCUA | National Credit Union Administration |
| NOAA | National Oceanographic and Atmospheric Administration |
| NSIIC | National Sheep Industry Improvement Center |
| SBA | Small Business Administration |
| RBS | Rural Business-Cooperative Service, Agriculture Department |
| RHS | Rural Housing Service, Agriculture Department |
| RUS | Rural Utilities Service, Agriculture Department |
| VBA | Veterans Benefits Administration, Veterans Affairs Department |

— CHAPTER 11 —

# Federal Marketing and Contracting Assitance

The federal government is the largest market in the world. It not only purchases more goods and services than anyone else, it also assists businesses that wish to sell directly to it and, through its contracting procedures, assists certain types of businesses to sell to its prime contractors.

This chapter discusses various types of assistance provided by the Small Business Administration (SBA) other than financial (which is reviewed in chapter 10): legal; business development; federal contracting; surety bond guarantees; and specific programs to help small, woman-owned, and minority-owned businesses to succeed as federal contractors. Also discussed are the SBA's various training and counseling programs.

## LEGAL ASSISTANCE

The SBA's Internet tool, www.BusinessLaw.gov, is designed to assist you with legal issues affecting your business such as choosing the right type of business entity, advising as to local, state, and federal regulations, preparing and inspecting contracts, obtaining financing, and offering advice on selected business problems. This is an easy-to-read, easy-to-use online tool that will help you start up a business or better operate an existing one. The Web site consolidates and indexes links to sources of information on thirty-nine topics ranging from basic ones, like licenses and permits, to highly specialized ones, like e-commerce and exporting.

There is, of course, no substitute for having your own attorney. The SBA recommends contacting your state or county bar association for referrals to individual lawyers whose practices focus on business issues, specifically the type of business you are engaged in. For example, if you are an exporter, your business will need an attorney specializing in international business; if you need to obtain a patent, you will require a patent lawyer.

A business lawyer will be an invaluable counselor and helper on a variety of issues, from filing papers to establish a partnership or corporation, to reviewing and possibly litigating contracts, to mergers and acquisitions. If you are short on funds, most counties have a Public Counsel; this is a nonprofit law firm that provides low-cost and, in some cases, no-cost assistance to small businesses having legal problems.

## MARKETING ASSISTANCE

The SBA serves as the federal government's focal point for providing marketing assistance for small disadvantaged firms. There are two programs: the 8(a) Program and the Small Disadvantaged Certification Program.[1] The 8(a) Program offers a broad range of assistance, including federal contracting assistance, while the certification program pertains only to federal procurement. Companies that are 8(a) qualified are automatically eligible for the certification program.

### The SBA's 8(a) Program

The most well-known element of the SBA's Minority Enterprise Development Program is the 8(a) Program, named from Section 8(a) of the Small Business Act. This is a business development program that provides its participants access to a variety of marketing services, including the opportunity to receive federal contracts on a sole-source or limited-competition basis.[2]

SBA's 8(a) Business Development Program has helped thousands of socially and economically disadvantaged entrepreneurs gain access to the U.S. business mainstream, which for many of them began as federal government contractors or subcontractors. In 2001, more than 6,400 firms participated in the 8(a) Program and were awarded $6.4 billion in federal contracts. The 8(a) Program has recently been improved, making it easier for non-minority firms to participate by proving they are socially disadvantaged and by adding the Mentor-Protégé Program to help start-up 8(a) firms learn the ropes from experienced businesspeople. The program is divided into two phases over nine years: a four-year development stage and a five-year transition stage.

*Major benefits.* There are five major benefits of the program, as follows:

1. Participants can receive sole-source federal contracts up to $3 million for goods and services and up to $5 million for manufacturing. The SBA encourages 8(a) companies to develop their competitive skills by competing for non–sole-source contracts while getting on their feet under the program.

2. Federal acquisition policies encourage U.S. agencies to award a certain percentage of their contracts to Small Disadvantaged Businesses (SDBs). The SBA has signed Memoranda of Understanding with twenty-five federal agencies allowing them to contract directly with 8(a) firms.
3. Companies qualifying for 8(a) are now permitted to form joint ventures and teams to bid on federal contracts, thus enhancing the ability of these firms to compete for and perform on larger prime contacts. The program also allows 8(a) firms to combine two or more contracts together to overcome the effects of contract bundling.
4. The SBA offers specialized business training, counseling, and marketing assistance, as well as high-level executive development opportunities.
5. These companies may also be eligible to obtain access to surplus government property and supplies, SBA-guaranteed loans, and bonding assistance.

There are numerous SBA controls and limits on the program. No single 8(a) company can be awarded more than $100 million of sole-source contracts or five times the value of its primary standard industrial classification (SIC) code. The SBA district offices monitor and measure each firm's progress through annual reviews, business planning, and systematic evaluations.

*Eligibility.* Eligibility requirements for the 8(a) Program are many. The firm must be owned and controlled by a socially and economically disadvantaged individual. Certain groups of business owners, under the SBA Act, are presumed to qualify: African American, Hispanic American, Asian/Pacific American, and Subcontinent Asian American. Other individuals can qualify for the program if they show through a "preponderance of the evidence" that they are disadvantaged because of race, ethnicity, gender, physical handicap, or they reside in an environment isolated from the mainstream of American society.

To meet the economic qualification of being disadvantaged, individuals must have a net worth of less than $250,000, excluding the value of the business and personal residence. Applicants must also meet the size standard for the type of small business they are in (see the section on eligibility in chapter 10), have been in business for at least two years, display reasonable success potential, and display good character. The two-year requirement can be waived, but the other requirements may not be waived while you are a participant in the program.

## The SBA's SDB Certification Program

The SBA's Small Disadvantaged Business Program (SDB), discussed in chapter 10, also contains the SDB Certification Program,[3] which pertains only to federal procurements. The SBA certifies SDBs to make them eligible for special bidding benefits on federal contracts. Specifically, valuation credits are available to prime contractors to boost subcontracting opportunities for certified SDBs. Firms that qualify for the 8(a) Program are automatically qualified for SDB certification.

There are two major benefits of the SDB Certification Program: (1) once certified, an SDB is eligible for price evaluation adjustments up to 10 percent when bidding on federal contracts in certain industries, and (2) the program provides evaluation credits to prime contractors who achieve SDB subcontracting targets. The program is intended to help federal agencies achieve the government-wide goal of 5 percent SDB participation in federal prime contracting.

When a business is certified, it is added to an online registry of SDB-certified firms that the SBA maintains in PRO-Net (discussed below). Certified companies remain on the register for three years. Contracting officers and large prime contractors can then search the online registry for potential SDB-certified suppliers. Eligibility requirements for SDB certification are the same as for the 8(a) Program.[4]

## GOVERNMENT CONTRACTING ASSISTANCE

The federal government bought $375 billion of all types of products and services in fiscal year 2000, both civil and military. Almost all of these procurements were from the private sector. The few exceptions were defense items made in the remaining federal arsenals, bases, and navy yards; coins made in the two federal mints and currency printed by the Treasury's Bureau of Engraving and Printing; and items made by prisoners in federal penitentiaries. Virtually everything else was purchased from businesses.

The list of civilian (i.e., nondefense) items procured by the government each year is quite long. Indeed, it fills a telephone book–size publication of the General Services Administration's Federal Supply Service and includes everything from autos to zinc. See appendix 11.1 for a small sample of federal civilian procurement items.

Once your company becomes a federal contractor, and particularly after it achieves $50,000 or more in sales to the government, it is required to comply with a long list of mandated activities, such as using fair employment practices, having an affirmative action program, paying "prevailing" wages, giving preference in procurements to American-made products, using recycled materials, and so on. For example, the Environmental Protection Agency's requirements for federal contractors are so extensive they are listed in its publication, "Comprehensive Procurement Guidelines"; these include regulations on carpets, cement, concrete, insulation, and the like. These federal procurement regulations were discussed in earlier chapters.

The SBA offers a number of programs to assist small businesses in becoming contractors to the federal government.[5] The SBA works closely with all federal departments and agencies, and with leading large businesses that are already federal prime contractors, to ensure that small businesses obtain a fair share of government sales/leases, prime contracts, and sub-contracts.

What has been their track record? In 2002, federal agencies awarded 22.6 percent of their $235 billion of contracts to small companies, just under the 23 percent goal set by law. The shortfall amounted to $900 million. The government awarded 4.4 percent of its contracts to disadvantaged businesses and 2.9 percent to women-owned businesses; the goal for both was 5 percent. The government feel far short of meeting its target of awarding 3 percent of all federal contracts to small businesses owned by disabled veterans. About 55 percent of the SBA's own contracts went to small businesses that year.[6]

## Prime Contracts Program

The SBA, through its Prime Contracts Program, helps small business increase its share of government contracts. Specifically, the program advocates the breakout of items to be purchased from single large procurement packages to a number of smaller packages to enable small business to bid on them through full and open competition.

SBA procurement center representatives (PCRs) are the individuals who work to expand contracting opportunities for small businesses in this manner. These individuals review contracting actions at major federal procurement centers, study their subcontracting plans, recommend contracting sources, and provide counseling.

There are two types of PCRs: traditional and breakout. Traditional PCRs work to increase the number of procurements set aside for small business. Breakout PCRs work to remove components or spare parts from sole-source procurements to make a number of new procurements through open competition, thus generating opportunities for small businesses to bid and to generate government savings through lower bids, which is typically the result. To learn more about PCRs and their activities, including a list of PCRs and buying installations nationwide, see www.sba.gov/gc.

## Subcontracting Assistance Program

The SBA's Subcontracting Assistance Program promotes maximum use of small businesses by the country's large prime contractors. The SBA's Commercial Market Representatives visit large businesses to identify and expand subcontracting opportunities for small firms.

Large prime contractors well understand the government's goal of achieving percentage targets for small businesses and SDBs in subcontracting. To ensure that these large primes comply with their small business subcontracting requirements, the commercial market reps conduct program reviews and counsel small businesses on how to market their products and services to these large primes.

## Size Determination Program

The SBA's Size Determination Program ensures that only small firms receive contracts and other benefits that are set aside exclusively for small business. When a company claims it is "small," it can be challenged, and the SBA size specialists make the determination that the company does or does not meet established SBA size standards. Size determinations may be made when requested in connection with other federal contracting programs.

## Certificate of Competency Program

This program allows a small business to appeal a contracting officer's determination that it is unable to fulfill the requirements of a specific government contract on which it is the apparent low bidder. Pursuant to this appeal, SBA industrial and financial specialists conduct a detailed review of the firm's capabilities to perform on the contract. If the business demonstrates the ability to perform, the SBA issues a Certificate of Competency to the contracting officer requiring the award of that contract to the small business.

## SUB-Net

There is no better example of how the Internet has changed marketing than the SBA's SUB-Net. SUB-Net is the Web site where federal prime contractors post their subcontracting needs. These solicitations become marketing opportunities for small business. In the past, small businesses had to use a shotgun approach to find bidding opportunities among prime contractors for products and services they provided in their areas of expertise.

Now, with SUB-Net, small businesses simply log onto this site and scroll down until they find solicitations appropriate to them and then make their bid for the work. This is a highly focused and sophisticated communication tool for primes to find appropriate subs and for subs to find marketing opportunities at primes.

Items posted by prime contractors on SUB-Net may not be exclusively solicitations for immediate subcontracting opportunities. These items may include announcements by primes who are seeking teaming partners or subcontractors for future contracts. Federal agencies, universities, nonprofit organizations, and even foreign governments use SUB-Net to read solicitations and notices posted by primes to compete for these opportunities.

## PRO-Net

This SBA Web site (www.pro-net.sba.gov/) is an electronic gateway for procurement information for small business, a search engine for contracting officers, a marketing tool for small business, and a link to procurement opportunities and other important information. As the SBA says, "it is designed to be a 'virtual' one-stop-procurement-shop."[7]

As a search engine, PRO-Net is an Internet database of information on more than 212,000 small, disadvantaged, 8(a), HUBZone (discussed later), and women-owned businesses. PRO-Net is open to and free for all small companies seeking federal, state, and private contracts, as well as to prime and other contractors seeking small business contractors, subcontractors and/ or partnership opportunities. Businesses are profiled on this search engine by NAIC and SIC codes, keywords, location, quality certifications, business type, ownership race and gender, EDI capability, and so on.

As a marketing tool, PRO-Net is an invaluable way for small businesses to market their capabilities to a wide audience. Each company listed on PRO-Net has placed its own profile in this database. These profiles are structured like executive summaries of the business and include data regarding the company's experience, capabilities, expertise, and management. These data are culled from the SBA's files, other databases, and additional business and marketing information on individual firms. It is the responsibility of each listed business to update its profile and keep the information current.

Profiles posted on PRO-Net give small businesses a first-class opportunity to market themselves to prime contractors and to seek teaming partners with other small businesses. Companies with their own Internet home pages can include a link in the profile to their own Web sites, making this a highly user-friendly marketing tool.

As a link to procurement opportunities, PRO-Net is an electronic gateway. It is linked to *Commerce Business Daily*, the federal government's "classified ad" for procurements, as well as to federal agencies' home pages and other sources of procurement opportunities. All small businesses desiring to do business with the federal government should contact the SBA and enter their profile on PRO-Net.

## HUBZone

The SBA's HUBZone Empowerment Contracting Program, begun in 1997, provides federal contracting opportunities for qualified small businesses located in distressed areas to revitalize these areas by creating jobs and attracting investment.[8] This program encourages economic development in historically underutilized business zones—hence the name—by giving federal procurement preferences for firms located in these areas.

To be eligible for the HUBZone Program, a small business must meet three criteria: be located in a "historically underutilized business zone," be owned and controlled by one or more U.S. citizens, and have at least 35 percent of its employees reside in the HUBZone.

*Definition.* A HUBZone is an area located in one or more of the following:

- a qualified census tract as defined in Sec. 42(d)(5)(C)(i)(I) of the Internal Revenue Code of 1986,
- a qualified "non-metropolitan county" as defined in Sec. 143(k)(2)(B) of the IRS Code of 1986 with a median household income of less than 80 percent of the state median household income or with an unemployment rate of not less than 140 percent of the statewide average, or
- land areas within the boundaries of federally recognized Indian reservations.

How does the HUBZone Program work? The SBA administers the program and

- determines which businesses are eligible to receive HUBZone contracts,
- maintains a list of qualified HUBZone small businesses that federal agencies can use as suppliers,
- adjudicates protests of eligibility to receive HUBZone contracts, and
- reports to Congress on the program's impact in HUBZone areas.

*Types of contracts.* There are two types of HUBZone contracts: competitive and sole source. Competitive contracts can be awarded if the contracting officer has a reasonable expectation that at least two qualified HUBZone small businesses will submit bids and that the contract can be awarded at a fair market price.

Sole-source contracts can be awarded if the contracting officer does not have a reasonable expectation that two or more qualified HUBZone small businesses will submit offers, determines that the qualified HUBZone small business is responsible, and determines that the contract can be awarded at fair market price. In either case, the government contract estimate cannot exceed $5 million for manufacturing requirements or $3 million for all other requirements.

A full and open competition contract can be awarded with a price evaluation preference. Bids by HUBZone small businesses will be considered lower than offers made by non-HUBZone bidders or non–small business bidders, providing that the offer of the HUBZone small business is not more than 10 percent higher.

### Women-Owned Business

Women own approximately 42 percent of all U.S. businesses, and the start-up rate for women-owned businesses is twice the rate for companies owned by men. The failure rate for women-owned firms is lower than for those owned by men—meaning that women are more successful.[9]

The SBA has numerous programs to help women entrepreneurs, who, in the administration's words, "still face unique obstacles in the world of business." The SBA's Office of Women's Business Ownership leads the way in this activity.[10] Some of these programs have been identified in previous chapters. One additional major advantage to women-owned business is that they are accorded extra points on their bids for federal contracts and subcontracts, as are prime contractors for having women-owned businesses as their subcontractors.

### Government Property Sales/Leases

The SBA's National Resources Sales Assistance Program is intended to ensure that small businesses obtain a fair share of government property sales and leases. This includes, when necessary, small business set-asides, that is, the designation of a certain percentage of the sale or lease property be made available only to qualified small businesses. The program also provides counseling and other assistance to small businesses concerning government sales and leases.[11]

## SURETY BOND PROGRAM

The SBA can guarantee bonds for contracts up to $2 million.[12] These guarantees cover bid, performance, and payment bonds for small and emerging contractors who cannot obtain surety bonds from normal commercial sources.

The SBA's guarantee provides sureties an incentive to provide bonding for eligible small business contractors and thereby strengthens their ability to obtain bonding and greater access to contracting opportunities. This SBA guarantee is an agreement between the administration and a surety company that the SBA will assume a predetermined percentage of loss if the contractor breaches the terms of the contract.

What is a surety bond? It is a surety bond is a three-party instrument between the contractor, a surety, and the project owner. The agreement binds the contractor to comply with the terms and conditions of a contract. If he or she is unable to successfully perform the contract, the surety assumes the contractor's responsibilities and ensures that the project is completed.

### Contract Bonds

There are four types of contract bonds that may be covered by an SBA guarantee:

- *Bid Bond*—guarantees that the bidder on a contract will enter into the contract and furnish the required payment and performance bonds;
- *Payment Bond*—guarantees payment from the contractor to persons who furnish labor, materials, equipment, and/or supplies for use in the performance of the contract;
- *Performance Bond*—guarantees that the contractor will perform the contract in accordance with its terms and conditions through to completion; these bonds are also called completion bonds or final bonds in certain areas; and
- *Ancillary Bonds*—guarantees items that are incidental but essential to the performance of the contract.

Companies eligible for SBA bond guarantees are contractors who qualify as a small business and meet the surety's bonding qualifications. Companies in construction and service industries can meet the SBA's size eligibility standards if their average annual receipts, including those of affiliates, for the last three fiscal years do not exceed $5 million.

Bid bonds and performance bonds are eligible for SBA guarantees if they are executed in connection with an eligible contract and are a type listed in the "Contract Bonds" section of the Surety Association of America's current *Manual of Rules, Procedures and Classifications*.

### How Does the System Work?

The SBA reimburses a participating surety company to the guarantee's specified amount for losses incurred as a result of a contractor's default on a guaranteed bid, payment, performance, or ancillary bond. This is accomplished through the Prior Approval Program of the Preferred Surety Bond Program.

*Prior Approval Program.* Under this program, an agent reviews the application package and recommends it to the surety company for approval. If the surety company agrees to issue a bond with the SBA guarantee, the package is forwarded to the appropriate local SBA office for further evaluation. If the applicant is determined to be qualified and approval is reasonable in light of the risks involved, the SBA may issue a guarantee to the surety company. The surety company then issues the bond to the contractor. The SBA guarantee agreement is with the surety company, not the small business contractor.

Any surety company certified by the U.S. Treasury to issue bonds may apply for participation in the Prior Approval Program, but the SBA will review and approve its bonds prior to their being issued. Contractors bonded under this program are generally smaller and less experienced than contractors bonded under the Preferred Surety Bond Program.

SBA guarantees 90 percent of the losses incurred on bonds up to $100,000 under the Prior Approval Program and for bonds to contractors that are socially and economically disadvantaged. SBA guarantees 80 percent of the losses incurred on all other bonds under this program.

*Procedure.* If you are a contractor desiring SBA surety bonds, you should apply directly to an agent or surety company of your choice for the type of bond you need. You will provide background information on your company, credit and financial information, and project information as required by the surety company and the SBA. Armed with this information, the surety company processes and underwrites the application in the same manner as any other contract bond application. The surety company may do one of the following: execute the bond without the SBA's guarantee, execute the bond with the SBA guarantee, or decline the bond even with the SBA guarantee.

If the surety company decides an SBA guarantee is required to provide the bond, it completes appropriate SBA forms and submits them to the area SBA office for review. The area office then determines whether the contractor and the surety company have provided sufficient information and documentation to warrant approval. If not, more information can be requested. After a careful review, the SBA area office may decide to approve, at which point an administration official signs a guarantee agreement and returns it to the surety company. If, however, after careful review, the SBA office determines that contractor's performance capacity cannot be reasonably assured, the administration rejects the application.

The SBA charges no application fee and no fee for a bid bond guarantee. If the SBA guarantees a performance bond, the contractor pays a guarantee fee equal to a certain percentage of the contract amount; the percentage is determined by the SBA and is published in the *Federal Register*. When the bond is issued, the small business pays the surety company's bond premium; this charge cannot exceed the level approved by the appropriate state regulatory body. The surety company pays the SBA a guarantee fee on each guaranteed bond (except bid bonds) based on a percentage of the bond premium; the SBA determines this percentage.

## TRAINING ASSISTANCE

The SBA offers training assistance in person at a local office, through its Web site for particular issues and topics of importance to you, and through its new digital classroom for general knowledge about business.

Local offices provide management and technical training through regular classroom programs and through regularly scheduled seminars and forums. You should contact your local SBA office for further information.

### Online Classroom

The SBA Classroom is an Internet learning tool that provides training for small companies in the changing global environment. This online classroom is designed to bring user-friendly electronic business courses to you 24/7 for your convenience. Resources available in the online classroom include:

- SBA online courses, including four new e-commerce courses,
- Cosponsored courses and resource areas,
- Library and online research materials,
- Business counselors,
- Comments and feedback to the SBA.

On this site, you can read articles, take courses, or perform research on such topics as business development and procurement programs. Through a Service Corps of Retired Executives (SCORE) Cyber-Chapter, you can access via e-mail business advice on topics of immediate importance to you. You can reach the online classroom at www.sba.gov/classroom.

## Management Training

SBA offers management training programs for small businesses through their Business Information Centers (BICs). The BIC concept began in 1991 in Seattle, as a joint venture between an SBA SCORE chapter and Microsoft. By 2001, there were eighty BICs located in major cities throughout the country. They have the latest in high-technology hardware, software, tele-communications equipment, and interactive videos to assist individuals in starting or building a business. These training programs cover all aspects of business management from pre–start-up to operating issues. BICs are an outstanding example of a successful public/private sector partnership. The service is free.

*Special training.* Special training programs are offered for specific circumstances. For small companies owned by socially and economically disadvantaged persons, there are workshops to assist these individuals in learning how to prepare an 8(a) loan application for certification. Another type of workshop is Entrepreneurs United, a business support group for men and women entrepreneurs and sales professionals that offers free marketing workshops, consulting services, and net-working opportunities within most major cities. The Women's Referral Service provides a networking organization, a referral service, and entrepreneurial train-ing for women.

*Seminars.* Special seminars and workshops are offered by local SBA offices and SCORE chapters across the country on such topics as Starting and Operating Your Own Business; Promoting and Protecting Your Invention; Publicity, Pro-motion, Advertising and You; Getting Financing for Your Business; and Tools of Retail Specialty Store Operation. These workshops and seminars are led by experienced professionals on a periodic basis. Some seminars charge a fee (usu-ally $20) and some are free. Call your local SBA office for a schedule of events and fee information.

The IRS also holds seminars and workshops on such topics as Record Keeping for Small Businesses, Running a Home-Based Business, and Introduction to State and Federal Payroll Tax. These are offered free of charge. Contact your local IRS or SBA office for a workshop schedule.

## Counseling

SBA offers counseling services for various types of small businesses, mostly through its development centers.

*Service Corps of Retired Executives (SCORE).* The SBA provides mentoring that is worth its weight in gold. This is accomplished through the SCORE Program. There are more than twelve thousand retired executives (average age is seventy-one) organized into four hundred chapters who volunteer throughout the United States to provide seasoned advise and counsel to small business owners.[13] There are more than fifty SCORE Counseling Centers in the greater Los Angeles area alone.

SCORE also has a Cyber-Chapter (www.score.org) that offers free e-mail counseling and mentoring to small companies, including pre–start-ups and inventors. There are more than eight hundred counselors online, and they are required to respond to your email within forty-eight hours.

These counselors have "been there, done that," and they offer their experience and wisdom to brash young start-ups and to older persons who are looking to make a career change. Whether the business is a restaurant, flower shop, dry cleaners, fast food franchise, day-care center, or heavy machinery manufacturing, there is a SCORE person somewhere within reach to help you avoid mistakes and capitalize on your strengths. Best of all, the service is free.

SCORE people will listen to your start-up idea and provide unbiased, impartial feedback to help you assess your probability of success or failure. For existing businesses, they provide counseling in such areas as planning, advertising, accounting, marketing, market and customer analysis, inventory control, cash and credit management, and other business functions. All of this counseling is designed to achieve one objective—to help your business succeed.

*Small Business Development Centers (SBDC).* The SBA has fifty-nine SBDCs located in major cities. These centers are the SBA's lead organizations providing administration contracts, loans, guaranteed loans, training, and technical assistance. This is a cooperative effort between the SBA, local government, educational institutions, and the private sector. This assistance is fee-based, but the fees are typically lower than those charged by colleges and universities for similar training.

SBDCs are organized to provide a wide variety of services to the small business community, including:

- *Finance Division*—to process loan applications,
- *Economic Development Division*—promoting SBA programs and services,
- *Legal Division*—maintaining legal order in the office's loan portfolio,
- *Information Resource Management Division*—keeping the office's computer network up-to-date,
- *Government Contracting Division*—assisting small firms apply for government contracts,
- *8(a) Business Development*—assisting small disadvantaged business to grow, and
- *Business Information Center*—helping entrepreneurs obtain needed SBA information.

*Women's Business Centers.* These centers are also available in many communities throughout the country to assist women-owned businesses. They are part of a national network of eighty educational institutions administered through the SBA.

*SBA District Offices.* These are in every major city. They are full-service operations that provide SBA publications, application forms, computer use for online services, and binders that have start-up information for virtually every type of business, both product and service. The staff personnel are quite knowledgeable and eager to assist an entrepreneur with start-up or expansion. This is a free service.

*Online SBA Programs.* These also assist small and medium-sized businesses. The SBA's Web site, BusinessLaw.gov, is a resource providing legal and regulatory information to small firms. The site is also a link to other federal, as well as state and local, information affecting business. The SBA Law Library provides valuable business information regarding forms, records, reports, laws and regulations, standard operating procedures, and the like for business.

### Scams that Target Small Business

There is an army of rip-off artists waiting to steal your profits and possibly your business. They are highly creative in devising ways to do it and are very slick in pulling it off. The cost to small firms is in the billions each year, but no one knows the actual figure because many companies that get taken are too embarrassed to report the crime. In some cases, firms are not even aware that they were taken.

The SBA's program to help small business owners avoid scams begins with awareness and prevention.[14] The administration has pamphlets and workshops devoted to spotting these frauds and, more importantly, on how to avoid being trapped into them. A perennial classic scam is a "consultant" who guarantees to get you an SBA loan for a 5 percent fee. There are two current favorite scams you should be aware of—phony invoices and long distance break-ins.

*Phony invoices.* Small companies place ads in newspapers all the time for various things: help wanted ads for new employees, ads for their products, ads announcing sales events, and so forth. The scam begins with a company placing a legitimate ad in a local newspaper or national trade magazine. Soon after, the company receives an invoice from another newspaper or magazine for a large sum of money; attached to the invoice is a page from the newspaper or magazine showing the ad. However, the company never placed the second ad. The scam artist simply cut out the genuine ad and carefully placed it on a legitimate page of another newspaper or magazine to create what appears to be an ad and then made a photocopy, which was attached to the invoice.

The variations on this scheme are endless: phony ads from classified phone directories that are different than the ones you use, a bill from an office supply company, an insurance premium, a trade magazine invoice, and the like—all bogus.

To catch these fake invoices and avoid paying the bills, your company needs to have sound business procedures in place. Every purchase should be preapproved and each invoice should bear a purchase order number or a specific contract reference. Bogus invoices will not have these numbers, but you have to have a procedure in place to catch them before your bookkeeper or accounts-payable clerk routinely pays the bill.

*Long-distance break-ins.* Using this scam, a thief obtains an outside telephone line from your company, uses it to make his own long-distance calls, and—worst of all—sells the outside telephone number to other thieves for a fee. The average cost to small businesses hit by this scam is $25,000. The worst case reported was by Mitsubishi Corporation, where over a two-month period they lost $450,000 to this scam.

How does it work? A scam artist calls your business and asks for a particular department. When he's connected, he says he has reached the wrong office and asks to be transferred back to the operator. At this point, the operator thinks the call originated inside the company, so when the thief requests an outside line, this seems normal. The perpetrator then makes long-distance calls at your company's expense.

Massive fraud comes with the unauthorized use of your 800 number. Thieves use personal computers, software designed to discover passwords, and random-number dialers to break into a system searching for an outside line. When they find it, they sell calls, especially international calls, through your line, usually from pay phones. A single setup into a company's phone system with two or three lines can net a thief as much as $150,000 per year.

What are your defenses against this? Telephone companies and their business customers work together to secure communications systems to safeguard against such fraud. For example, you can limit access to outside lines through the voice mail system to certain times of day or to certain people with special passwords. Awareness and prevention, says the SBA, are the key steps to prevent these frauds.

## Small Business Advocate/Ombudsman

In Washington, D.C., and in every state capital there is a small business advocate, an employee of the SBA who brings the voice of small business to policymakers in the nation's capital and state capitals. The advocate works to reduce regulatory burdens that government policies impose on small businesses and to maximize benefits small businesses receive from government.

The SBA's National Ombudsman Program is a major service to small business. When small firms experience excessive federal regulatory enforcement action, such as repeated audits or investigations and excessive fines, they can appeal to the national ombudsman for help. They can file a comment, appeal to a regulatory fairness board, or contact the local congressperson through the ombudsman.

## CONCLUSION

The Small Business Administration offers a wide variety of programs to assist small business in getting stated and in expanding. Many of these programs are tailored for small disadvantaged businesses, women-owned businesses, and minority-owned businesses. They provide marketing assistance to the federal government and contracting help both as prime contractors and subcontractors. Other forms of help include technical training, management training, and counseling by seasoned retired executives through the SCORE Program. They even have a fraud prevention program.

Chapter 12 looks at ways state and local governments have to help entrepreneurs start and grow their businesses.

## APPENDIX 11.1

### Sample of Federal Civilian Procurement Items[15]

| | |
|---|---|
| Alarm systems | Office furniture and decorations |
| Cattle guards | Office machines and supplies |
| Chemicals and chemical products | Paint |
| Cleaning supplies | Photography equipment and supplies |
| Conveyors and forklifts | Record equipment |

Data processing equipment

Dental equipment and supplies

Drugs and pharmaceutical supplies

Fire-fighting equipment

Industrial machinery

Internet products

Law enforcement equipment

Marine equipment

Medical supplies

Musical instruments

Recreational equipment

Relocation services

Road maintenance

Shipping, packaging, and supplies

Storage tanks

Telecommunications and media supplies

Tires

Transportation services

Water purification and sewer equipment

Wheeled and tracked vehicles

# — CHAPTER 12 —

# State and Local
# Government Assistance

State and local governments combined represent a market that is even larger than the federal government in contract dollar value. States and municipalities provide incentives and various forms of assistance to companies to locate within their jurisdictions. And state and local governments offer businesses within their areas marketing support in Washington, D.C.

This portion of the U.S. business/government relationship is one of the largest, most dynamic arenas of economic activity in the world, and yet little attention is paid to it. In this chapter, state and local assistance to business is discussed from several standpoints: marketing, financing and contracting assistance, location incentives, and political support in Washington, D.C. Other forms of assistance, such as employee training, utility and franchise fee waivers, and export/import help, are discussed under the larger headings.

## STATE AND LOCAL GOVERNMENT AS A MARKET

While the federal government is the world's largest single market, the combined value of procurements made by the nation's fifty states and their various counties and cities is, in fact, larger. In 2000, state and local governments as a group represented 57 percent of all government procurements in the United States versus 43 percent by the federal government. The dollar value of these state and local purchases was $489 billion versus $375 billion by the federal government.[1]

The nature of the purchases is also vastly different: the largest single type of procurement by the federal government is defense equipment, while state and local governments spend their procurement dollars on nondefense items.

Another way of expressing the federal versus state/local difference is high-tech equipment versus civilian goods and services. State and local governments buy many of the same types of commodities and services as do companies, making state and local government a natural marketing target.

There are nearly 90,000 state and local governments in the United States. Each of these governmental units is a market, which buys products and services from the private sector for their administrative offices, public schools and universities, courthouses, fire and police stations, health facilities, parks, highway construction, beaches, and so on.

Demand for these goods and services increases with the public's increasing demand for governmental services, which has been the long-term trend for the past half century. Therefore, state/local government is a growth market that is stable, has well-established procurement procedures that are almost always highly competitive and fair to all bidders, and the funding behind these procurements is usually solid. New York City purchases over $7 billion in goods and services annually.[2] Even during an extreme situation like the largest county bankruptcy in U.S. history—Orange County, California, in 1995—the county continued to buy essential products and services and pay its bills.

The state and local government marketplace is subdivided into four major categories of procurements, as summarized in Table 12.1.[3]

The "Durable goods" category includes such items as road-building equipment, trucks and autos, heavy machinery and equipment for state and county buildings, computers and other office equipment, and the like. "Nondurable goods" includes pens, pencils, paper, uniforms, cleaners and solvents, and so forth. "Construction," the largest part of the market, includes building structures, such as office buildings, schools, hospitals, fire stations, and city halls. This also includes building state highways, bridges, port facilities, dams, and other infrastructure projects. "Services" refers to such contracted activities as communications services (telephone, Internet, etc.), legal and consulting services, cleaning services, and security guards.

**Table 12.1**
**State and Local Government Market, 2000**

| Types of Items Procured | $ Billions |
| --- | --- |
| Durable goods | 74 |
| Nondurable goods | 111 |
| Construction (structures) | 165 |
| Services | 139 |
| **Total** | **$489** |

## FINANCIAL ASSISTANCE

Virtually all states, counties, and cities have programs to assist businesses in getting started and expanding. These programs usually involve a mixture of federal funds with state and local money, together with an investment by the entrepreneur. Not unexpectedly, these programs require the firm to be sited in the county and the city providing the funds—to provide tax revenue, jobs, and possibly technology development as a *quid pro quo* for local government financial support.

The following examples of state and local financial assistance are from California: the state, its largest county, its largest city, and one medium-size city (Long Beach). These California programs are at best modest and represent a minimum level of governmental involvement offered to attract and retain business. Many other states and their counties and cities offer much more assistance, as the next section on location incentives illustrates.

### State of California

Every state has some type of development program to lure businesses to it or to keep them there. California is typical of states that offer a limited number of such programs. It offers enterprise zones, which are usually administered by counties or municipalities, certain tax incentives, and job services that are of use to businesses. Job services are mentioned here because they financially benefit businesses insofar as companies using these services do not need to pay for their own employee training.

California's Employment Development Department (EDD) provides the following:[4]

- *Job Service Program*—serves the state's 850,000 employers and about 1 million job seekers who register for its computer-based CalJobs system. This system electronically cross-references qualified job applicants with employers' job openings.
- *Employment Training Panel*—trains employees and may offer cash reimbursements averaging $1,000 to $1,500 for each employee trained a minimum of forty hours and retained on a job for at least ninety days.
- *Center for Business Training*—local colleges provide consulting and customized training designed to meet specific workforce and management training needs. By using this service, qualified companies may be eligible for state funding to offset training costs.

Another agency, California Statewide Communities Development Authority, has funding from $250,000 available to qualifying manufacturers and solid waste processors and recyclers for financing new facilities, expanding existing facilitates, or upgrading equipment. This agency specializes in issuing tax-exempt financing for public and private agencies for industrial, housing, nonprofit, and other tax-exempt facilities.[5]

The state also has a foreign trade zone at the Port of Los Angeles. This is an area where foreign and domestic merchandise is considered to be outside U.S. Customs territory. Merchandise may be admitted into a foreign trade zone without formal Customs entry, thereby deferring payment of duty or excise taxes until the product is legally entered into the United States or eliminating duty altogether if the product is reexported. The Port of L.A. has developed an open zone concept to make its foreign trade zone program more accessible to companies of varying types and sizes.[6]

California, like a number of states whose economies are deeply involved in international trade and investment, had a Technology, Trade & Commerce Agency until the 2003 budget crisis eliminated it for reasons of cost and inefficiency. This state agency had twelve overseas trade offices, an export financing office, and a technology investment partnership program that funded start-up high-tech companies that were exporters.

Critics of the elimination of this agency argue that the nation's leading exporting and importing state requires this type of governmental support for sustained success, while acknowledging that the agency had been poorly managed. One critic said the blame for shuttering the agency "should be laid at the feet of Governor Gray Davis, who packed the Agency with political appointees and inexperienced people with virtually no business experience or acumen."[7]

### Los Angeles County

Every major county and city has an economic development agency, by whatever name it is called. The task of these offices is to attract businesses to their community, help provide funding if available, and to help clear a path through bureaucratic red tape to enable a firm to get started or to expand in their area. Some are better at it than others.

Los Angeles County's development agency is typical of many found in larger counties throughout the country. The county has a Workforce Investment Board, the main purpose of which is to help displaced workers retool their skills and find new jobs. For companies, the board provides financial incentives to qualified employers and saves them time and money through a variety of no-fee placement, training, and information services, including job training and tax credit certification. In 2002, the board's programs were funded at $300 million.[8]

*Community Development Commission.* The county also has a Community Development Commission whose mission is to assist business primarily through three programs: loans, incubators, and enterprise zones.

First, the commission funnels federal, state, and county money through a variety of low-interest loans to large and small businesses of all types, commercial to industrial, that might not qualify for commercial financing. These loans range from the Micro Loan Program, involving small dollar amounts for relatively short periods, to the Float Loan Program that lends up to $15 million for longer terms. From 1993 to 2003, the commission provided more than $70 million in business loans that created or retained more than two thousand jobs.[9]

Second, the commission assists very young entrepreneurial companies that show promise of future economic success to get on their feet by putting them in one of six incubators. This program is called the L.A. County Incubator Network or IN-NET. These incubators focus on high technology and emerging industry clusters that range from software to advanced medical services and devices. IN-NET member companies have access to the County Technology Loan Program, a seed capital fund available only to businesses located in incubators that are part of IN-NET.

Each incubator focuses on a different area of specialization: health care, industrial design, technology transfer from aerospace/defense to commercial markets, service technologies, and biomedical. Local colleges and universities and specific county agencies are introduced to these incubator companies to provide them with technology, contacts, and marketing leads.[10]

Third, the commission administers two state enterprise zones: the Mid-Alameda Corridor Enterprise Zone and the Altadena Enterprise Zone. In these economically depressed zones, along with one of its own in Lancaster/Palmdale, the commission offers special tax incentives to stimulate development and hiring.[11]

In an enterprise zone, all companies are given the following tax incentives:[12]

- reduced property tax rates;
- the 8.25 percent sales/use tax paid on purchases of machinery, manufacturing equipment, computers, telecommunications equipment, and the like can be claimed as a tax credit;
- 6 percent investment tax credit is given to manufacturers for machinery and equipment in addition to the sales tax credit;
- 15 percent R&D tax credit is provided for work performed in-house or 24 percent for R&D work that is outsourced;
- hiring tax credit of $26,895 over a five-year period can be claimed for each qualified employee hired;
- 25 percent five-year electrical discount is offered for new and expanding businesses in zones located within the city of Los Angeles;
- up to $20,000 can be deducted from the cost of new equipment before depreciation; and
- 100 percent net operating loss carry forward is permitted for lenders, meaning net interest can be deducted from income earned on loans made in an enterprise zone.

Finally, the Community Development Commission also networks other state and county programs with its own programs to provide assistance to business. An example is linking the County Earthquake Loan Program with commission incentives to provide a $650,000 low-interest loan to the International Boardwalk at Redondo Beach Pier.[13] Another example is Three D Plastics, Inc., a Burbank-based maker of highway signs and hardware, which received $500,000 in low-interest loans from the commission and the California Integrated Waste Management Board, which promotes the use of recycled materials.[14]

### City of Los Angeles

The city of Los Angeles offers businesses three types of financial assistance through its Community Development Department: low-interest loans, tax-exempt bonds, and Section 108 loans for real estate acquisition.[15]

*Low-interest loans.* These fund projects in state enterprise zones, federal empowerment zones, and other low- and moderate-income communities. These loans are offered through the city's Industrial and Commercial Division, and range from $500,000 to $10 million. The city's stated purpose is "to create jobs and increase the availability of goods and services."

*Industrial development bonds.* These provide manufacturing businesses up to $10 million for property acquisition, machinery and equipment purchases, building improvements, and construction. This agency is the issuing authority for tax-exempt and taxable private activity bonds. Typical bond issues range from $2 to $6 million. Interest paid to investors who purchase these bonds is exempt from federal and state income tax. The borrower benefits from reduced interest rates, lowering the cost of funds. Taxable financing is a way for companies to finance other parts of their project not covered by the tax-exempt component.

*Section 108 loans.* These offer gap financing up to $5 million for real estate acquisition, construction or renovation, cost of fixtures and equipment, and soft costs such as legal and loan fees. Funds also finance assembled land for project redevelopment, relocation of businesses to the city, and development of incubators or industrial parks. For a project to qualify, it must include a minimum 10 percent owner equity participation, a commercial loan component, and gap financing up to 30 percent, which is the city's maximum loan contribution.

The city of Los Angeles also provides business tax incentives and tax reductions for firms located in seven economically depressed areas of the city that have been designated as eligible for these benefits: South Central, Watts, Boyle Heights, Eastern Section, Pacoima, Hollywood, and North Hollywood.[16]

## City of Long Beach

The city of Long Beach (population 462,000) has an aggressive financial assistance program for business development. Through its Community Development Department, the city has been highly successful in the past several years turning blighted urban areas into an already thriving new downtown/waterfront business district.

In the early 1990s, the city lost 50,000 high-paying jobs when the Long Beach Naval Base was closed and McDonnell Douglas, the city's largest employer, downsized about 75 percent of its workforce. The city's major recovery strategy was through retail expansion because of retail's ability to generate sales tax revenue.

To implement the strategy, the city undertook to redevelop much of its downtown area. Entire city blocks of shuttered business buildings were demolished to make space for urban mall-type stores and mixed-use structures with convenient parking in secure structures. Other areas on the Pacific Ocean waterfront were rezoned to permit retail, residential, and mixed-use structures, replacing vacant land, boarded-up buildings, and derelict hangouts. Some of these areas benefit from coastline views of the Pacific Ocean, taking advantage of physical settings that were previously ignored.

Altogether, over the past decade, nine major projects were planned and completed with a value well in excess of $500 million, with more on the way. These projects were financed by a combination of federal funds (primarily HUD for housing), city general fund investments, city development authority investments, city-backed revenue and lease revenue refund bonds, federal and state enterprise zones, sales tax rebate program, reduced utility taxes and franchise fees, job training, and reduced business license fees for companies moving to development areas.[17]

## New York City

By comparison, New York City, through its Economic Development Corporation, offers more than fifty business incentive programs, including financing through a number of bond programs, grants for industrial relocation, a Women's Venture Fund, Small Industry Incentive Program (waiver of sales tax on construction materials, waiver of mortgage recording tax, and a twenty-five-year property tax abatement and exemption), the Empire (Enterprise) Zone Program for selected depressed areas of the city, and the Lower Manhattan Economic Revitalization Plan.[18]

## LOCATION INCENTIVES

Many state governments offer incentives to companies to locate within their borders. These incentives range from very modest assistance in helping to find appropriate greenfield or brownfield sites, existing buildings, or other structures, to a full array of enticements including tax incentives, employee training, and the like. The Boeing Company received an incentive package from Illinois worth $41 million to relocate its small corporate headquarters staff to Chicago from Seattle, primarily for prestige reasons.[19]

### Auto Assembly Plant Incentives

Three examples regarding auto assembly plants illustrate large-scale incentive programs offered by states to obtain these trophy investments.

*BMW.* This Munich-based company decided in the early 1990s to build its first auto factory outside of Europe.[20] They chose to establish a production operation in the United States, their largest export market, believing this would help the company "maintain, secure, and build up its position in the U.S. luxury-car market, the world's biggest."[21] With this objective in mind, the company evaluated 215 possible locations and narrowed its choices to a short list of four finalists. In the end, management announced in 1992 their choice of Spartanburg, South Carolina as the location of their first non-European assembly plant.

This South Carolina location beat the others partly because of an attractive incentive package from the state government, a key component of which concerned import duties. The new plant was granted free-trade status as part of the Greenville-Spartanburg airport's free-trade zone. The effect of this was that U.S. duties on parts imported from Germany and elsewhere would not have to be paid unless the final product was sold in the United States. Because a large percentage of production was planned for export to Europe and other areas, no duties would be paid until the auto reached its final destination. Moreover, for cars staying in the U.S. market, no duties had to be paid until the auto was assembled and left the factory, thus reducing financing costs.

Other portions of South Carolina's incentive package included reduced building and infrastructure costs. The site also provided easy access to highways and rail, was minutes from an international airport, and it was close to the large seaport of Charleston. The cost of living in the area was considerably lower than other areas of the United States. And a major attraction was that South Carolina had a "right to work" law, meaning that labor unions would not have to be brought into the plant. BMW's labor rates in Germany were the highest in the world.

In return for its incentives, South Carolina became the U.S. home of BMW manufacturing. BMW's investment totaled $600 million, with a $400 million initial cost for construction of a 1.2 million square foot plant, followed by a $200 million investment in tooling. The plant was designed to build three hundred Z3 roadsters a day, with expansion to four hundred per day if the market demanded it. The plant was built in two years. A few years later, BMW decided to build more models at the plant and expanded its capacity by

300,000 square feet at a cost of $200 million more. In the end, BMW joined 329 other foreign companies in choosing South Carolina and added 4,700 new high-skill, high-paying jobs to the South Carolina tax base.[22]

*Mercedes and Nissan.* DaimlerChrysler followed a similar scenario when it decided to build its first U.S. Mercedes-Benz assembly plant in Alabama to produce SUVs. Similarly, Nissan, which received $363 million in state incentives, opened a new $1.43 billion, 3.5 million square foot plant in 2003 in Canton, Mississippi, to produce minivans, light trucks, SUVs, and a sedan. The Nissan factory employed 5,300 well-paid workers in 2004, as it achieved full-rate production.[23]

## Northrop Grumman

In the early 1990s, Northrop Corporation (later Northrop Grumman) needed to find a plant location to produce a new tactical missile for the Defense Department.[24] This would be a factory requiring special layout and facilities and would employ well over one thousand high-skilled, highly paid workers.

The company had existing facilities in Southern California that could be adapted for use, but the state of California was largely indifferent to the opportunity to add this activity to its high technology and employment base. The cost of doing business in the Los Angeles area was already among the highest in the country, and there was an added problem of finding enough trained or willing-to-be-trained workers who met critical qualifications: U.S. citizenship, basic literacy, and pass a mandatory drug test. Given the high operating costs, tight labor market, and no state incentives, the company looked elsewhere.

More than two dozen states asked to make presentations to the company. Approximately one dozen were selected as realistic candidates, primarily due to labor market and operating cost issues, and these were visited by a team to inspect potential sites and receive presentations from state officials. The short list of finalists were all in the South: South Carolina, Georgia, Alabama, and Mississippi. A site near Macon, Georgia, was finally chosen.

Why Macon, Georgia? This state offered an incentive package and other positive factors that were quite similar to the others nearby, but it had a few extras that were quite attractive. Their package included the following actions by the state of Georgia:

- buy the acreage needed for the greenfield site and lease back to the company at a very nominal rate over a ten-year period, after which the company could purchase it at market price;
- improve the land, grade it, and make it construction-ready at no expense to the company;

- install all utility lines, sewer connections, and hookups at no expense to the company;
- pay for and build an Interstate Highway connector ramp to the plant;
- recruit the one thousand–person workforce from the immediate area or bring in skilled labor from other locations in the state; and
- provide transitional training for all production employees at no company expense.

In addition to these tangible incentives, Georgia also had "right to work" laws, low cost of living, and a solid work ethic that produced quality products. Finally, Georgia was represented in the U.S. Senate at that time by an individual who was chairman of the Senate Armed Services Committee; this relationship would augur well for continued funding for the Defense Department's missile program.

### Incentive Programs—Cities

Most major cities offer incentives to bring businesses to their community or to keep them there if they intend to expand. Long Beach's incentive for a major cruise line is illustrative of a creative approach.

*Carnival Cruise Line.* A unique incentive program was created by the city of Long Beach, California, to make its port the Carnival Cruise Line's West Coast home port.[25]

For years, Carnival had used the adjacent Port of Los Angeles to pick up and return passengers for its Southern California-originated cruises to Mexico. That port was not particularly attractive, being primarily a container and freight complex, had inadequate and unsecured parking, and no customer-friendly embarkation/debarkation facilities or overnight accommodations.

The city of Long Beach owned a 30,000-square foot empty dome-shaped building adjacent to the city-owned Queen Mary floating hotel that had been the display hanger for Howard Hughes's Spruce Goose airplane, which had left the area.

Creative people at Long Beach City Hall got the idea to lure Carnival to their port, literally a half-mile away, and use the first-class facility the dome-shaped building represented, located at the water's edge next to a large parking structure, for passenger check-in, immigration, and customs. For $40 million, Carnival would build and own the new port facility, the first in the country to be built and owned by a cruise operator. Carnival, not having an extra $40 million, needed help with both the financing and with clearing away municipal red tape regarding zoning, construction permits, environmental issues, and other regulations.

City Hall was happy to help with all aspects of the move. The key incentive was financial: the city, with its excellent credit rating, underwrote a $32 million bond issue by Carnival at the city's discounted interest rate to build a pier jutting out from the dome structure long enough to handle two Carnival cruise ships at a time. As a result, Long Beach became the West Coast home port for two Carnival cruise liners, the Ecstasy and the Elation, each carrying up to 2,052 passengers, many of whom spend at least one night before or after their cruise at the Queen Mary. Over 600,000 passengers annually were projected to use this port.

This was a win/win for Long Beach and for Carnival; both got what they wanted. For Long Beach, they got use of their empty domed building, more hotel nights at the Queen Mary, and economic development activity in their port facility. Carnival obtained a first-class passenger facility, ample and secure parking for their customers, an adjacent hotel for passenger convenience, and a low interest rate on long-term bonds with little out-of-pocket cost. The entire deal took less than one year to accomplish.

*Auto dealerships.* When they are motivated, cities can be very creative to provide unusually attractive incentives to bring business to their communities. A typical example is an automobile dealership. This is a real prize for a city, and many will offer much to land one.

Why is a dealership viewed as a trophy win? The reasons are tangible and intangible. The tangible win is tax revenue, both sales tax and income tax. A vehicle is the biggest "big ticket" purchase the average person makes, except for a house. Cities especially crave the 1 percent sales tax revenue each car sale brings them via the state collecting activity. The intangible reason is the prestige a major dealership brings to a city—being home to such a business is a real feather in the cap of a community.

Major shopping malls, like auto dealerships, are a huge plus for any city, and you can expect hard bargaining to take place to obtain one. Again, the main benefits to the community are sales tax revenue and prestige, acting as a magnet to attract other businesses.

## POLITICAL SUPPORT IN WASHINGTON, D.C.

No business is immune to laws and regulations enacted in the nation's capital, and no company wants to defend itself alone in that arena. All seek the very real help and support that an active and committed congressional delegation can provide to prevent the enactment of legislation that is harmful to business or to overturn such legislation if already enacted. Occasionally companies request and receive the proactive support of their delegation to achieve a positive result. Not all state delegations are equal; some do a far better job of helping their home-based companies than others.

### Political Willingness and Effectiveness

Owing to the fact that all states have two senators and one or more congresspeople in the House of Representatives, based on their state's population, there are two real issues of their political effectiveness: whether their senators and congresspeople serve on particular committees having jurisdiction over your business' activities and whether or not even one congressperson or senator will make the effort to champion your cause and use his or her power and connections to make a difference. They have to be persuaded that the cause is justified, the result will produce jobs (or prevent their loss) in their home state, and that the effort and political capital needed to persuade their colleagues is worth it to them politically.

*Why some are unwilling.* For some senators and members of Congress, championing the needs of business is ideologically repulsive, and they therefore eschew any such role. Other members simply are unwilling to lift a finger for any but a few favorite causes, usually funded by a special-interest group representing those causes, or possibly because their seats are so secure there is no need to make the effort.

For others, playing the role of champion is confined to those economic and business areas politically, intellectually, and ideologically acceptable to their viewpoint. For example, some of California's representatives will not support defense issues, while others are strongly positive on national defense. One senator, while refusing to do anything regarding defense, did nevertheless champion a defense company's efforts to win funding for a public transit vehicle's development.[26]

Other key variables are whether the state's delegation has members in the majority, whether they have members in the leadership, and whether key members are of the same party as the president. For the 108th Congress, 2003–2004, the Republican Party had a majority in both the House and Senate and had the presidency; this is the exact reverse of a decade earlier when the Democratic Party held all three of these positions.

*Federal flow of funds.* A measure of how effective a particular congressional delegation is in serving its state's interests in Washington, D.C., is the federal flow-of-funds analysis: is the state a winner in gaining back more than it pays in taxes, or is it a loser, paying more taxes than it receives in federal largesse? The biggest winner of all (in 2002) was the District of Columbia: for every $1.00 it paid in federal taxes, it received $6.44 in federal grants-in-aid, contracts, and programs. The biggest loser was New Jersey, receiving only $0.62 for each tax dollar donated.

In 2002, only six states received less in federal funds than they paid in federal taxes. Number six on the list was the largest tax-paying state— California. In 2002, California received only 76 cents in federal expenditures for every dollar paid in federal taxes. A decade earlier, by comparison, the state received 93 cents in federal expenditures on each taxable dollar. See table 12.2 for a list of the largest winners and losers.[27]

Table 12.2
Highest Federal Tax Donor and Recipient States. 2002

| Highest Donor States | | Highest Recipient States | |
| --- | --- | --- | --- |
| New Jersey | $.62 | District of Columbia | $6.44 |
| Connecticut | .65 | New Mexico | 2.37 |
| New Hampshire | .66 | North Dakota | 2.07 |
| Nevada | .74 | Alaska | 1.91 |
| Massachusetts | .75 | Mississippi | 1.89 |
| California | .76 | West Virginia | 1.82 |

The unique status of the District of Columbia, being essentially a ward of the Congress, partially explains its federal bounty. New Mexico's is partly explained by the fact that it is the location of numerous federal projects and programs, and its two senators, one Republican (Pete Domenici) and one Democrat (Jeff Bingaman), are chair and ranking member of the Senate Committee on Energy and Natural Resources. Domenici is also a senior member of the Appropriations and Budget committees, and Bingaman is a senior member of the Finance Committee. These committee assignments provide powerful leverage, and the two senators are willing to use it to powerfully benefit their state.

### California's Congressional Delegation

The largest congressional delegation is of course California's, with fifty-three congresspeople and two senators, giving it fifty-five electoral votes.[28] Does this mean that California has more political muscle than any other state? The short answer is: far from it. There are two reasons: this enormous delegation has traditionally not worked together to achieve legislative objectives, and, because in the past there had been frequent turnover of members, other states that returned their representatives with obdurate regularity had more seniority and therefore more committee chairmanships. This has changed in recent years as a result of redistricting, producing so many "safe seats" that election turnover is rare.

Why do some delegations not work together? In California's case, the answer is that the delegation is divided in many ways:

- by party affiliation, having thirty-three Democrats versus twenty Republicans in 2003;
- by ideology, with representatives from the Far Left, Far Right, and political center;

- by interest, with some members favoring certain issues (such as social services) or industries (such as defense) that other members regularly vote against; and
- by region, with members from agricultural districts having little in common with inner-city members and their constituents' concerns.

*Power of congressional committees.* Further, with Republicans in the majority in the 108th Congress (2003–2004) and with California having mostly Democrats in Congress, one might conclude that the state had limited opportunities to gain committee chairmanships, which is where the real power lies. Both of the state's senators (Feinstein and Boxer) are Democrats, and so they held no chairmanships. Nevertheless, in the 108th Congress, five House committee chairmanships were held by California Republicans, the most of any state: Armed Services (Duncan Hunter), Resources (Richard Pombo), Rules (David Dreier), Ways and Means (William Thomas), and the Select Committee on Homeland Security (Christopher Cox).

Three of these are viewed as among the most powerful of all committees: Armed Services, which authorizes funds for all Pentagon procurements; Rules, which has great bargaining power because it determines which bills will go to the House floor for debate and passage; and Ways and Means, which is the committee of origination for all tax legislation. The importance of Homeland Security has yet to be tested, but it is potentially important because it authorizes a substantial budget.

*Powerful chairmanships.* Four additional committees generally are viewed as great powers: Appropriations, chaired by Bill Young of Florida; Energy and Commerce, chaired by Billy Tauzin of Louisiana; Financial Services, chaired by Michael Oxley of Ohio; and International Relations, chaired by Henry Hyde of Illinois. Of these, Appropriations is clearly the most important.

California, thus, has three of the seven most powerful chairmanships. However, generally speaking, this does not make a difference for California's citizens and businesses because these chairman are for the most part so focused on the specific work of their committees that they do not "log-roll" or "trade off" their votes with other powerful members to achieve state-oriented objectives. The needs of the home state are usually put second to the work of the federal government.

California has one leadership position: Nancy Pelosi is House minority leader. However, because of her short tenure in the position, it has yet to be determined if she uses this powerful position to benefit California.

## Other States' Delegations

What state delegation is viewed as the most effective for its own citizens? Texas is the clear winner. There is an old political saying in the Lone Star State: "Keep Texas Green," referring to the color of U.S. currency. Every

Texas congressman and senator has a mission in Washington, D.C.—to bring back to Texas every dollar of federal appropriations and every job that might go with it that he or she can. Few other states have delegations that are so single-minded in their pursuit of federal largesse.

Moreover, in 2003–2004, Texas has two Republican senators (the current majority), and its House delegation, the second largest in Congress, is nearly evenly divided with seventeen Democrats and fifteen Republicans. Texas also has the House majority leader, Tom DeLay. When an opportunity to benefit Texas comes before the House or Senate, that delegation works as a team, regardless of party or ideology, like no other to "bring home the bacon."

In 2003–2004, the state with the least political clout is Vermont. This is because one of Vermont's two senators is a Democrat (Patrick Leahy) and is therefore in the minority, and the other is an independent (James Jeffords), who bolted the Republican Party and is therefore not trusted by either party. The one congressman from Vermont, Bernard Sanders, is also an independent and therefore has no possibility of gaining a chairmanship or influencing legislation within either party's political councils.

### States' Lobbying Activities

Most of the large states conduct lobbying activities in Washington, D.C. Many states maintain an office usually near Capitol Hill to track congressional activities that may impact their state, and they lobby for their state on federal funding and other issues of state importance. As usual, some states are more effective at this than others, and the success of their effort largely depends on the cooperation and support of their congressional delegation, as well as the approachability of state officials for help with problems.

On generic issues of federalism and especially the increasing role of states in taking responsibility for implementing federally mandated programs, the Council of State Governments provides assistance. This is an association of all fifty states whose national headquarters is located in Lexington, Kentucky, but whose focus of activity is Washington, D.C. This office monitors federal government developments and trends, and evaluates the impact of federal activities on states. It also provides a voice for state leaders to Congress. Through its four regional offices, the council also helps promote intergovernmental cooperation on regional issues and multistate solutions to regional problems.[29]

Some states' governors or mayors have national political standing and may also be influential in Washington, D.C., to help achieve state objectives. When Ronald Reagan was California's governor, he frequently visited the nation's capital to lobby for state programs and positions. Governor Nelson Rockefeller of New York did the same for his state.

Today, other than Governor Arnold Schwarzenneger of California, there are no "celebrity" governors like Reagan and Rockefeller, but Governor Pataki of New York has a national following, largely because of his post-9/11 work, and can be influential in Washington, as can former New York City mayor Rudi Giuliani. Generally speaking, however, few governors and mayors have the clout to get much done at the federal level. Indeed, most have little influence on their own congressional delegations. Usually only large coalitions of mayors and governors working as a team have any impact on federal policymakers.

## CONCLUSION

States' and municipalities' aggregated procurements are the largest in the world, and this robust market is not ignored by the private sector. States and local government procurement and contracting policies and procedures are clear-cut and well established, and offer businesses a major opportunity.

States provide assistance to business in numerous ways: through financing packages, tax incentives, enterprise zones, employee training grants and subsidies, and by providing political support in Washington, D.C. Many states also offer comprehensive packages of incentives to lure companies to their state. The larger the company's operation, the larger the incentive program.

How companies can use state-provided political support is a subject of the final chapter on business/government interaction.

# — PART IV —

# Business/Government Interaction

This final part presents a range of options for business to deal with government. Each company must face the fact that government is a major part of its external environment and impacts the business at many levels of its operations. Finding realistic and effective ways to deal with this powerful external force is a major leadership challenge for every company, regardless of size and type of industry.

# — CHAPTER 13 —

# How Business Can Deal with Government

The previous chapters have presented an assessment of governmental involvement in the life of every business, from the smallest start-up to the largest multinational corporation. To this point, the discussion has been almost entirely one-way: government impacts on business. Now the question needs to be asked: what, if anything, can business do about it?

Certainly business has to comply with governmental regulations or face enforcement penalties. Aside from mere compliance, does business have any options for taking action toward government, and does it have a right to do so? Indeed it does. Business is an interest group that should think of government strategically.

This chapter presents a range of options for companies to deal with government: passive, reactive/confrontational, participatory, and aggressive. These options take into account that business has bargaining chips of its own to influence governmental outputs. Each of these business-to-government strategies is discussed briefly. Some basic principles of business/government relationships are then summarized.

## BUSINESS AS AN INTEREST GROUP

Companies, like individuals, have a Constitutional right to present their views to government under the First Amendment—free speech and redress of grievance. It is a mistake for businesses to think they cannot or should not undertake such activities as lobbying, forming political action committees, and presenting "white papers" to congressional committees and independent agencies.

These activities are not improper or unseemly; they are just as legitimate as producing and marketing products and services. They are the same activities as those engaged in by other interest groups or pressure groups such as organized labor, state governments, citizen groups organized for particular causes, and the like.

The differences among them are points of access, purpose and focus of activities, sustainability, and multiple areas of interest. One could argue that business not only has a right to present its case to public officials, it has a duty because in our representative democracy elected officials need to know constituents' views.[1]

## Managing Political Strategies

Given the web of interrelated governmental activities and the complexity of most public policy issues, it is imperative that larger businesses organize their government relations activities on a professional basis. Just as company experts manage the firm's technical activities, their marketing, contracts, and legal departments, so too are experienced professionals needed to organize and manage their government relations program, which is essentially political marketing.

These professionals, working with top management, should take the lead in crafting government relations strategies that are both defensive and offensive. Defense strategies seek to prevent harm to the company from new laws and to protect gains already won—keeping contracts in-house, keeping funding for them flowing from Congress, keeping regulatory agencies from upsetting important business relationships that are working well, and keeping the competitive playing field level.

Offensive strategies are those that seek to create a competitive advantage for your firm and do the reverse for your competitors by suggesting new laws and regulations that would undermine their business or jeopardize their standing with regulatory agencies.

Government relations should be understood as a strategic battlefield, and your firm's professionals are the strategists and the foot soldiers under your command. Just remember, your competitors may be thinking the same way.

What is being described is the essence of political marketing. Whether defensive or offensive, this involves crafting, packaging, and communicating a company's position on public policy issues of importance to the firm. This process involves tactical decisions regarding where and how to make your point and who should deliver the message. This function should be performed by a senior corporate officer who is also the head of the company's Washington office and who sits in the company's highest councils that make broad strategy decisions affecting all aspects of the business.

Businesses of any size have four basic strategic options for dealing with government: passive, reactive/confrontational, participative, and aggressive.

## PASSIVE STRATEGY

Many small firms and even large ones simply acquiesce in the face of federal, state, and municipal rules, regulations, and taxes in the belief that there is nothing they can do about them. The classic statement is "that's the way it is," and we will just have to live with it. What these companies are doing by abdicating any activist role is letting others carry the burden of fighting for them. Other companies do undertake the effort to organize and lobby for changes in governmental policies to lift the weight of government's burden not only from themselves, but also for others as well. Passive companies take a free ride, benefiting from the work of others that improves their own situation.

Often, passive firms, especially start-ups, do not have the time or resources to undertake anything beyond the immediate tasks of getting their business up and running. This is understandable. Once the firm is established and running smoothly, its owners and managers need to face the decision of whether or not to deal with the largest issue in their company's environment—other than their immediate competition—the role of government. As we have seen, government can make or break a company with taxation and regulations that can undermine a firm's profit stream by raising operating costs and siphoning off profits. At some point in your firm's growth, you must face this issue.

"Managers who ignore the actions of government do so at great risk." There should be "no mistake about it: the rule-making game is every bit as competitive as selling products and services. It just takes place in a different arena and with a different set of players. . . ."[2] To sustain your business, you must play the game—and play effectively. It really is not a game because it is played for keeps. Government is an arena of mortal combat, a battlefield with winners and losers, victors and vanquished.

Many companies, reaching the end of their rope in the face of deteriorating business conditions, simply leave the field. Half of all start-ups that shut down their businesses within the first year do so because they were not prepared for the heavy burden of government regulations and taxation. Other firms leave communities that are oppressive, seeking greener pastures elsewhere. This is exactly what the Boeing Company did when it moved its headquarters from Seattle to Chicago, tiring of waging a losing war against the antibusiness climate in Seattle, Washington.

## REACTIVE/CONFRONTATIONAL STRATEGY

The first "activist" role companies often play is one of reaction, confronting a situation to try to defeat it. A company sitting passively for months or years will suddenly be awaked one day by reading about a new law, regulation, or tax that is being considered at the federal or state level that will dig into its business with profound impact. At that point, it reacts—it gets angry and wants to do something about it. Reactive strategies often start with letters to legislators or the governor complaining about the impact this new proposal will have on the company. This is useful and important—exercise your First Amendment right of free speech and the right to petition the government for redress of grievance.

The same reactive activities increase in effectiveness if they are grouped with those of other companies similarly impacted. This is most typically accomplished through business and community associations, such as the Chamber of Commerce or a trade association representing your industry. Organizing and working with others increases your impact dramatically.

An example of this type of reactive undertaking will illustrate the point. In the early 1980s in California, then-governor Jerry Brown supported a proposed law to tax corporations headquartered in the state on their business earnings produced in other states and other countries. This was called the Universal Tax. The effect of this would be that companies with factories and other production operations out-of-state would be taxed twice—in the state where the factory produced the goods and in California, the state where the firm's headquarters is located.

One of the industries that would have been severely impacted was aerospace and defense. Executives from those companies concluded that individually these companies, even though they were among the largest employers in the state, would have little impact working alone. Under the leadership of one company, Northrop, the fifteen largest companies in that industry organized the California Aerospace Alliance. This group represented 5 percent of the state's gross product and 15 percent of its employees. Having organized under this one banner, the alliance began lobbying in Sacramento to derail the Universal Tax bill. Working also with established organizations, such as the California Chamber of Commerce, California Taxpayers Association, and the California Manufacturers and Technology Association, the allies and its associates were successful.[3]

This "reactive" strategy worked, and it was decided to continue the alliance, fearing that other types of legislation damaging to the industry might surface later. The reactive strategy thus morphed into a participatory strategy.

## PARTICIPATORY STRATEGY

Companies that participate day-to-day in the workings of their cities, states, and national governments are in a good position to get early warning signals of potential threats to their businesses and are often able to deal with them before they become monster issues. Working through trade associations and business organizations is an easy, cost-effective, and reliable way to keep abreast of developments and take action early.

Large companies also have their own contract lobbyists and their own offices in state capitals and in Washington, D.C., to monitor and deal with emerging issues, as well as to promote their company's own competitive interests, such as winning government contracts. More than five hundred companies have Washington, D.C., offices to maintain a presence, keep contacts alive, represent the company to trade and other associations and to the federal government, and to provide marketing assistance to the firm's operating units.[4]

An example of a large-scale lobbying activity in Washington, D.C., is the pharmaceutical industry's effort to defeat a bill that would allow the importation of prescription drugs from less expensive foreign sources. The industry had about $150 billion in U.S. sales in 2002 and, in the first half of 2003, spent more than $29 million through their trade association, the Pharmaceutical Research and Manufacturers of America, to defeat the bill. In addition, individual drug companies undertook their own lobbying activities: Eli Lilly spent $2.9 million, Bristol-Myers Squibb $2.6 million, Johnson & Johnson $2.2 million, and Pfizer $1.8 million.[5]

At the state level, roughly 35,000 organizations were registered in 1997 as lobbyists. Over half of these, 53 percent, were registered in only one state. Of those companies and specialized interests registered in multiple states, only a few were registered in many states, with the mean being just six states. Looking at companies' registration profiles, a few large corporations are registered in most states: Anheuser-Bush in fifty states, American Insurance Association in forty-eight, Brown and Williamson Tobacco in forty-seven, AT&T in forty-five, Pfizer in forty-three, National Federation of Independent Businesses in forty-two, and American Cancer Society in forty. Businesses represented 77 percent of all registrations at the state level in 1999.[6]

By regularly and continually participating with business and industry groups and associations, firms are well served by receiving a steady supply of information on trends in government regulations and legislation, on upcoming hearings and rule-making sessions, and equally importantly they will have a collective voice to speak for them on issues concerning their business. Companies rarely want to have to take center stage to oppose threatening issues; trade associations provide useful political cover. These associations include the U.S. Chamber of Commerce, National Association of Independent Business, National Association of Manufacturers, and specialized trade associations like the Aerospace Industries Association and the American Automobile Manufacturers Association.

### Relationships Mean Access

Through regular participation, companies can establish relationships with policymakers. This is the first-level goal. Without relationships, you typically cannot gain access. Without access, your message cannot be delivered except through the media, where it is often lost in the clutter of a myriad of other messages. Relationships equal access. That is the critical first step.

The second step is crafting your message so that it can be grasped quickly and easily, makes intellectual sense to the policymaker, and is packaged in ways that coincide with his or her own agenda. In other words, let the policymaker know in clear terms what your message is and what he or she will get out of supporting your cause.

## The Calculus of Politics

The third step is understanding the calculus of politics. All degrees of political support—from a legislator simply cosigning a letter to undertaking a full-scale effort—come with political cost to policymakers. You have to help the policymaker make the calculation that by supporting your cause he/she will possibly lose some support, say, with environmentalists, but that the gains, for instance, in support from workers and consumers, will exceed those losses. These types of political calculations occur every day in every arena of government, and businesspeople have to get used to making them or their message will not be heard, support will not be provided, and their cause will not succeed.

Government relations professionals understand these calculations, as well as the rules that govern their profession. Such rules include the registration of lobbyists, periodic reports on their work, their financial activities and contributions, filing of reports on company political action committee activities and contributions, and a myriad of other details. These regulations pertain to federal, state, and local governmental units, with very few exceptions. Failure to comply can result in severe penalties for the firm and for the individual lobbyist.[7]

Contract lobbyists make a business of representation-for-hire. These are independent companies, much like law firms, that sell their services to businesses needing to establish or maintain relationships with key politicians or regulators and to companies needing immediate help on a one-time basis, like getting an appropriations line item passed. Certain firms specialize in working with Democratic or Republican legislators, and others specialize in particular public policy areas, such as FCC or FAA regulations. The sons and daughters of powerful congressional committee chairmen and senior members of key committees have formed their own lobbying firms or have joined previously established firms; their "access" to these committees is of course guaranteed, and they can easily deliver the message of their employer.[8]

## AGGRESSIVE STRATEGY

The most effective approach is to work together with other companies that share your interest, but there are times when an individual company has no choice but to strike out on its own to defend or promote its particular interest. This happens when other companies in the same trade or business associations have a view different from yours, or other firms in the associations conclude that the issue in question is of marginal importance to the bulk of the association's membership and is therefore not worthy of expending political capital. Yet, your firm's very life might be at stake, and so you have no choice but to mount a solo campaign.

Examples of such individual company initiatives abound. AT&T is a member of electronic and communications associations, as well as the U.S. Chamber of Commerce. Yet, it had to strike out on its own, lobbying the FCC and Congress, to protect its vital business interests against the "baby bells" who were lobbying to undercut AT&T's virtual monopoly of long-distance service by working to gain approval to offer long-distance service in addition to local telephone service.

Meanwhile, the "baby bells" organized a lobbying effort "to end government management of competition" for local communication service. SBC Communications, Verizon, BellSouth, and other local phone service providers launched a three-year campaign to change government regulations requiring them to lease lines to other providers at regulated costs. They are enlisting the support of equipment suppliers, like Lucent Technologies and Motorola, as well as their own trade group, the U.S. Telecom Association, to lobby for these changes. "Their purpose is clearly economic—to destroy the competitors," said a former FCC general counsel.[9]

Consumer groups fought bitterly against the Bush administration's intention to raise tariffs on imported steel, arguing that higher steel prices would increase prices of consumer goods by raising the cost of imported steel. Farm interests also lobbied against steel tariffs fearing the European Union would retaliate against U.S. farm exports. Bush raised the tariffs anyway with support from United States Steel and the steelworkers' union. He later rescended the tariff under pressure from the World Trade Organization and the European Union.

Taking aggressive action can include a whole range of activities, from individual lobbying contacts; making campaign contributions through the company's Political Action Committee; mobilizing your company's stakeholders (employees, retirees, unions, investors, community activists, etc.); activating industry and trade associations; organizing grassroots involvement; advertising on radio, television, and through print media; and speaking out at public forums and industry venues. Coca-Cola, for example, has an aggressive ongoing campaign to repeal state laws that require deposits on beverage containers.

## Costs of Involvement

Aggressive involvement has costs, both in money and time, that are greater than any other strategy. Companies adopting this strategy generally hire professional lobbying firms to work with their own in-house lobbyists to craft tactics and to work the halls of government. Mailings to employees, retirees, suppliers, and others are expensive and carry certain public relations risks to the firm—if some of the target stakeholders have views different from the one the firm is touting. For consumer product companies, this can cost sales. For any company, an aggressive strategy may have reputational costs, the prevention of which requires tight controls on the activity by the CEO. The cost of not undertaking a political marketing strategy may, however, be greater.

This is a lesson learned the hard way by Wal-Mart, the world's largest company. Sam Walton, the founder, eschewed politics, and his legacy lasted until 1998, when the company changed its apolitical stance to an aggressive strategy. What happened? That year Wal-Mart learned its plans for large-scale expansion in China were thwarted by the terms of the U.S.–China trade deal limiting Americans to a 30 store agreement, far below the company's plans. Today, Wal-Mart has the second largest Political Action Committee in Washington, D.C., was the largest donor to parties and candidates in 2003, and has five in-house lobbyists and a stable of contract lobbyists that are the cream of profession. Wal-Mart is still learning the ropes in federal and state politics, but what it has learned is that it has to look out for itself,having so much at stake.[10]

Management's time and attention will be required to participate and oversee political marketing activities, taking energy away from core business operations. Top executives may have to take a crash course in government to be effective. In a recent survey of government relations professionals at *Fortune* 100 companies, 77 percent rated typical top executives as having a mediocre—or worse—grasp of the way governmental processes work.[11] Many corporate executives are genuinely uncomfortable working the hustings as well as the back rooms of politics. Often, politicians want to meet with the CEO to be certain the company is truly committed to this aggressive course of action. If you adopt an aggressive strategy, get used to being on the firing line personally.

## PRINCIPLES FOR INFLUENCING GOVERNMENT

Whatever form of involvement your firm adopts for protecting and promoting its interests in governmental arenas, there are a few principles that sum up what needs to be clearly understood:[12]

- *Never discount the potential impact of government.* When government intervenes, it can be decisive—either for you or against you. Working with government is far more productive than fighting it, and by being on the scene you increase your probability of success.
- *Effective influence is built on a foundation of relationships.* Those relationships cannot be built overnight—on the spur of the moment, when a governmental

action is about to be announced that will hurt your company. Then, it is too late. You have to invest the time and resources to steadily build relationships to be able to cash in that political capital when it becomes urgently needed.

- *To shape the rules, you have to build coalitions.* Small to medium-size companies lack the resources and experience to make an impact alone. They need partners, usually lots of them, to even be heard by public officials. This is why trade and industry associations are ubiquitous—many companies belong to several. One survey of the nation's largest companies (*Fortune* 100 firms) found that these companies belong to an average of twenty-eight trade associations, with some belonging to as many as three hundred, excluding informal groups and short-term teams formed for specific actions.[13] Building coalitions requires finding other companies with complementary goals and a willingness to work with others. Not even the largest companies go it alone—unless they are forced to.

- *Where you play is as important as how you play.* Choosing where to play the political game is of equal importance to how you go about it. Selecting the right arena of combat—whether the House, Senate, a regulatory agency, a state administrative body, or the courts—will as much as any later activity influence the outcome. Whether you are playing offense or defense, identifying the right forum is vital to influencing governmental outputs. For companies with activities in many states, the preferred forum is the federal government—to minimize cost, time, and to achieve maximum impact.

- *The ability to influence rule making is a weapon in the competitive game.* If a company cannot beat another in the marketplace, it may try to torpedo it in the rule-making arena. Microsoft accused Netscape of exactly that strategy when the latter filed an antitrust complaint with the Justice Department. Some companies will always be active in the governmental arena, and the result of their actions may help or harm your company's competitive standing. This is particularly important when basic industry rules are being created, such as e-commerce, or are changing, such as telecommunications. Your company's best interests may not be protected unless you are actively involved in the development of your firm's competitive governmental strategy. Some firms having close relationships with key congressional committees or staffers actively participate in the drafting of legislation and provide expert testimony on various public policy issues.[14]

- *The influence game is never over.* There is no rest for the weary. Or, looked at from a lobbyist's perspective, this is a guaranteed full-employment profession because government is growing, and its role in business is deepening. Battles may be won or lost, but the war never ends. Perpetual vigilance is the price of sustaining success.

## CONCLUSION

Business has the right to present its views to government at all levels. In a representative democracy, this is also an obligation. Truly effective representation can be achieved only over time by establishing and sustaining relationships with public officials. Various techniques for achieving successful relationships have been presented.

Large companies need to have a government relations officer in their highest executive councils to craft and execute political marketing strategies that promote company programs and defend company interests in the face of government regulations and regulators.

A vigorous government relations program is an essential component of any firm's activities, regardless of company size. Once an entrepreneurial start-up has achieved critical mass and is operating smoothly, this function requires the owner's attention, just as it is a critical responsibility of a major corporation's CEO.

# Notes

## CHAPTER 1

1. For information on how to write a business plan, see Wesley B. Truitt, *Business Planning: A Comprehensive Framework and Process* (Westport, CT: Quorum Books, 2002).

2. For a discussion of the external business environment, see ibid., chapter 4. See also George A. Steiner and John F. Steiner, *Business, Government, and Society: A Managerial Perspective*, 10th ed. (New York: McGraw-Hill/Irwin, 2003), chapter 2; and C. W. Roney, *Assessing the Business Environment: Guidelines for Strategists* (Westport, CT: Quorum Books, 1999).

3. James E. Anderson, *Politics and the Economy* (Boston: Little, Brown, 1966), 1–2.

4. This discussion is based on Alfred Chandler, Jr., "Government vs. Business: An American Phenomenon," in *Business and Public Policy*, ed. John T. Dunlop (Boston: Division of Research, Graduate School of Business Administration, Harvard University, 1980).

5. Alfred Chandler, Jr., "Government vs. Business: An American Phenomenon," *Harvard Business Review*, March 1982, 21.

6. For a discussion of the populist and progressive movements, see Samuel Eliot Morison and Henry Steele Commager, *The Growth of the American Republic*, 4th ed. (New York: Oxford University Press, 1958) vol. II, 105–73 and 236–65, respectively.

7. Chandler, "Government vs. Business," 22.

8. For other reasons why people have a critical attitude toward business, see Steiner and Steiner, *Business, Government, and Society*, 89–112. In their view, the fundamental source of criticism is that businesspeople prioritize profit over more worthy values (truth, honesty, justice, etc.) and that economic development imposes strains on societies.

9. This discussion is based on Murray L. Weidenbaum, *Business and Government in the Global Marketplace*, 6th ed. (Upper Saddle River, NJ: Prentice Hall, 1999), 6–7.

10. In *Dartmouth College v. Woodward*, 4 Wheaton 519 (1819), the Court sided with business against arbitrary state power when the legislature of New Hampshire amended the Charter of Dartmouth College, attempting to change it from a private to a state school. The Supreme Court ruled that Dartmouth's Charter is a contract, "the obligation of which cannot be impaired without violating the Constitution of the United States."

11. Weidenbaum, *Business and Government*, 7.

12. For a brief discussion, see Steiner and Steiner, *Business, Government, and Society*, 288–90.

13. Cited in Weidenbaum, *Business and Government*, 32.

14. *U.S. v. Standard Oil Co.*, 221 U.S. 1 (1911); *U.S. v. American Tobacco Co.*, 211 U.S. 106 (1911).

15. Anderson, *Politics and the Economy*, 14.

16. Ibid., 14.

17. Preceding data in this section is from Richard Bolling and John Bowles, "Regulations Have Dulled America's Competitive Edge but They Needn't," *Los Angeles Times*, August 9, 1981, VI 3.

18. Adapted from Lawrence Mosher, "Environmentalists Question Whether to Retreat or Stay on the Offensive," *National Journal*, December 13, 1980, 2120.

19. Weidenbaum, *Business and Government*, 32–35.

20. See the classic study of this trend by Adolph A. Berle, Jr. and Gardner C. Means, *The Modern Corporation and Private Property* (New York: Macmillan, 1932).

21. This section is largely based on Steiner and Steiner, *Business, Government, and Society*, 278–80. The Council of Economic Advisors states the two reasons for demand for regulation somewhat differently: to address market imperfections and address specific interests, both of which generate cost because "resources will be allocated to or captured in less productive uses than would have been the case absent the regulation." Council of Economic Advisors, *Economic Report of the President* (Washington, DC: U.S. Government Printing Office, 2003), 138; see also 139–42.

22. *Los Angeles Times*, March 28, 2003, C5; May 10, 2003, C1; May 14, 2003, C1.

23. *Wall Street Journal*, June 3, 2003, A1; *Los Angeles Times*, January 23, 2004, A14.

24. For a discussion of the Motor Carrier Act of 1980 (PL96-296), see *Congressional Quarterly Almanac, 1980*, 242–43. See also Bob Gatty, "New Horizons in Trucking," *Nation's Business*, October 1980, 40–46.

25. For more information on rule-making procedures, see Cornelius M. Kerwin, *Rulemaking: How Government Agencies Write Law and Make Policy*, 2nd ed. (Washington, DC: CQ Press, 1999).

26. *Wall Street Journal*, October 22, 2003, A6.

27. Council of Economic Advisors, *Economic Report of the President*, 157.

28. The U.S. Supreme Court established these standards, known as the Chevron Doctrine, in a well-known case, *Chevron U.S.A. v. Natural Resources Defense Council, Inc.*, 467 U.S. 843 (1984).

## CHAPTER 2

1. Appendix 2.1 is adapted from Murray L. Weidenbaum, *Business and Govern-*

*ment in the Global Marketplace*, 7th ed. (Upper Saddle River, NJ: Pearson Prentice Hall, 2004), 15.

2. See chapter 10.

3. Cited in George A. Steiner and John F. Steiner, *Business, Government, and Society: A Managerial Perspective*, 10th ed. (New York: McGraw-Hill Irwin, 2003) 294–5.

4. Maurice McTigue, *Federal Times*, January 15, 2003.

5. Susan Dudley, Mercatus Center, George Mason University, presentation to President's Economic Forum, Waco, Texas, 2001.

6. Lawrence Mosher, "Big Steel Says It Can't Afford to Make the Nation's Air Pure," *National Journal*, July 5, 1980, 1088.

7. "Deregulation," *Business Week*, March 9, 1981, 65–66.

8. The 1976 study was by economist Robert DeFina; the 1980 study was by Murray Weidenbaum, who a year later became chairman of the Council of Economic Advisors. Cited in "Deregulation," *Business Week*, March 9, 1981, 66. See also Murray Weidenbaum, "Regulation: How Washington Will Switch," *Nation's Business*, February 1981, 26–30.

9. EPA's FY-2002 appropriation was $7.840 billion; *The Budget of the United States Government, Fiscal Year 2004* (Washington, DC: U.S. Government Printing Office, February 2003).

10. Survey conducted for the National Association of Manufacturers (NAM) by Mercatus Center, George Mason University, Virginia.

11. U.S. Small Business Administration, "The Changing Burden of Regulation, Paperwork, and Tax Compliance on Small Business: A Report to Congress," October 1995, www.sba.gov/advo/laws/archive/law_brd.html.

12. Ibid., 3.

13. Ibid., 15.

14. *Los Angeles Times*, July 22, 2002, A1; and February 19, 2003, C4.

15. Lawrence Mosher, "With EPA's New Air Pollution Penalties, It's Never Cheaper to Pay the Fine," *National Journal*, January 24, 1981, 133, 135.

16. *Los Angeles Times*, June 27, 2002, C1; May 6, 2003, C3. *Wall Street Journal*, June 10, 2003, A1. Samuel Waksal, former ImClone chairman, was sentenced to seven years and three months in federal prison and fined $3 million for obstruction of justice and insider trading, *Wall Street Journal*, June 11, 2003, A2.

17. *Los Angeles Times*, August 31, 2002, C1.

18. *Wall Street Journal*, June 18, 2003, A3.

19. Ibid.; April 29, 2003, A1, C1. See also "Partners in Crime," *Fortune*, October 27, 2003, 79–100.

20. *Wall Street Journal.*, October 10, 2002, B10.

21. *Los Angeles Times*, March 6, 2003, C1, C6.

22. *Wall Street Journal*, July 25, 2003, A3.

23. *Los Angeles Times*, October 24, 2002, C7.

24. *Wall Street Journal*, July 25, 2003, C1.

25. *Los Angeles Times*, February 24, 2003, C4.

26. Ibid.

27. For a discussion of corporate governance in the post–Sarbanes-Oxley period, see Paul F. Kocourek, Christian Burger, and Bill Birchard, "Corporate Governance: Hard Facts about Soft Behaviors," *Strategy+Business*, Spring 2002, 59–69. See also

*Economic Report of the President*, (Washington, DC: U.S. Government Printing Office, 2003), 73–108.

28. *Wall Street Journal*, January 22, 2003, C1.

29. *Los Angeles Times*, May 19, 2003, C1, C5.

30. Interview with a Hughes senior vice president, March 1983.

31. *Economic Report of the President* (Washington, DC: U.S. Government Printing Office, 2003), Table B-79, 370.

32. Ibid., Table B-80, 371.

33. Ibid., 175.

34. Susan Dudley and Melinda Warren, *Regulatory Spending Soars: An Analysis of the U.S. Budget for Fiscal Years 2003 and 2004*, Joint Study of Weidenbaum Center at Washington University and Mercatus Center at George Mason University, 2003.

35. Homeland Security Bill, *Los Angeles Times*, November 26, 2002, A18.

36. Preceding fiscal year data are total on-budget obligations, *The Budget of the United States Government, Fiscal Year 2004* (Washington, DC: U.S. Government Printing Office, 2003). Outlays were projected to rise to $2.1 trillion in FY-2008.

37. *The Budget of the United States Government, Fiscal Year 2004.*

38. These phenomena may not occur due to projected reduced levels of federal deficit and the enormous size of the international bond market; see Anna Bernasek, "Duking It Out Over the Deficit," *Fortune*, May 26, 2003, 40.

39. Homeland Security Bill, *Los Angeles Times*, November 26, 2002, A18, including data in table 2.1. FY-2002 actual budget authority for Homeland Security was $30.4 billion; *The Budget of the United States Government, Fiscal Year 2004.*

40. For more information on deregulation, see Weidenbaum, *Business and Government in the Global Marketplace*, 6th ed. (Upper Saddle River, NH: Prentice-Hall, 1999), 143–63.

41. For airline deregulation, see Melvin A. Brenner, "Is U.S. Deregulation a Failure? Here's How to Find Out," *Airline Executive*, September 1980, 22–23; "Sky Wars: The Airlines Enter a New Age," *Dun's Review*, February 1981, 28–34; and Michael Wines, "Verdict Still Out on Deregulation's Impact on U.S. Air Travel System," *National Journal*, March 6, 1982, 404–9.

42. For telecommunications, see Shaifali Puri, "Deals of the Year," *Fortune*, February 17, 1997, 102; and *Fortune*, January 11, 1999, 72.

43. Financial services deregulation began in 1980 with the Depository Institutions Deregulation and Monetary Control Act; see "America's New Financial Structure," *Business Week*, November 17, 1980, 138–44. For the 1999 act, see Annual Report of the Council of Economic Advisors, *Economic Report of the President* (Washington, DC: U.S. Government Printing Office, 2003), 144–45.

44. Council on Competitiveness, *Legacy of Regulatory Reform* (Washington, DC: U.S. Government Printing Office, 1992).

45. Mercatus Center, George Mason University, Virginia.

46. Council of Economic Advisors, *Economic Report of the President* (Washington, DC: U.S. Government Printing Office, 2002), 162–63.

47. For a discussion of mergers and acquisitions, see Donald DePamphilis, *Mergers, Acquisitions, and Other Restructuring Activities* (San Diego: Academic Press, 2001), especially 40–44, 54–86.

48. John D. Williams, "Rail-Rate Increases Due for Early Arrival Thanks to New Law," *Wall Street Journal*, October 14, 1980, 1.

49. Michael Wines, "Three Years After Deregulation, Railroads Leaner, More Competitive," *National Journal*, December 10, 1983, 2560–65.

50. U.S. Census Bureau, *Statistical Abstract of the United States, 2002* (Washington, DC: U.S. Government Printing Office, 2002), Tables 473 and 475, 320–21. Data exclude intelligence agencies.

51. The National Bureau of Economic Research, the independent group that makes determinations regarding recessions, declared in July 2003 that the 2001 recession began in March and ended in November 2001 and was "relatively mild," with economic activity contracting just 0.6 percent, the second smallest output loss on record. *Wall Street Journal*, July 18, 2003, A2.

52. Labor Department data; *Los Angeles Times*, September 23, 2001, A1, A20.

53. James Flanigan, "Far-Off Terrorism Cuts Close to Home," *Los Angeles Times*, October 20, 2003, C1, C3.

54. *Los Angeles Times*, April 13, 2003, A29.

55. Peter G. Gosselin and Jube Shiver, Jr., "'New Economy' Is a Thing of the Past," *Los Angeles Times*, September 23, 2001, A1.

56. All airline data and the quotations are from Cait Murphy, "A No-Fly Zone," *Fortune*, April 14, 2003, 56.

57. See www.firstgov.gov/Agencies/Federal/Independent.shtml.

## CHAPTER 3

1. This tripartite grouping was suggested by Dr. Donald DePamphilis.

2. U.S. Census Bureau, *Statistical Abstract of the United States: 2002* (Washington, DC: U.S. Government Printing Office, 2002), 320, table 473, hereinafter cited as *Statistical Abstract*.

3. General Electric and IBM data from *Fortune*, April 14, 2003, F-1.

4. *Statistical Abstract*, 326, 331, tables 485, 494.

5. Ibid., 312, 320, tables 461, 474.

6. Murray L. Weidenbaum, *Business and Government in the Global Marketplace*, 7th ed. (Upper Saddle River, NJ: Pearson Prentice Hall, 2004), 9.

7. *Statistical Abstract*, 716.

8. Ibid., 306–307, tables 452–53.

9. E. I. du Pont de Nemours & Company, *2002 Review*, 1.

10. The USAF proposed a lease/buy arrangement for one hundred Boeing 767 jets for $16 billion to use as air refueling tankers, *Los Angeles Times*, May 24, 2003, C1. This proposal, however, ran into apolitical fire-storm later.

11. *Economic Report of the President* (Washington, DC: U.S. Government Printing Office, February 2003), 46.

12. For information on macroeconomics, including fiscal policy, see Peter Kennedy, *Macroeconomic Essentials*, 2nd ed. (Cambridge, MA: MIT Press, 2001).

13. U.S. Constitution, Article I, Section 8.

14. *Economic Report of the President*, 52–53.

15. Tax data are from the Tax Foundation: www.taxfoundation.org/taxfreedomday.html.

16. *Economic Report of the President*, 54–57.

17. *Budget of the United States Government, Fiscal Year 2001* (Washington, DC: U.S. Government Printing Office, 2000).

18. Social Insurance Payroll Taxes include Social Security taxes, Medicare taxes, unemployment insurance taxes, and federal employee retirement payments. This category grew from 2 percent of GDP in 1955 to 6.8 percent in 2001. *Budget of the United States Government, Fiscal Year 2001.*

19. *Economic Report of the President,* 54. FY-2002 revenues of $1.95 trillion were reported in *The Budget of the United States Government, 2004* (Washington, DC: U.S. Government Printing Office, 2003), 59.

20. U.S. Department of Housing and Urban Development, www.hud.gov/news/release docs/homeowning.cfm.

21. Heritage Foundation study, June 2003, www.heritage.org.tax/.

22. *Economic Report of the President,* 53–54; see also Kathy M. Kristof, "New Tax Breaks Offer a Lifeline to Businesses," *Los Angeles Times,* March 16, 2003, C3.

23. U.S. Constitution, Article I, Section 8; capitalization as shown in original document.

24. Libertarians still take a strict constructionist position; see Larry Elder, *Showdown* (New York: St. Martin's Press, 2002).

25. *Budget of the United States Government, Fiscal Year 2001.* Totals may not add due to rounding. The President's budget for FY-2005 calls for $2.4 trillion in spending; *Wall Street Journal,* February 3, 2004, A1.

26. Ben Bernanke, a Federal Reserve governor, believes deflation in the United States is unlikely; see his "Deflation: Making Sure 'It' Doesn't Happen Here," *Federal Reserve Bulletin,* November 2002.

27. The twelve district Federal Reserve Banks are in Atlanta, Boston, Chicago, Cleveland, Dallas, Kansas City, Minneapolis, New York, Philadelphia, Richmond, San Francisco, and St. Louis.

28. Fed chairmen are appointed for four-year terms. For Greenspan's influence on monetary policy, see Bob Woodward, *Maestro, Greenspan's Fed and the American Boom* (New York: Simon & Schuster, 2000).

29. *Wall Street Journal,* June 26, 2003, A1.

30. *Economic Report of the President,* 51.

31. Report to Congress by the Treasury Department and the Federal Reserve, *Los Angeles Times,* March 15, 2003, A21.

32. www.FederalReserveEducation.org. See also *Los Angeles Times,* May 20, 2003, C4.

33. For a discussion, see Kennedy, *Macroeconomic Essentials,* 218–19.

34. John Dillon, "Will Evian Refresh World Trade?" *Wall Street Journal,* June 3, 2003, B2.

35. *Foreign Investment: Implications of Exon-Florio and Related Amendments* (Washington, DC: General Accounting Office, 1995).

36. *Statistical Abstract,* 785, 788, tables 1267, 1272.

37. *Wall Street Journal,* July 16, 2003, A4; February 13, 2004, A4.

38. *Economic Report of the President,* 46.

39. U.S. Census Bureau, *U.S. International Trade in Goods and Services,* Series FT-900 (01-12); www.census.gov/foreign-trade/Press-Release/2001pr/FinalRevisions2001.

40. For more information on exchange rates, see John D. Daniels and Lee H. Radebaugh, *International Business: Environments and Operations,* 9th ed. (Upper Saddle River, NJ: Prentice Hall, 2001), chap. 9, 10.

41. *Budget of the United States Government, Fiscal Year 2004* (Washington, DC: U.S. Government Printing Office, 2003); and *Statistical Abstract*, 307, table 453.

42. U.S. Census Bureau, www.census.gov/population/www/projections/np_p2.gif.

43. As an example, the Advanced Technology Transit Bus was funded on this basis. See Jose de la Torre and Wesley B. Truitt, "Northrop Grumman and the Advanced Technology Transit Bus Program," in Jose de la Torre, Yves Doz, and Timothy Devinney, *Managing the Global Corporation: Case Studies in Strategy and Management*, 2nd ed. (New York: Irwin/McGraw Hill, 2001), 259–71.

44. Weidenbaum, *Business and Government in the Global Marketplace*, 244–50.

45. For New York City, the federal credit program consisted of short-term direct loans in 1975 and with loan guarantees in 1978; in turn, the city pledged to balance its budget by 1982, which it did in 1981; see "New York City: On the Comeback Trail," *Morgan Guaranty Survey*, April 1981, 10–15. For Chrysler, see Lee Iacocca, *Iacocca: An Autobiography* (New York: Bantam Books, 1984). Chrysler Corp. paid off $600 million in debt at 30 cents on the dollar and laid off 40 percent of its workers.

46. Weidenbaum, *Business and Government in the Global Marketplace*, 256–58.

47. Murray L. Weidenbaum, "Paying the Price of Federal Bailouts," *Los Angeles Times*, October 28, 1980, IV, 3.

48. Weidenbaum, *Business and Government in the Global Marketplace*, 253.

49. *Budget of the United States Government, Fiscal Year 2004* (Washington, DC: U.S. Government Printing Office, 2003).

50. *Wall Street Journal*, August 26, 2003, A2; *Los Angeles Times*, December 5, 2003, A1.

51. *Los Angeles Times*, August 27, 2003, C3.

52. *Budget of the United States Government, Fiscal Year 2004.*

## CHAPTER 4

1. U.S. Census Bureau, *Statistical Abstract of the United States, 2002* (Washington, DC: U.S. Government Printing Office, 2002), 260–61, tables 405–406. Hereinafter cited as *Statistical Abstract*.

2. *Statistical Abstract*, 268, table 414.

3. Interview with Robert S. Torrez, CFO, City of Long Beach, April 2003. See www.longbeach.gov/citygov/budget.htm.

4. The Tax Foundation, http://www.taxfoundation.org/corporateincometaxrates.html.

5. State tax data are from the Tax Foundation, www.taxfoundation.org/statelocal02.html. See also *Wall Street Journal*, April 8, 2004, D1.

6. The Tax Foundation, www.taxfoundation.org/pr-businesstaxclimate.html.

7. *Los Angeles Times*, May 4, 2003, A1; and *Statistical Abstract*, 276, table 422, 1999 revenue.

8. *Statistical Abstract*, 269, table 416.

9. Murray L. Weidenbaum, *Business and Government in the Global Marketplace*, 7th ed. (Upper Saddle River, NJ: Pearson Prentice Hall, 2004), 261, 263.

10. *Statistical Abstract*, 22, 272, 274, tables 18, 420–21. Bureau of Economic Analysis, U.S. Commerce Dept., www.ntanet.org. For additional state data, see

National Association of State Budget Officers, "Fiscal Survey of States," November 2002, http://www.nasbo.

11. U.S. Census Bureau, *U.S. International Trade in Goods and Services*, Series FT-900.

12. *Statistical Abstract*, 32–34, 294–95, tables 30, 439–40; see www.census.gov.

13. Ibid., 292–93, tables 437–38; see www.census.gov.

14. State economic data from Bureau of Economic Analysis, U.S. Commerce Department, www.ntanet.org and international data from OECD.org.

15. The Customs District of Los Angeles is the nation's largest, with $214.3 billion in trade in 2002; *Los Angeles Times*, May 19, 2003, C1, C6.

16. *Statistical Abstract*, 519, 523–24, tables 787, 796–97.

17. U.S. Census Bureau, *Annual Survey of Manufacturers, Geographic Area Statistics*. Series M00 (AS)-3. See also Los Angeles Times, January 21, 2004, C2 for L.A. county data.

18. U.S. Census Bureau www. Guidefacts.census.gov/qfd/states/00000.html.

19. www.sba.gov/advo/stats/profiles/02ca.

20. *The Economist*, April 19, 2003, 26–27, and conversations with Boeing officials.

21. *Wall Street Journal*, July 18, 2003, A2.

22. Wells Fargo Bank, reported in *USA Today*, August 11, 2003, A1.

23. Data in this section is from UCLA Anderson School Forecast, *Los Angeles Times*, June 5, 2003, C1, C11.

24. *Los Angeles Times*, August 26, 2003, C1; April 27, 2004, C2.

25. Shawn Tully, "Postcards from the Edge," *Fortune*, August 11, 2003, 34.

26. Workers' Compensation Research Institute, *Wall Street Journal*, August 18, 2003, A10.

27. *Los Angeles Times*, August 28, 2003, C1, C11; March 26m, 2004, B1.

28. *USA Today*, August 11, 2003, A1.

29. "State Business Tax Climate Index Ranks State Tax Systems on How Friendly They Are to Business," Tax Foundation, http://www.taxfoundtion.org/pr-businesstaxclimate.html.

30. For its "Business Tax Burden Study," see Council on State Taxation, http://www.statetax.org/COSThome.cfm.

31. California Employment Development Department, http://www.edd.ca.gov/direp/diindtx.htm.

32. California Economic Development Department, http://www.edd.ca.gov/direp/diflatx.htm.

33. Tully, "Postcards from the Edge," 34.

34. *Los Angeles Times*, August 29, 2003, B1.

35. Ibid., October 6, 2003, A1, A19.

36. Benjamin Zycher, "State's Profligate Short-Timers," *Los Angeles Times*, June 9, 2003, B11.

37. The Tax Foundation, http://www.taxfoundation.org/states/california.

38. *Wall Street Journal*, August 18, 2003, A10.

39. Jack M. Stewart, "Does California Mean Business Anymore?" *Cal-Tax Digest*, March 2003.

40. As reported in *Desert Sun*, June 25, 2003, A1.

41. http://www.taxfoundation.org/ff/factsonCA.html.

42. John Kincaid, "Trends in Federalism: Is Fiscal Federalism Fizzling?" in *The Book of the States*, 2003 ed. (Lexington, KY: Council of State Governments, 2003), 26.

43. http://www.taxfoundation.org/pr-businesstaxclimate.html, 2.

44. Zycher, "State's Profligate Short-Timers," B11.

45. Bureau of Economic Analysis, U.S. Department of Commerce; Bureau of Labor Statistics, U.S. Department of Labor; National Association of State Budget Officers, http://www.nasbo.org.

46. National Conference of State Legislatures, *The Economist*, May 24, 2003, 27.

47. *Los Angeles Times*, June 26, 2003, A28.

48. Ibid., April 13, B1; May 4, 2003, A1; August 3, 2003, A1.

49. *Wall Street Journal*, August 18, 2003, A10.

50. *Los Angeles Times*, June 2, 2003, B8.

51. Ibid., August 23, 2003, A20.

52. Ibid., June 6, 2003, B1; June 13, 2003, C9.

53. *Wall Street Journal*, July 15, 2003, C1.

54. Ibid., July 25, 2003, C11.

55. *Los Angeles Times*, June 21, 2003, B1.

56. *Wall Street Journal*, August 28, 2003, A1. Gov. Schwarzenegger rescinded this tax on his first day in office.

57. *Los Angeles Times*, July 30, 2003, A1, and August 3, 2003, A1.

58. *Wall Street Journal*, August 5, 2003, C15.

59. "The Lady's in a Straitjacket," *The Economist*, February 22–28, 2003, 29–30.

60. "The Homeless Governor," *The Economist*, February 22–28, 2003, 30.

61. *Los Angeles Times*, June 2, 2003, B8.

62. *Wall Street Journal*, July 2, 2003, A10, and July 15, 2003, A14.

63. *Los Angeles Times*, August 3, 2003, A22.

64. Ibid., May 25, 2003, B1.

65. Ibid., June 4, 2003, B3; see also June 28, 2003, B3.

66. This discussion is based on Michael Hiltzik, "Assessing a Commercial Property Showdown in San Francisco," *Los Angeles Times*, May 22, 2003, C1, C5.

67. Bob Taylor, "Pension Crisis Swamps Cities and Counties," *Cal-Tax Special Report*, May 20, 2003.

68. *Orange County Register*, February 14, 2003, A1.

69. *San Diego Union-Tribune*, March 13, 2003, B1.

70. *Los Angeles Times*, July 4, 2003, A1; *Wall Street Journal*, January 16, 2004, A7.

71. Zycher, "State's Profligate Short-Timers," B11.

72. U.S. Department of Education, National Assessment of Educational Progress Report, http://www.nces.ed.gov/nationsreportcard/states/profile.asp.

73. U.S. Department of Education, National Assessment of Educational Progress Report, 2002, *Los Angeles Times*, June 20, 2003, A1, A32; seven states did not administer the test: Alaska, Colorado, Illinois, New Hampshire, New Jersey, South Dakota, and Wisconsin. Twelfth-graders taking the test included both public and private schools.

74. U.S. Department of Education Budget Series, http://www.NoChildLeftBehind.gov.

75. *Los Angeles Times*, June 14, 2003, A1, A25.
76. Larry McCarthy, "Competition Killers: More Delays, Less Infrastructure," *Cal-Tax Commentary*, http://www.caltax.org/member/digest/may2001.
77. *Wall Street Journal*, June 26, 2003, A3–4.
78. Jack M. Stewart, "Does California Mean Business Anymore?" *Cal-Tax Digest*, http://www.caltax.org/member/digest/M.../3.2003.Stewart.
79. Tully, "Postcards from the Edge," 33–34.

## CHAPTER 5

1. U.S. Small Business Administration, "The Changing Burden of Regulation, Paperwork, and Tax Compliance on Small Business: A Report to Congress," October 1995, 1, www.sba. gov/advo/laws/archive/law_brd.html.
2. See www.sba.gov/starting_business/startup/guide4.
3. U.S. Small Business Administration, "The Changing Burden of Regulation, Paperwork, and Tax Compliance on Small Business," 12, 15.
4. This section is based on Henry R. Cheeseman, *The Legal and Regulatory Environment*, 2d ed. (Upper Saddle River, NJ: Prentice Hall, 2000), chap. 12, 13; and Frank B. Cross and Roger LeRoy Miller, *West's Legal Environment of Business*, 5th ed. (Mason, OH: Thomson/South-Western, 2004), chap. 16–18.
5. Mark Diener, "Seeking Counsel," *Entrepreneur*, January 2003, 69.
6. "Patton Boggs Helping Hawaiians," *National Journal*, May 31, 2003, 1707.
7. Steven C. Bahls and Jane Ester Bahls, "Feeling Woozy?" *Entrepreneur*, August 2002, 68.
8. Mark Henricks, "The Winner Is . . . ," *Entrepreneur*, October 2003, 21–24.
9. See www.sba.gov/starting_business/startup/guide4.html, 5.
10. See www.eeoc.gov/small/otherissues.html, 1.
11. This section is based on U.S. Equal Employment Opportunity Commission, "An Overview of the EEOC and Small Business," www.eeoc.gov/small/overview.html.
12. 117 S. Ct. 660 (1997); EEOC Notice No. 915.002, May 2, 1997; www.eeoc.gov/docs/metropol.html.
13. For further information, see EEOC's *Facts about Employment Discrimination*.
14. See www.eeoc.gov/ada/adahandbook.
15. See U.S. Department of Labor, www.dol.gov/dol/ofccp.
16. Steven C. Bahls and Jane Easter Bahls, "Under the Radar?" *Entrepreneur*, November 2002, 88.
17. U.S. Small Business Administration, "The Changing Burden of Regulation, Paperwork, and Tax Compliance on Small Business," 12.
18. U.S. Department of Labor, OSHA Standard 1904.1(a)(1)&(2), www.osha.gov.
19. U.S. Department of Labor, "OSHA Handbook for Small Businesses," OSHA 2209, 1996 (Rev.), vii.
20. Reported in U.S. Small Business Administration, "The Changing Burden of Regulation, Paperwork, and Tax Compliance on Small Business," 10.
21. 66 FR 6122, January 19, 2001, www.owadisp.show_document?p_table =STANDARDS.

## CHAPTER 6

1. 29 U.S.C. Section 201 et seq.
2. See also EEOC, www.eeoc.gov/small/overview.html.
3. 26 U.S.C. Sections 3301–11.
4. 26 U.S.C. Section 1001 et seq.
5. See Department of Labor, http://www.dol.gov/dol/asp/public/programs/handbook/fmla.htm.
6. 29 U.S.C. Section 151 et seq.
7. For more information, contact the Department of Labor, www.dol.gov/dol/. The AFL/CIO also has a useful Web site: www.aflcio.org.
8. Attributed to the late John K. Northrop, founder of Northrop Corporation, now Northrop Grumman. For labor union data, see *Los Angeles Times*, August 31, 2003, C1.
9. See EEOC's "Facts About Sexual Harassment," www.eeoc.gov/facts/fs-sex.html.
10. See EEOC's "Questions and Answers about Employer Responsibilities concerning the Employment of Muslims, Arabs, South Asians, and Sikhs," www.eeoc.gov/facts/backlash- employer.html.
11. U.S.C. Sections 651–78.
12. Railroad workers and employees in the mining industry have their own regulations.
13. See *Code of Federal Regulations* (CFR) for maritime: 29 CFR 1915–19; agriculture: 29 CFR 1928; construction: 29 CFR 1926; and general industry: 29 CFR 1910.
14. U.S. Labor Department, "OSHA Handbook for Small Businesses," OSHA 2209, 1996 (Rev.), 51–53.
15. 42 U.S.C. Section 4321 et seq.
16. See www.epa.gov/epahome/lawregs.
17. For proposed rules on your industry, see www.epa.gov/ebitpages/industry.
18. 33 U.S.C. Section 1251 et seq.
19. 42 U.S.C. Section 4901.
20. 7 U.S.C. Section 135 et seq., and 15 U.S.C. Section 2601 et seq.
21. See www.epa.gov/ebtpages/pollutants.
22. See www.epa.gov/ebitpages/pesticides.
23. 15 U.S.C. Section 2051.
24. See www.cpsa.gov/smallbus/info.
25. See www.ftc.consumer.
26. 15 U.S.C. Section 1451 et seq.
27. *Wall Street Journal*, June 26, 2003, B1, B7.
28. *Wall Street Journal*, August 1, 2003, B1.
29. Jane Ester Bahls, "Better Safe . . ." *Entrepreneur*, July 2003, 76.
30. 15 U.S.C. Section 2301 et seq.
31. 21 U.S.C. Section 301.
32. See www.fda.gov/ora/fed_state/Small_Business/sb_guide.
33. 15 U.S.C. Sections 41–51.
34. See www.ftc.gov/consumer.

35. 39 U.S.C. Section 3009.

36. This section is largely based on Henry R. Cheeseman, *The Legal and Regulatory Environment: Contemporary Perspectives in Business,* 2d ed. (Upper Saddle River, NJ: Prentice Hall, 2000), 151–84.

37. This section is largely based on www.sec.gov/info/smallbus/reachsec.

38. For the text, see www.law.uc.edu/CCL/sldtoc.html.

39. This discussion is largely based on www.sec/gov/about/whatwedo.

40. www.sec.gov/about/whatwedo.

41. *Wall Street Journal,* November 5, 2003, A3.

42. Steven C. Bahls and Jane Ester Bahls, "Witness Protection," *Entrepreneur,* April 2003, 78.

43. www.sec.gov/info/smallbus/sbforum.

44. www.irs.ustreas.gov.

45. U.S. Treasury Department, IRS Publication 15, "Circular E, Employer's Tax Guide."


## CHAPTER 7

1. For a discussion, see Wesley B. Truitt, *Business Planning: A Comprehensive Framework and Process* (Westport, CT: Quorum Books, 2002), 45–48.

2. For a discussion of using M&A to gain customers, see Larry Selden and Geoffrey Colvin, "M&A Needn't Be a Loser's Game," *Harvard Business Review,* June 2003, 70–79.

3. *Los Angeles Times,* July 9, 2003, C4; and *Wall Street Journal,* July 1, 2003, C14; first half of 2003 deals totaled only about 3,600, valued at roughly $162 billion.

4. Samuel Eliot Morison and Henry Steele Commager, *The Growth of the American Republic* (New York: Oxford University Press, 1958), vol. II, 137–38.

5. Donald DePamphilis, *Mergers, Acquisitions, and Other Restructuring Activities* (San Diego: Academic Press, 2001), 85–86.

6. Shaifali Puri, "Deals of the Year," *Fortune,* February 17, 1997, 102.

7. This section is based on FTC, "An Antitrust Primer," www.ftc.gov/bc/compguide/antitrst; Henry R. Cheeseman, *The Legal and Regulatory Environment,* 2d ed. (Upper Saddle River, NJ: Prentice Hall, 2000), 568–86; and Frank B. Cross and Roger LeRoy Miller, *West's Legal Environment of Business,* 5th ed. (Mason, OH: Thomson/South-Western, 2004), chap. 26–27.

8. 15 U.S.C. Section 1; for the full text of these four acts, see "Statutes Enforced by the Antitrust Division," www.usdoj.gov/atr/foia/divisionmanual/ch2.

9. 15 U.S.C. Section 15.

10. 15 U.S.C. Sections 41–51.

11. 15 U.S.C. Section 13.

12. www.ftc.gov/bc/.

13. www.usdoj.gov/atr/enforcement.

14. Morison and Commager, *The Growth of the American Republic,* 534–37.

15. For a full discussion, see the Department of Justice, www.usdoj.gov/atr/index and www.ftc.gov/bc/compguide/illegal.

16. 15 U.S.C. Section 18.

17. Clayton Act, Section 7.

18. *Los Angeles Times*, July 17, 1998, C1.

19. This section is based on FTC, "Mergers," www.ftc.gov/bc/compguide/mergers.htm; and Cheeseman, *The Legal and Regulatory Environment*, 568–86.

20. Jack Welch, *Jack: Straight from the Gut* (New York: Warner Books, 2001), chap. 23.

21. 259 U.S. 200, 42 S. Ct. 465.

22. Adapted from Cross and Miller, *West's Legal Environment of Business*, 605.

23. This procedure section is based on FTC, "Pre-merger Notification and Instructions: A Menu of Guidelines, Forms and Rules," www.ftc.gov/80/bc/hsr.htm; FTC, "An Antitrust Primer," www.ftc.gov/bc/compguide/antitrst.htm; and DePamphilis, *Mergers, Acquisitions, and Other Restructuring Activities*, 60–66.

24. 374 U.S. 321.

25. For a discussion and summary of reporting requirements, see DePamphilis, *Mergers, Acquisitions, and Other Restructuring Activities*, 55–65.

26. *Wall Street Journal*, June 26, 2003, B1; *Los Angeles Times*, June 11, 2003, C2 and June 28, 2003, C2.

27. This discussion is largely based on DePamphilis, *Mergers, Acquisitions, and Other Restructuring Activities*, 79–83.

28. *Wall Street Journal*, July 17, 2003, B2.

29. *Los Angeles Times*, July 17, 1998, C1.

30. Securities and Exchange Commission, "The Laws that Govern the Securities Industry," www.sec.gov/about/laws.shtml.

31. This section is largely based on DePamphilis, *Mergers, Acquisitions, and Other Restructuring Activities*, 83.

32. *Wall Street Journal*, July 10, 2003, A1.

33. This section is largely based on DePamphilis, *Mergers, Acquisitions, and Other Restructuring Activities*, 82–83.

32. Cheeseman, *The Legal and Regulatory Environment*, 552–53.

## CHAPTER 8

1. "Divestiture" in this chapter refers to terminating the business in its entirety, not a partial sell-off of portions of a business, as discussed in Lee Dranikoff, Tim Koller, and Antoon Schneider, "Divestiture: Strategy's Missing Link," *Harvard Business Review*, May 2002, 74–83. This discussion does not include bankruptcy, for which there are special rules.

2. For a discussion of business entities, see chapter 5.

3. 29 U.S.C. Section 1001 et seq.

4. The General Accounting Office (GAO) and United quotations are from *Wall Street Journal*, July 24, 2003, A2; see also October 15, 2003, A2 and January 29, 2004, A2.

5. The pension and contribution discussion is largely based on U.S. Pension Benefit Guaranty Corporation, *2002 Annual Report* (Washington, DC: U.S. Pension Guaranty Corporation, 2003); and David Wessel, "The Politics of Pension Promises," *Wall Street Journal*, July 17, 2003, A2.

6. 26 U.S.C. Section 1161 (a).

7. The Comprehensive Environmental Response, Compensation, and Liability Act, 42 U.S.C. Section 9601 et seq.

## CHAPTER 9

1. www.sba.gov/starting_business/startup/guide4.html; and for California: www.calgold.
2. See chapter 5 for a discussion of business entities.
3. This is the case nationwide and in the city of Long Beach, California, as reported by Melanie Fallon, director, Department of Community Development; interview, April, 2003.
4. EEOC, "State and Local Agencies," www.eeoc.gov/small/stateandlocal. html.
5. Shawn Tully, "Postcards from the Edge: What Message is California Sending to Companies? Get Lost!" *Fortune*, August 11, 2003, 34. "Labor Law update," California Chamber of Commerce, February, 2004, 4.
6. State Code Sec. 1280(c), www.leginfo.public.ca.gov/cgi.../displaycode?section=uic&group=00001-01000&file=675-687.2.
7. Tully, "Postcards from the Edge," 34.
8. *Wall Street Journal*, August 18, 2003, A10.
9. www.edd.ca.gov/direp/diindtx.htm.
10. www.edd.ca.gov/direp/disditx.htm.
11. www.edd.ca.gov/direp/diflatx.htm.
12. www.scif.com.
13. www.dir.ca.gov/DOSH/consultation.html.
14. Available from the California Chamber of Commerce, www. calchamberstore.com.
15. Specialty posters can be obtained from Cal/OSHA, www.dir.ca.gov/occupational _safety.
16. These can be obtained from www.calchamberstore.com.
17. State Board of Workers' Compensation, www.ca.gov.
18. For Cal/OSHA, see www.dir.ca.gov/DOSH/consultation.
19. www.naco.org/Template.cfm?Section=Codes_and_Ordinances& Templat.../codes_srch.
20. *Wall Street Journal*, August 18, 2003, A10.
21. This tax discussion is largely based on SBA, "Regulations," www.sba.gov/starting_business/startup/guide4.html; and, for California, Peri H. Pakroo, *The Small Business Start-Up Kit for California*, 4th ed. (Berkeley, CA: NOLO Press, 2002), 8/11–8/17.
22. City of Los Angeles, Office of Finance, "Business and Other Taxes," May 2002.
23. Ibid., 18–19.
24. This discussion is partially based on Donald DePamphilis, *Mergers, Acquisitions, and Other Restructuring Activities* (San Diego, CA: Academic Press, 2001), 77–79.
25. For an analysis of states' antitrust laws, see William J. Hayes, Jr., *State Antitrust Laws* (Washington, DC: Bureau of National Affairs, 1989).
26. David P. Baron, *Business and Its Environment*, 4th ed. (Upper Saddle River, NJ: Prentice Hall, 2003), 293.
27. *Wall Street Journal*, August 1, 2003, A2.

28. *Wall Street Journal,* August 28, 2003, A4.

29. *Wall Street Journal,* July 15, 2003, C1; and July 25, 2003, C1.

30. National Association of Counties, Washington, DC, www.naco.org/Template.cfm?Section=Codes_and_Ordinances&Templat.../codes_srch.cf.

31. City of Los Angeles, Office of Finance, "Business and Other Taxes," May 2002.

## CHAPTER 10

1. www.sba.gov/financing/preparation/eligibility.html.

2. SBA, *Small Business Resource Guide,* 2002 edition, 14–15.

3. www.whitehouse.gov/omb/grants/spoc.html.

4. See Charles A. Goldman and T. Williams, *Paying for University Research Facilities and Administration* (Santa Monica, CA: RAND Study MR-1135-1, 2000). *Wall Street Journal,* April 20, 2004, D5.

5. Scott Hassell, Scott Florence, and Emile Ettedqui, *Summary of Federal Construction, Building, and Housing Related Research & Development in FY1999* (Santa Monica, CA: RAND Study MR-1390, 2001).

6. www.gsa.gov/Portal/home.jsp.

7. www.sba.gov/financing/basics/grants.html.

8. For more information on SBIR and STTR programs, see www.sba.gov/sbir/indexsbir.html.

9. www.sba.gov/sbir/indexfast.html.

10. www.cfda.gov/public/browse_typast.asp?catcode=E.

11. U.S. Small Business Administration, "SBA's Role in Providing Financial Assistance to America's Small Businesses," www.sba.gov/financing/basics/sbarole.html.

12. Forms for any SBA type of financing are available at www.sba.gov/library/forms.html.

13. SBA, *Small Business Resource Guide,* 2002 edition, 14–20.

14. Interview with Richard Ginsburg, SBA, Washington, DC, May 7, 2001.

15. For more information, see www.sba.gov/financing/fr7aloan.html.

16. For more information, see www.sba.gov/financing/frmicro.htm.

17. Interview with Richard Ginsburg, SBA.

18. For more information, see www.sba.gov/financing/sbaloan/cdc504.html.

19. Small Business Administration, "2002 American Business Profile: United States," www.sba.gov/adv/stats/profiles/02nation.

20. www.cfda.gov/public/viewprog.asp?progid=1466.

21. www.sba.gov/starting/indexspecial.html.

22. 7 U.S.C. 1932, Sec. 310(B), www.cfda.gov/public/viewprog.asp? progid=120.

23. Murray L. Weidenbaum, *Business and Government in the Global Marketplace,* 7th ed. (Upper Saddle River, NJ: Pearson Prentice Hall, 2004), 246.

24. Samuel Eliot Morison and Henry Steele Commager, *The Growth of the American Republic* (New York: Oxford University Press, 1958), vol. II, 621–22.

25. For a discussion of the pros and cons of debt versus equity financing, see Wesley B. Truitt, *Business Planning: A Comprehensive Framework and Process* (Westport, CT: Quorum Books, 2002), 155–57.

26. www.sba.gov/financing/basics/equity.html.

27. www.sba.gov/INV/.

28. www.sba.gov/INV/NMVC/index.

29. www.sba.gov/ss/ss8 and www.sba.gov/ss/ss5.

30. SBA, *Small Business Resource Guide*, 2002 edition, 16, 18–19.

31. www.opic.gov/pressreleases/.

32. Interview with OPIC's Robert O'Sullivan, associate general counsel, and Joan Edwards, director, investment services, in Washington, DC, May 6, 2001.

33. www.sba.gov/financing/basics/applyloan.html.

34. www.sba.gov/financing/preparation/borrowing.html.

35. This section is based on the author's personal experience in this industry.

36. www.irs.gov/businesses/small/article/o,,id=100688,00.

37. Adapted from Weidenbaum, *Business and Government in the Global Marketplace*, 279, Office of Management and Budget Data.

38. www.sba.gov/adv/stats/profiles/02nation.

## CHAPTER 11

1. www.sba.gov/8abd/; and SBA, *Small Business Resource Guide*, 2002 edition, 29–30.

2. www.sba.gov/starting/indexspecial.

3. www.cfda.gov/public/viewprog.asp?progid=1466.

4. For more information, see www.sba.gov/sdb, or call (800) 558-0884.

5. www.sbaonline.sba.gov/GCI; and SBA, *Small Business Resource Guide*, 2002 edition, 30.

6. *Wall Street Journal*, June 26, 2003, B8. Veteran data is for 2003; January 13, 2004, B1.

7. SBA, *Small Business Resource Guide*, 2002 edition, 32.

8. www.sba.gov/starting/indexspecial; and SBA, *Small Business Resource Guide*, 2002 edition, 32–33.

9. Interview with Robert Ginsburg, SBA, Washington, DC, May 7, 2001.

10. www.sba.gov/starting/indexspecial.

11. www.sba.gov/starting/indexspecial.

12. www.sba.gov/wa/seattle/seabgk.html; and SBA, *Small Business Resource Guide*, 2002 edition, 30–32.

13. Interview with Robert Ginsburg, SBA.

14. SBA publication, "Scams that Target Small Businesses," available from SBDC, Los Angeles, undated.

15. Adapted from Murray L. Weidenbaum, Business and Government in the Global Marketplace, 7th ed. (Upper Saddle River, NJ: Pearson Prentice-Hall, 2004), p. 261.

## CHAPTER 12

1. Murray L. Weidenbaum, *Business and Government in the Global Marketplace*, 7th ed. (Upper Saddle River, NJ: Pearson Prentice Hall, 2004), 260–61.

2. www.nyc.gov.

3. Adapted from Weidenbaum, *Business and Government in the Global Marketplace*, 263.

4. www.southbaypartnership.com/business_assistance.cfm.
5. www.cacommunities.com.
6. www.portla.com/zone.htm.
7. The CalTrade Report: www.caltradereport.com/eWeb...ebPages/front-page-1059827805.
8. www.wib.co.la.ca.us/about.htm; and www.wib.co.la.ca.us/employer02.htm.
9. www.lacdc.org/economic/business/index.shtm.
10. www.lacdc.org/economic/incubators/innet.shtm.
11. www.lacdc.org/economic/business/index.shtm.
12. www.cityofla.org/cdd/icd/.
13. www.lacdc.org/economic/business/index.shtm.
14. www.ciwmb.ca.gov/Grants/; and James Flanigan, "Despite Thorns, State Is Still Fertile Ground," *Los Angeles Times*, August 27, 2003, C1.
15. www.lacity.org/CDD/business/lending.
16. City of Los Angeles, Office of Finance, "Business and Other Taxes," May 2002, 24.
17. This discussion is based on interviews with city of Long Beach officials, April 2003: Robert Torres, Melanie Fallon, and Eugene Fong. See also www.longbeach.gov/citygov/ budget.htm.
18. www.newyorkbiz.com/Business_Incentives/; and www.nycedc.com.
19. "Going, Boeing . . . ," *The Economist*, April 19, 2003, 26–27.
20. This discussion is based on Sibel Berzeg, Michael Maier, and Juan Carlos Paez, "BMW: Globalizing Manufacturing Operations," in Jose de la Torre, Yves Doz, and Timothy Devinney, *Managing the Global Corporation: Case Studies in Strategy and Management*, 2d ed. (New York: Irwin/McGraw-Hill, 2001), 427–42.
21. Ibid., 431.
22. *Los Angeles Times*, November 11, 2003, A18.
23. *Los Angeles Times*, May 26, 2003, C3.
24. This discussion is based on the author's personal experiences as a Northrop Grumman executive at the time of the case.
25. This discussion is based on interviews with officials at the city of Long Beach: Melanie S. Fallon, director, Department of Community Development, and Robert S. Torrez, CFO/director, Department of Financial Management, April 2003; and *Los Angeles Times*, April 13, 2003, L3.
26. Jose de la Torre and Wesley B. Truitt, "Northrop Grumman and the Advanced Technology Transit Bus Program," in de la Torre, Doz, and Devinney, *Managing the Global Corporation*, 259–71.
27. www.taxfoundation.org/taxingspending.html.
28. Data from "U.S. Congress Handbook: 108th Congress, First Session, 2003," Washington, DC, 2003.
29. www.csg.org/CSG/Regional+Offices/default.htm.

## CHAPTER 13

1. The classic study of interest groups was by David B. Truman, *The Governmental Process* (New York: Knopf, 1951).
2. Michael Watkins, Mickey Edwards, and Usha Thakrar, *Winning the Influence Game* (New York: Wiley, 2001), 1.

3. This discussion is based on the author's experience as founding chairman of the California Aerospace Alliance.

4. Murray L. Weidenbaum, *Business and Government in the Global Marketplace*, 7th ed. (Upper Saddle River, NJ: Pearson Prentice Hall, 2004), 299.

5. *Wall Street Journal*, October 13, 2003, A15.

6. Virginia Gray and David Lowery, "Trends in Lobbying in the States," *The Book of the States* (Lexington, KY: The Council of State Governments, 2003), 260–61.

7. This discussion is partly based on the author's experience as a registered lobbyist for Northrop Grumman Corporation.

8. *Los Angeles Times*, May 27, 2003, A1; and June 22, 2003, A1, A26–27.

9. *Los Angeles Times*, October 28, 2003, C1, C5.

10. *Wall Street Journal*, March 24, 2004, A1, A15.

11. Watkins, Edwards, and Thakrar, *Winning the Influence Game*, 10.

12. This discussion is adapted from ibid., 13–27.

13. Ibid., 19.

14. For example, over the years, I have worked with the U.S. Senate Foreign Relations Committee and the House International Relations Committee to draft legislation affecting his company's overseas operations. At the state level, the author served on a Governor's commission regarding federal spending, and at the local level, he lobbied the Los Angeles City Council and L.A. County Board of Supervisors and testified before those bodies on company issues and programs.

# Selected Bibliography

## ARTICLES

Abramson, Jill. "The Business of Persuasion Thrives in Nation's Capital." *New York Times*, September 29, 1998.

Ackelsburg, Robert, and Peter Arlow. "Small Businesses Do Plan and It Pays Off." *Long Range Planning*, October 1985.

"America's New Financial Structure." *Business Week*, November 17, 1980.

Argenti, John. "Stakeholders: The Case Against." *Long Range Planning*, June 1997.

Badaracco, Joseph L., Jr., and David B. Yoffie. "Industrial Policy: It Can't Happen Here." *Harvard Business Review*, November–December 1983.

Bahls, Jane Ester. "Better Safe . . ." *Entrepreneur*, July 2003.

Bahls, Steven C., and Jane Ester Bahls. "Feeling Woozy?" *Entrepreneur*, August 2002.

———. "Under the Radar?" *Entrepreneur*, November 2002.

———. "Witness Protection." *Entrepreneur*, April 2003.

Baron, David P., and John A. Ferejohn. "Bargaining in Legislatures." *American Political Science Review*, December 1989.

Beal, Reginald M. "Competing Effectively: Environmental Scanning, Competitive Strategy, and Organizational Performance in Small Manufacturing Firms." *Journal of Small Business Management*, January 2000.

Becker, Gary S. "A Theory of Competition and Pressure Groups for Political Influence." *Quarterly Journal of Economics* 98 (1983).

Bernanke, Ben. "Deflation: Making Sure 'It' Doesn't Happen Here." *Federal Reserve Bulletin*, November 2002.

Bernasek, Anna. "Duking It Out over the Deficit." *Fortune*, May 26, 2003.

Berzeg, Sibel, Michael Maier, and Juan Carlos Paez. "BMW: Globalizing Manufacturing Operations." In Jose de la Torre, Yves Doz, and Timothy Devinney, *Managing the Global Corporation: Case Studies in Strategy and Management*. 2nd ed. New York: Irwin/McGraw-Hill, 2001.

Bhide, Amar. "How Entrepreneurs Craft Strategies that Work." *Harvard Business Review*, March/April 1994.

Birley, Sue, and Paul Westhead. "A Taxonomy of Business Start-Up Reasons and Their Impact on Firm Growth and Size." *Journal of Business Venturing*, January 1994.

Birnbaum, Jeffrey H. "Power Player." *Fortune Small Business*, October 2001.

Block, Zenas, and Ian C. MacMillan. "Milestones for Successful Venture Planning." *Harvard Business Review*, September–October 1985.

Bolling, Richard, and John Bowles. "Regulations Have Dulled America's Competitive Edge but They Needn't." *Los Angeles Times*, August 9, 1981.

Bordwin, Milton. "Your Company and 'THE LAW,'" *Management Review*, January 2000.

Bower, Joseph L. "A Primer on Politics and Government Management in the United States." Boston: Harvard Business School, Case No. 9-302-100, March 2002.

Bracker, Jeffrey S., Barbara W. Keats, and John N. Pearson. "Planning and Financial Performance among Small Firms in a Growth Industry." *Strategic Management Journal* 9 (1988).

Bracker, Jeffrey S., and John N. Pearson. "Planning and Financial Performances in Small Mature Firms." *Strategic Management Journal* 7 (1986).

Bradley, Gene E. "How to Work in Washington: Building Understanding for Your Business." *Columbia Journal of World Business*, Spring 1994.

Brenner, Melvin A. "Is U.S. Deregulation a Failure? Here's How to Find Out." *Airline Executive*, September 1980.

Bruno, Albert V., Joel K. Leidecker, and Joseph W. Harder. "Why Firms Fail." *Business Horizons*, March/April 1987.

Calingaert, Michael. "Government-Business Relations in the European Community." *California Management Review*, Winter 1993.

Carter, Nancy M., William B. Gartner, and Paul D. Reynolds. "Exploring Start-Up Event Sequences." *Journal of Business Venturing*, May 1996.

Chandler, Alfred, Jr. "Government vs. Business: An American Phenomenon." *Harvard Business Review*, March 1982.

Cooper, Arnold C. "Challenges in Predicting New Firm Performance." *Journal of Business Venturing*, May 1993.

Covin, Jeffrey G., and Dennis P. Slevin. "New Venture Strategic Posture, Structure, and Performance: An Industry Life Cycle Analysis." *Journal of Business Venturing*, March 1990.

de la Torre, Jose, and Wesley B. Truitt. "Northrop Grumman and the Advanced Technology Transit Bus Program." In Jose de la Torre, Yves Doz, and Timothy Devinney, *Managing the Global Corporation: Case Studies in Strategy and Management*. 2nd ed. New York: Irwin/McGraw Hill, 2001.

"Deregulation: A Fast Start for the Reagan Strategy." *Business Week*, March 9, 1981.

Diener, Mark. "Seeking Counsel." *Entrepreneur*, January 2003.

Dillon, John. "Will Evian Refresh World Trade?" *Wall Street Journal*, June 3, 2003.

DiLorenzo, Thomas J. "The Origins of Antitrust: An Interest Group Perspective." *International Review of Law and Economics* 5 (1985).

Dranikoff, Lee, Tim Koller, and Antoon Schneider. "Divestiture: Strategy's Missing Link." *Harvard Business Review*, May 2002.

Drucker, Peter F. "The Global Economy and the Nation-State." *Foreign Affairs*, September–October 1997.

Duck, Jeanie Daniel. "Managing Change: The Art of Balancing." *Harvard Business Review*, November–December 1993.

E. I. du Pont de Nemours & Company. *2002 Review*, 2003.

Flanigan, James. "Far-Off Terrorism Cuts Close to Home." *Los Angeles Times*, October 20, 2002.

Friedman, Milton. "The Social Responsibility of Business Is to Increase Its Profits." *New York Times Magazine*, September 13, 1970.

"The Future of the State." *The Economist*, September 20, 1997.

Gale, Jeffrey, and Rogene A. Buchholtz. "The Political Pursuit of Competitive Advantage: What Business Can Gain from Government." In *Business Strategy and Public Policy*, edited by Alfred A. Marcus, Allen M. Kaufman, and David R. Beam. New York: Quorum Books, 1987.

Gatty, Bob. "New Horizons in Trucking." *Nation's Business*, October 1980.

"Going, Boeing . . ." *The Economist*, April 19, 2003.

Goldsmith, Stephen. "Can Business Really Do Business with Government?" *Harvard Business Review*, May–June 1997.

Gosselin, Peter G., and Jube Shiver, Jr. "'New Economy' Is a Thing of the Past." *Los Angeles Times*, September 23, 2001.

Gray, Virginia, and David Lowery. "Trends in Lobbying in the States." In *The Book of the States*. 2003 ed. Lexington, KY: Council of State Governments, 2003.

Groseclose, Timothy, and James M. Snyder, Jr. "Buying Supermajorities." *American Political Science Review*, June 1996.

Ha, Yao-Su. "Global Corporations Are National Firms with International Operations." *California Management Review*, Winter 1992.

Hagstrom, Jerry. "From the K Street Corridor." *National Journal*, May 3, 1997.

Hall, Richard L., and Frank W. Wayman. "Buying Time: Moneyed Interests and the Mobilization of Bias in Congressional Committees." *American Political Science Review* 84 (1990).

Hanks, Steven H., and L. R. McCarrey. "Beyond Survival: Reshaping Entrepreneurial Vision in Successful Growing Ventures." *Journal of Small Business Strategy*, Spring 1993.

Henricks, Mark. "The Winner Is . . ." *Entrepreneur*, October 2003.

Hiltzik, Michael. "Assessing a Commercial Property Showdown in San Francisco." *Los Angeles Times*, May 22, 2003.

Hulse, David S., and Thomas R. Pope. "The Effect of Income Taxes on the Preference of Organizational Form for Small Businesses in the United States." *Journal of Small Business Management*, January 1996.

Huntington, Samuel P. "The Erosion of American National Interests." *Foreign Affairs*, September–October 1997.

Ibrahim, A. Bakr. "Strategy Types and Small Firm's Performance: An Empirical Investigation." *Journal of Small Business Strategy*, Spring 1993.

Inglehart, Richard. "Globalization and Postmodern Values." *Washington Quarterly*, Winter 2000.

Ireland, R. Duane, and Michael A. Hitt. "Achieving and Maintaining Strategic Competitiveness in the 21st Century: The Role of Strategic Leadership." *Academy of Management Executives* 13, no. 1 (1999).

Jacobson, Louis, and Brody Mullins. "The GOP's New Bridge to K Street." *National Journal*, May 5, 2001.

Jordan, Don D. "The Deregulation Dilemma." *Chief Executive*, January–February 1997.

Kanter, Rosabeth Moss. "Thriving Locally in the Global Economy." *Harvard Business Review*, September–October 1995.

Karakaya, Fahri, and Bulent Kobu. "New Product Development Process: An Investigation of Success and Failure in High Technology and Non-High Technology Firms." *Journal of Business Venturing*, January 1994.

Kaufmann, Patricia J. "Franchising and the Choice of Self-Employment." *Journal of Business Venturing*, July 1999.

Keim, Gerald D. "Corporate Grassroots Programs in the 1980s." *California Management Review*, Fall 1985.

Kincaid, John. "Trends in Federalism: Is Fiscal Federalism Fizzling?" In *The Book of the States*. 2003 ed. Lexington, KY: Council of State Governments, 2003.

Kocourek, Paul F., Christian Burger, and Bill Birchard. "Corporate Governance: Hard Facts about Soft Behaviors." *Strategy+Business*, Spring 2003.

Kristof, Kathy M. "New Tax Breaks Offer a Lifeline to Businesses." *Los Angeles Times*, March 16, 2003.

Krugman, Paul. "Competitiveness: A Dangerous Obsession." *Foreign Affairs*, March–April 1994.

Laitinen, Erkki K. "Prediction of Failure of a Newly Founded Firm." *Journal of Business Venturing*, July 1992.

Lang, James R., Roger J. Calantone, and Donald Gudmundson. "Small Firm Information Seeking as a Response to Environmental Threats and Opportunities." *Journal of Small Business Management*, January 1997.

Lodge, George C. "Top Priority: Renovating Our Ideology." *Harvard Business Review*, September–October 1970.

Lord, Michael D. "Corporate Political Strategy and Legislative Decision Making." *Business & Society*, March 2000.

Lussier, Robert N. "A Nonfinancial Business Success versus Failure Prediction Model for Young Firms." *Journal of Small Business Management*, January 1995.

Marx, Thomas G. "Integrating Public Affairs and Strategic Planning." *California Management Review*, Fall 1986.

Matthews, Charles H., and Susanne G. Scott. "Uncertainty and Planning in Small and Entrepreneurial Firms: An Empirical Assessment." *Journal of Small Business Management*, October 1995.

McCarthy, Larry. "Competition Killers: More Delays, Less Infrastructure." *Cal-Tax Commentary*, www.caltax.org/member/digest/may2001.

McKay, Betsy. "Coke to Help Fight Aids in Africa." *Wall Street Journal*, June 20, 2001.

McTigue, Maurice. *Federal Times*, January 15, 2003.

"Memo to U.S. Inventors: File Early." *Business Week*, January 29, 1996.

Milyo, Jeffrey, David Primo, and Timothy Groseclose. "Corporate PAC Campaign Contributions in Perspective." *Business and Politics* 2 (2000).

Mintzberg, Henry. "Managing Government, Governing Management." *Harvard Business Review*, May–June 1996.

Mosakowski, Elaine. "A Resource-Based Perspective on the Dynamic Strategy-Performance Relationship: An Empirical Examination of the Focus and Differentiation Strategies in Entrepreneurial Firms." *Journal of Management* 19, no. 4 (1993).

Mosher, Lawrence. "Big Steel Says It Can't Afford to Make the Nation's Air Pure." *National Journal*, July 5, 1980.

———. "Environmentalists Question Whether to Retreat or Stay on the Offensive." *National Journal*, December 13, 1980.

———. "With EPA's New Air Pollution Penalties, It's Never Cheaper to Pay the Fine." *National Journal*, January 24, 1981.

Murphy, Cait. "A No-Fly Zone." *Fortune*, April 14, 2003.

Naffziger, Douglas W., and Donald F. Kuratko. "An Investigation into the Prevalence of Planning in Small Business." *Journal of Business and Entrepreneurship*, October 1991.

Nehemkis, Peter. "Business Payoffs Abroad: Rhetoric and Reality." *California Management Review*, Winter 1975.

"New York City: On the Comeback Trail." *Morgan Guaranty Survey*, April 1981.

Nye, Joseph, Jr. "Globalization's Democratic Deficit." *Foreign Affairs*, July–August 2001.

O'Brian, Bridget. "Government Sets New Standards for Ways to Get Properly Pickled." *Wall Street Journal*, September 25, 1991.

Olson, Philip D., and Donald W. Bokor. "Strategy Process-Content Interaction: Effects on Growth Performance in Small, Startup Firms." *Journal of Small Business Management*, January 1995.

O'Neill, Hugh M. "How Entrepreneurs Manage Growth." *Long Range Planning*, February 1983.

Orpen, Christopher. "The Effects of Long-Range Planning on Small Business Performance: A Further Examination." *Journal of Small Business Management*, January 1985.

Osborne, Richard L. "Planning: The Entrepreneurial Ego at Work." *Business Horizons*, January/February 1987.

"Partners In Crime." *Fortune*, October 27, 2003.

"Patton Boggs Helping Hawaiians." *National Journal*, May 31, 2003.

Porter, Michael E. "Knowing Your Place—How to Assess the Attractiveness of Your Industry and Your Company's Position in It." *Inc.*, September 1991.

———. "What Is Strategy?" *Harvard Business Review*, November–December 1996.

"Privatization on a Roll." *The American Enterprise*, November–December 1997.

Robinson, Richard B., Jr. "The Importance of Outsiders in Small Firm Strategic Planning." *Academy of Management Journal*, March 1982.

Robinson, Richard B., Jr., and John A. Pearce II. "Product Life-Cycle Considerations and the Nature of Strategic Activities in Entrepreneurial Firms." *Journal of Business Venturing*, Spring 1986.

———. "Research Thrusts in Small Firm Strategic Planning." *Academy of Management Review*, January 1984.

Rothchild, Ronald D. "Making Patents Work for Small Companies." *Harvard Business Review*, July–August 1987.

Rue, Leslie W., and Nabil A. Ibrahim. "The Relationship between Planning Sophistication and Performance in Small Business." *Journal of Small Business Management*, October 1998.

Salmon, Walter J. "Crisis Prevention? How to Gear Up Your Board." *Harvard Business Review*, January–February 1993.

Selden, Larry, and Geoffrey Colvin. "M&A Needn't Be a Loser's Game." *Harvard Business Review*, June 2003.

Sexton, Donald L., and Philip Van Auken. "A Longitudinal Study of Small Business Strategic Planning." *Journal of Small Business Management*, January 1985.

Shrader, Charles B., Charles L. Mumford, and Virginia L. Blackburn. "Strategic and Operational Planning, Uncertainty, and Performance in Small Firms." *Journal of Small Business Management*, October 1989.

Shuman, Jeffrey C., John J. Shaw, and Gerald Sussman. "Strategic Planning in Smaller Rapid Growth Companies." *Long Range Planning*, December 1985.

"Sky Wars: The Airlines Enter a New Age." *Dun's Review*, February 1981.

Snyder, James. "Campaign Contributions as Investments: The U.S. House of Representatives 1980–1986." *Journal of Political Economy* 98 (1990).

Stevenson, Howard H., and David E. Gumpert. "The Heart of Entrepreneurship." *Harvard Business Review*, March–April 1985.

Stewart, Jack M. "Does California Mean Business Anymore?" *Cal-Tax Digest*, March 2003.

"Taxes for a Cleaner Planet." *The Economist*, June 28, 1997.

Taylor, Bob. "Pension Crisis Swamps Cities and Counties." *Cal-Tax Special Report*, May 20, 2003.

Taylor, Jeffrey, and Warren Getler. "U.S. Examines Alleged Price-Fixing on Nasdaq." *Wall Street Journal*, October 20, 1994.

Tsai, William Ming-Hone, Ian C. MacMillan, and Murray B. Low. "Effects of Strategy and Environment on Corporate Venture Success in Industrial Markets." *Journal of Business Venturing*, January 1991.

Tully, Shawn. "Postcards from the Edge." *Fortune*, August 11, 2003.

Van Cise, Jerrold G. "Regulation—By Business or Government?" *Harvard Business Review*, March–April 1965.

Wartick, Steven L., and Robert E. Rude. "Issues Management: Corporate Fad or Corporate Function." *California Management Review*, Fall 1986.

Watkins, Michael. "Government Games: Understanding the Role of Government in Business Strategy." *Harvard Business Review Note*, June 28, 2002.

Weidenbaum, Murray. "Regulation: How Washington Will Switch." *Nation's Business*, February 1981.

———. "Paying the Price of Federal Bailouts." *Los Angeles Times*, October 28, 1980.

———. "Regulatory Process Reform: From Ford to Clinton." *Regulation*, Winter 1997.

———. "The U.S. Defense Industry After the Cold War." *Orbis*, Fall 1997.

Wessel, David. "The Politics of Pension Promises." *Wall Street Journal*, July 17, 2003.

Williams, John D. "Rail-Rate Increases Due for Early Arrival Thanks to New Law." *Wall Street Journal*, October 14, 1980.

Wilson, James Q. "The Corporation as a Political Actor." In *The American Corpo-*

*ration Today*, edited by Carl Kaysen. New York: Oxford University Press, 1996.

Wines, Michael. "Three Years after Deregulation, Railroads Leaner, More Competitive." *National Journal*, December 10, 1983.

———. "Verdict Still Out on Deregulation's Impact on U.S. Air Travel System." *National Journal*, March 6, 1982.

Wolf, Charles, Jr. "A Theory of Nonmarket Failure." *Journal of Law and Economics*, April 1979.

Wolf, Martin. "Will the Nation-State Survive Globalization?" *Foreign Affairs*, January–February 2001.

Yochelson, John. "Can the U.S. Compete?" *Chief Executive*, June 1997.

Yoffie, David B. "Corporate Strategies for Political Action: A Rational Model." In *Business Strategy and Public Policy*, edited by Alfred A. Marcus, Allan M. Kaufman, and David R. Beam. Westport, CT: Quorum Books, 1987.

———. "How an Industry Builds Political Advantage." *Harvard Business Review*, May–June 1988.

Zahra, Shaker A. "Environment, Corporate Entrepreneurship, and Financial Performance: A Taxonomic Approach." *Journal of Business Venturing* 8 (1993).

———. "The Changing Rules of Global Competitiveness in the 21st Century." *Academy of Management Executive* 13, no. 1 (1999).

———. "K Street's Top 10: The Shifting Lineup." *National Journal*, October 20, 2001.

Zycher, Benjamin. "State's Profligate Short-Timers." *Los Angeles Times*, June 9, 2003.


## BOOKS

Adams, P. *155 Legal Do's (and Don'ts) for the Small Business*. New York: John Wiley, 1996.

Anderson, James E. *Politics and the Economy*. Boston: Little, Brown, 1966.

Areeda, Philip, and Louis Kaplow. *Antitrust Analysis*. 5th ed. New York: Aspen Law and Business, 1997.

Asch, Peter. *Consumer Safety Regulations*. New York: Oxford University Press, 1988.

Bacon, Jeremy. *Corporate Boards and Corporate Governance*. New York: Conference Board, 1993.

Bagley, Constance E. *Managers and the Legal Environment: Strategies for the 21st Century*. 3rd ed. St. Paul, MN: West Publishing, 1999.

Baron, David P. *Business and Its Environment*. 4th ed. Upper Saddle River, NJ: Prentice Hall, 2003.

Berenbeim, Ronald. *Regulation: Its Impact on Decision Making*. New York: Conference Board, 1981.

Berle, Adolph A., Jr., and Gardner C. Means. *The Modern Corporation and Private Property*. New York: Macmillan, 1932.

Blair, John M. *Economic Concentration, Structure, Behavior and Public Policy*. New York: Harcourt Brace, 1973.

Blum, Laurie. *Free Money from the Federal Government for Small Businesses and Entrepreneurs*. 2nd ed. New York: John Wiley, 1996.

*The Book of the States*. 2003 ed. Council of State Governments. Lexington, KY: 2003.

Bork, Robert H. *The Antitrust Paradox.* New York: Basic Books, 1978.
Bothwell, James L. *Government Sponsored Enterprises (GSEs).* Washington, DC: U.S. General Accounting Office, 1997.
Bouchoux, Deborah E. *Protecting Your Company's Intellectual Property.* New York: AMACOM, 2001.
Bozeman, Barry. *All Organizations Are Public: Bridging Public and Private Organizational Theories.* San Francisco: Jossey-Bass, 1987.
Brayman, Harold. *Corporate Management in a World of Politics: The Public, Political, and Governmental Problems of Business.* New York: McGraw-Hill, 1967.
Buchholz, Rogene A. *Business Environment and Public Policy: Implications for Management.* 5th ed. Upper Saddle River, NJ: Prentice Hall, 1995.
Calvin, Robert J. *Entrepreneurial Management.* New York: McGraw-Hill, 2002.
Cheeseman, Henry R. *The Legal and Regulatory Environment.* 2nd ed. Upper Saddle River, NJ: Prentice Hall, 2000.
Cohen, Linda R., and Roger G. Noll. *The Technological Pork Barrel.* Washington, DC: Brookings Institution, 1991.
*Congressional Quarterly Almanac, 1980.* Washington, DC: CQ Press, 1981.
Cross, Frank B., and Roger LeRoy Miller. *West's Legal Environment of Business.* 5th ed. Mason, OH: Thomson/South-Western, 2004.
Daniels, John D., and Lee H. Radebaugh. *International Business: Environments and Operations.* 9th ed. Upper Saddle River, NJ: Prentice Hall, 2001.
DePamphilis, Donald. *Mergers, Acquisitions, and Other Restructuring Activities.* San Diego: Academic Press, 2001.
Drew, Elizabeth. *The Corruption of American Politics.* Woodstock, NY: Overlook Press, 1999.
Drier, Peter, et al. *Place Matters: Metropolitics for the Twenty-First Century.* Lawrence, KS: University Press of Kansas, 2001.
Drucker, Peter F. *Innovation and Entrepreneurship: Practices and Principles.* New York: HarperCollins, 1985.
Dudley, Susan, and Melinda Warren. *Regulatory Spending Soars: An Analysis of the U.S. Budget for Fiscal Years 2003 and 2004.* Joint Study of the Weidenbaum Center at Washington University and Mercatus Center at George Mason University, 2003.
Dunlop, John T., ed. *Business and Public Policy.* Boston: Division of Research, Graduate School of Business Administration, Harvard University, 1980.
Dunning, John H., ed. *Governments, Globalization, and International Business.* New York: Oxford University Press, 1999.
Eismeier, Theodore J., and Philip H. Pollock III. *Business, Money and the Rise of Corporate PACs in American Elections.* Westport, CT: Quorum Books, 1988.
Elder, Larry. *Showdown.* New York: St. Martin's Press, 2002.
Emmons, Willis. *The Evolving Bargain: Strategic Implications of Deregulation and Privatization.* Boston: Harvard Business School Press, 2000.
Epstein, Edwin M. *The Corporation in American Politics.* Englewood Cliffs, NJ: Prentice Hall, 1969.
Faris, Jack. *The Americans with Disabilities Act.* Washington, DC: National Legal Center for the Public Interest, 1996.

Fox, J. Ronald. *Managing Business-Government Relations: Cases and Notes on Business-Government Problems.* Homewood, IL: Irwin, 1982.

Frey, Robert S. *Successful Proposal Strategies for Small Business: Using Knowledge Management to Win Government, Private-Sector, and International Contracts.* 3rd ed. Boston: Artech House, 2002.

Furchgott-Roth, Diana, and Christine Stalba. *Women's Figures: The Economic Progress of Women in America.* Arlington, VA: Independent Women's Forum, 1996.

Garten, Jeffrey E. *The Politics of Fortune: A New Agenda for Business Leaders.* Boston: Harvard Business School Press, 2002.

Gilder, George. *The Spirit of Enterprise.* New York: Simon & Schuster, 1984.

Gilpin, Robert. *The Challenge of Global Capitalism.* Princeton, NJ: Princeton University Press, 2000.

Goldman, Charles A., and T. Williams. *Paying for University Research Facilities and Administration.* Santa Monica, CA: RAND Study MR-1135-1, 2000.

Gollner, Andrew B. *Social Change and Corporate Strategy: The Expanding Role of Public Affairs.* Stamford, CT: iap 1983.

Green, Charles H. *The SBA Loan Book: How to Get a Small Business Loan, Even with Poor Credit, Weak Collateral, and No Experience.* Holbrook, MA: Adams Media Corp. 1999.

Greer, Douglas E. *Business, Government, and Society.* 3rd ed. Upper Saddle River, NJ: Prentice Hall, 1993.

Greider, William. *Secrets of the Temple: How the Federal Reserve Runs the Country.* New York: Touchstone Books, 1989.

Grove, Andrew S. *High-Output Management.* New York: Random House, 1983.

Hall, Bronwyn. *R and D Tax Policy during the Eighties: Success or Failure.* Cambridge, MA: National Bureau of Economic Research, 1992.

Hall, Craig. *The Responsible Entrepreneur: How to Make Money and Make a Difference.* Franklin Lakes, NJ: Career Press, 2001.

Handler, Edward, and John R. Mulkern. *Business and Politics.* Lexington, MA: Lexington Books, 1982.

Handlin, Oscar, and Mary Flug Handlin. *Commonwealth; A Study of the Role of Government in the American Economy: Massachusetts, 1774–1861.* New York: New York University Press, 1947.

Hassell, Scott, Scott Florence, and Emile Ettedqui. *Summary of Federal Construction, Building, and Housing Related Research & Development.* Santa Monica, CA: RAND Study MR-1390, 2001.

Hay, Robert D., and Edmund R. Gray. *Business & Society: Cases and Text.* Cincinnati, OH: South-Western Publishing, 1981.

Hayes, William J., Jr. *State Antitrust Laws.* Washington, DC: Bureau of National Affairs, 1989.

Hines, James. *Forbidden Payments: Foreign Bribery and American Business After 1977.* Cambridge, MA: National Bureau of Economic Research, 1996.

Hisrich, Robert D., and Michael P. Peters. *Entrepreneurship.* 5th ed. New York: McGraw-Hill/Irwin, 2002.

Hopkins, Thomas. *Regulatory Costs in Profile.* St. Louis: Washington University, Center for the Study of American Business, 1996.

Huntington, Samuel P. *The Clash of Civilizations and the Remaking of World Order.*
New York: Simon and Schuster, 1996.

Iacocca, Lee. *Iacocca: An Autobiography.* New York: Bantam Books, 1984.

Jacoby, Neil H. *Corporate Power and Social Responsibility.* New York: Macmillan,
1973.

Jacoby, Neil H., Peter Nehemkis, and Richard Eells. *Bribery and Extortion in World
Business.* New York: Macmillan, 1977.

Jenkins, Michael D. *Starting and Operating a Business in the U.S.* Palo Alto, CA:
Running "R" Media Publisher, 1999.

Karten, David C. *When Corporations Rule the World.* W. Hartford, CT: Kumarian
Press, 1995.

Kaysen, Carl, ed. *The American Corporation Today.* New York: Oxford University
Press, 1996.

Kellerman, Barbara. *Reinventing Leadership: Making the Connection between Politics
and Business.* Albany, NY: State University of New York Press, 1999.

Kennedy, Peter. *Macroeconomic Essentials: Understanding Economics in the News.* 2nd
ed. Cambridge, MA: MIT Press, 2001.

Kerwin, Cornelius M. *Rulemaking: How Government Agencies Write Law and Make
Policy.* 2nd ed. Washington, DC: CQ Press, 1999.

Kettl, Donald F. *The Global Public Management Revolution: A Report on the Trans-
formation of Governance.* Washington, DC: Brookings Institution, 2000.

Klitgaard, Robert. *Controlling Corruption.* Berkeley: University of California Press,
1988.

Kuratko, Donald F., and Harold P. Welsch. *Entrepreneurial Strategy.* Fort Worth,
TX: Dryden Press, 1994.

Lebne, Richard. *Government and Business: American Political Economy in Comparative Perspective.* London: Chatham House Publishers, 2001.

Leonard, Jonathan S. *The Impact of Affirmative Action Goals.* Cambridge, MA:
National Bureau of Economic Research, 1984.

Lindblom, Charles E. *The Market System.* New Haven: Yale University Press, 2001.

Lodge, George Cabot. *Comparative Business-Government Relations.* Upper Saddle
River, NJ: Prentice Hall, 1990.

Lusterman, Seymour. *Managing Federal Government Relations.* New York: Conference Board, 1988.

MacAvoy, Paul. *Industry Regulation and the Performance of the American Economy.*
New York: W. W. Norton, 1992.

Mack, Charles S. *Business Strategy for an Era of Political Change.* Westport, CT:
Quorum Books, 2001.

Maidment, Frederick, and William Eldridge. *Business in Government and Society:
Ethical, International Decision-Making.* Upper Saddle River, NJ: Prentice
Hall, 2000.

Mancuso, Joseph R. *How to Start, Finance and Manage Your Own Small Business.*
Englewood Cliffs, NJ: Prentice-Hall, 1978.

Marcus, Alfred A. *Adversary Economy: Business Responses to Changing Governmental Requirements.* Westport, CT: Quorum Books, 1984.

Marcus, Alfred A., Allen M. Kaufman, and David R. Beam, eds. *Business Strategy and Public Policy: Perspectives from Industry and Academia.* New York: Quorum Books, 1987.

Margos, Alice H., ed. *Small Business Financing: How and Where to Get It.* Chicago: Commerce Clearing House, 1998.

McDonald, Forrest. *We the People: The Economic Origins of the Constitution.* Chicago: University of Chicago Press, 1963.

McGuire, E. Patrick. *The Impact of Product Liability.* New York: Conference Board, 1988.

McMillan, John. *Reinventing the Bazaar: The Natural History of Markets.* New York: W. W. Norton, 2002.

Megginson, Leon C., Mary Jane Byrd, and William L. Megginson. *Small Business Management: An Entrepreneur's Guidebook.* 4th ed. New York: McGraw-Hill, 2003.

Miller, Roger LeRoy, and Frank B. Cross. *The Legal Environment Today.* St. Paul, MN: West, 1996.

Miller, Roger LeRoy, and Gaylord A. Jentz. *Business Law Today.* 4th ed. St. Paul, MN: West, 1997.

Milling, Bryan E. *How to Get a Small Business Loan: A Banker Shows You Exactly What to Do to Get a Loan.* 2nd ed. Naperville, IL: Sourcebooks Trade, 1998.

Mitchell, Neil J. *The Conspicuous Corporation: Business, Public Policy and Representative Democracy.* Ann Arbor, MI: University of Michigan Press, 1997.

Mokry, Benjamin W. *Entrepreneurship and Public Policy: Can Government Stimulate Business StartUps?* Westport, CT: Quorum Books, 1988.

Moore, Mark H. *Creating Public Value: Strategic Management in Government.* Boston: Harvard University Press, 1997.

Morison, Samuel Eliot, and Henry Steele Commager. *The Growth of the American Republic.* 4th ed. New York: Oxford University Press, 1958.

Morrison, Catherine. *Managing Corporate Political Action Committees.* New York: Conference Board, 1986.

Moss, David A. *When All Else Fails: Government as the Ultimate Risk Manager.* Boston: Harvard University Press, 2002.

Mourdoukoutas, Panos, and Stratos Papadimitriou. *Nurturing Entrepreneurship: Institutions and Policies.* Westport, CT: Quorum Books, 2002.

Norman, Jan. *What No One Ever Tells You About Starting Your Own Business: Real Life Start-up Advice from 101 Successful Entrepreneurs.* Chicago: Upstart Publishing Co., 1999.

O'Hara, Patrick D. *SBA Loans: A Step-by-Step Guide.* New York: John Wiley, 2002.

Olson, Dean F., and Omar L. Carey. *Opportunity Management: Strategic Planning for Smaller Businesses.* Reston, VA: Reston, 1985.

O'Reilly, James. *Administrative Rulemaking.* Colorado Springs: Shepard's/McGraw-Hill, 1983.

Osborne, David, and Peter Plastrik. *The Reinventor's Fieldbook: Tools for Transforming Your Government.* San Francisco: Jossey-Bass, 2000.

Pakroo, Peri H. *The Small Business Start-Up Kit for California.* 4th ed. Berkeley, CA: NOLO Press, 2002.

Pollitt, Christopher, and Geert Bouckaert. *Public Management Reform: A Comparative Analysis.* Oxford, England: Oxford University Press, 2000.

Porter, Michael E. *The Comparative Advantage of Nations.* New York: Free Press, 1990.

Post, James, Anne Lawrence, and James Weber. *Business and Society: Corporate Strategy, Public Policy, Ethics.* 10th ed. New York: McGraw-Hill/Irwin, 2002.

Reinhardt, Forest L., and Richard H. K. Victor. *Business Management and the Natural Environment: Cases and Text.* Cincinnati, OH: South-Western College Publishing, 1996.

Resnick, Paul. *Everything You Need to Know to Start Your Own Small Business.* New York: John Wiley, 1998.

Roney, C. W. *Assessing the Business Environment: Guidelines for Strategists.* Westport, CT: Quorum Books, 1999.

Rosecrance, Richard. *The Rise of the Virtual State.* New York: Basic Books, 1999.

Russo, Michael V. *Environmental Management: Readings and Cases.* Boston: Houghton Mifflin, 1999.

Ryan, J. D., and Gail Hiduke. *Small Business: An Entrepreneur's Business Plan.* 6th ed. Cincinnati, OH: South-Western College Publishing, 2003.

Sabato, Larry J. *PAC Power: Inside the World of Political Action Committees.* New York: W.W. Norton, 1984.

Salamon, Lester M., ed. *The Tools of Government: A Guide to the New Governance.* New York: Oxford University Press, 2002.

Schollhammer, Hans, and Arthur H. Kuriloff, *Entrepreneurship and Small Business Management.* New York: John Wiley, 1979.

Schultze, Charles L. *The Public Use of Private Interest.* Washington, DC: Brookings Institution, 1977.

Shenefield, John H., and Irwin N. Stelzer. *The Antitrust Laws: A Primer.* Lanham, MD: American Enterprise Institute Press, 1993.

Shienbaum, Kim Ezra. *American Shockwave: Entrepreneurial Capitalism and Its Global Impact.* Westport, CT: Praeger Publishers, 2002.

Shipper, Frank, and Marianne M. Jennings. *Business Strategy for the Political Arena.* Westport, CT: Quorum Books, 1984.

Shugart, William F., II. *Antitrust Policy and Interest-Group Politics.* Westport, CT: Quorum Books, 1990.

Steiner, George A., and John F. Steiner. *Business, Government and Society: A Managerial Perspective.* 10th ed. New York: McGraw-Hill/Irwin, 2003.

Steingold, Fred S. *Legal Guide for Starting and Running a Small Business.* 7th ed. Berkeley, CA: Nolo Press, 2003.

Stiglitz, Joseph E. *Globalization and Its Discontents.* New York: W.W. Norton, 2002.

Sullivan, E. Thomas, ed. *The Political Economy of the Sherman Act.* New York: Oxford University Press, 1991.

Swank, Duane. *Global Capital, Political Institutions, and Policy Change in Developed Welfare States.* London: Cambridge University Press, 2002.

Thorne McAllister, Debbie, O. C. Ferrell, and Linda Ferrell. *Business and Society: A Strategic Approach to Corporate Citizenship.* Boston: Houghton Mifflin, 2003.

Tolchin, Susan J., and Martin Tolchin. *Dismantling America: The Risk to Deregulation.* New York: Oxford University Press, 1983.

Truitt, Wesley B. *Business Planning: A Comprehensive Framework and Process.* Westport, CT: Quorum Books, 2002.

Truman, David M. *The Governmental Process.* New York: Knopf, 1951.

Tullock, Gordon et al. *Government Failure: A Primer in Public Choice.* Washington, DC: Cato Institute, 2002.

Vernon, Heidi. *Business and Society: A Managerial Approach.* 6th ed. New York: McGraw-Hill, 1998.

Vernon, Raymond. *In the Hurricane's Eye.* Cambridge, MA: Harvard University Press, 1998.

Vesper, Karl H. *New Venture Strategy.* Englewood Cliffs, NJ: Prentice-Hall, 1980.

Viscusi, W. Kip. *Regulating Consumer Product Safety.* Washington, DC: American Enterprise Institute, 1984.

Vogel, David. *Fluctuating Fortunes: The Political Power of Business in America.* New York: Basic Books, 1989.

Wachter, Michael L., and Susan M. Wachter, eds. *Toward a New Industrial Policy?* Philadelphia: University of Pennsylvania Press, 1981.

Ward, Ralph D. *Improving Corporate Boards.* New York: John Wiley, 2000.

Wartick, Steven L., and Donna J. Wood. *International Business and Society.* Malden, MA: Blackwell Business, 1998.

Watkins, Michael, Mickey Edwards, and Usha Thakrar. *Winning the Influence Game: What Every Business Leader Should Know about Government.* New York: John Wiley, 2001.

Weidenbaum, Murray L. *Business and Government in the Global Marketplace.* 7th ed. Upper Saddle River, NJ: Pearson Prentice Hall, 2004.

———. *Government Mandated Price Increases.* Washington, DC: American Enterprise Institute, 1975.

———. *The Future of Business Regulation.* New York: Amacon, 1980.

Welch, Jack. *Jack: Straight from the Gut.* New York: Warner Books, 2001.

Weston, J. Fred. *Concentration and Efficiency: The Other Side of the Monopoly Issue.* Croton-on-Hudson, NY: Hudson Institute, 1978.

Wilson, Ian. *The New Rules of Corporate Conduct: Rewriting the Social Charter.* Westport, CT: Quorum Books, 2000.

Wilson, James Q., ed. *The Politics of Regulation.* New York: Basic Books, 1980.

———. *Bureaucracy: What Government Agencies Do and Why They Do It.* New York: Basic Books, 1989.

Woodward, Bob. *Maestro: Greenspan's Fed and the American Boom.* New York: Simon & Schuster, 2000.

Worthington, Margaret et al. *Contracting with the Federal Government.* 4th ed. New York: John Wiley, 1998.

Yergin, Daniel, and Joseph Stanislow. *The Commanding Heights: The Battle between Government and the Marketplace that Is Remaking the Modern World.* New York: Simon & Schuster, 1998.

## PUBLIC DOCUMENTS

*The Budget of the United States Government, Fiscal Year 2004.* Washington, DC: U.S. Government Printing Office, February 2003.

Census Bureau. *Annual Survey of Manufacturers, Geographic Area Statistics.* Series MOO(AS)-3.

———. *Statistical Abstract of the United States, 2002.* Washington, DC: U.S. Government Printing Office, 2002.

———. *U.S. International Trade in Goods and Services.* Series FT-900(01-12).

City of Los Angeles, Office of Finance. "Business and Other Taxes." May 2002.

Congressional Budget Office. *Resolving the Thrift Crisis.* Washington, DC: U.S. Government Printing Office, 1993.

Council of Economic Advisors, *Economic Report of the President.* Washington, DC: U.S. Government Printing Office, 2003.

Council on Competitiveness. *Legacy of Regulatory Reform.* Washington, DC: U.S. Government Printing Office, 1992.

General Accounting Office, *Foreign Investment: Implications of Exon-Florio and Related Amendments.* Washington, DC: U.S. Government Printing Office, 1995.

Occupational Safety and Health Act, P.L. 91-596.

Office of the U.S. Trade Representative. *Foreign Trade Barriers.* Washington, DC: U.S. Government Printing Office, 1993.

U.S. Congress, Joint Economic Committee. *The Economic Impact of Environmental Regulations.* Washington, DC: U.S. Government Printing Office, 1974.

U.S. Labor Department, Bureau of Labor Statistics. *Workplace Injuries and Illnesses in 1995.* Washington, DC: U.S. Department of Labor, 1997.

———. "OSHA Handbook for Small Business." OSHA 2209, 1996 (Rev.).

U.S. Pension Benefit Guaranty Corporation, *2002 Annual Report.* Washington, DC: U.S. Government Printing Office, 2003.

U.S. Small Business Administration. "The Changing Burden of Regulation, Paperwork, and Tax Compliance on Small Business: A Report to Congress." October 1995.

U.S. Treasury Department, IRS Publication 15, "Circular E, Employer's Tax Guide."

## WEB SITES

### Commercial and Not-for-Profit

AFL/CIO, www.aflcio.org

Biz Filings Inc., www.bizdilings.com/index.html

Biz Starters Online, www.bizstarters.com/

Biz Women, www.bizwomen.com

Business Resource Center, www.morebusiness.com

California Department of Industrial Relations, www.dir.ca.gov/

California Chamber of Commerce, www.calchamber.org

Council on State Taxation, www.statetax.org

California Taxpayers Association, www.caltax.org

Council of State Governments, www.csg.org

Dunn & Bradstreet Information Service, www.dnb.com

Entrepreneur's Electronic Resource Center, www.enterprise.org/enet/index.html

Findlaw, www.findlaw.com/

Heritage Foundation, www.heritage.org

Internet Legal Resource Guide, www.ilrg.com/
Interstate Labor Standards Association, www.ilsa.net/
Inventor Information, www.patentcafe.com/smallbiz/cafe/index.html
ISO Online, www.iso.ch
ISO 9000, www.praxiom.com/iso-intro.htm
Manufacturing, www.manufacturing.net/
National Association of Counties, www.naco.org
National Association of Government Labor Officials, www.naglo.org/
National Association of State Budget Officers, www.nasbo.org
National Conference of State Legislatures, www.ncsl.org
NOLO Law for All, www.nolo.com/indx.html
Organization for Economic Cooperation and Development, www.oecd.org
Small Business Advisor, www.openmarket.com/
Tax Foundation, www.taxfoundation.org
Venture Economics, www.ventureconomics.com
Workers' Compensation Law, www.law.cornell.edu/topics/workers_compensation.html
World Wide Yellow Pages, www.yellow.com

## U. S. Government and State/Local Government

California, State of, www.calgold
    Employment Development Department, www.edd.ca.gov
    Community Development Authority, www.cacommunities.com
    Compensation Insurance Fund, www.scif.com
    Safety and Health, www.dir.ca.gov/DOSH/consultation
    Unemployment Law, www.leginfo.public.ca.gov/cgi.../displaycode?section =uic
Catalogue of Federal Direct Assistance, www.cfda.gov/public/browse_typast.asp?
    catcode
Commerce Department, www.doc.gov
    Bureau of Economic Analysis, www.ntanet.org
    Census Bureau, www.census.gov
Education Department, www.doe.gov
    Budget Series, www.NoChildLeftBehind.gov
    National Assessment of Educational Progress, www.nces.ed.gov/nationsreportcard/
        states/profile.asp
Environmental Protection Agency, www.epa.gov
    EPA Laws, www.epa.gov/epahome/lawregs
    E-Rule Making, www.regulations.gov
    EPA Pesticides, www.epa.gov/ebitpages/pesticides
    EPA Pollution, www.epa.gov/ebtpages/pollutants
    EPA Proposed Rules, www.epa.gov/ebitpages/industry
Equal Employment Opportunity Commission, www.eeoc.gov/home
    Americans with Disabilities Act, www.eeoc.gov/ada/adahandbook
    Facts About Arabs and Muslims, www.eeoc.gov/facts/backlash-employer
    Overview, www.eeoc.gov/small/overview.html
    Sexual Harassment, www.eeoc.gov/facts/fs-sex.html
    State and Local Agencies, www.eeoc.gov/small/stateandlocal.html

Federal Deposit Insurance Corporation, www.fdic.gov
Federal Reserve Board, www.federalreserve.gov
    Rulemaking, www.federalreserve.gov/boarddocs/legaldevelopments/rulemaking/
Federal Trade Commission, www.ftc.gov
    Antitrust, www.ftc.gov/bc/compguide/antitrst
    Consumer, www.ftc.consumer
    Mergers, www.ftc.gov/bc/compguide/mergers.htm
    Pre-Merger Forms and Rules, www.ftc.gov/80/bc/hsr.htm
    Sherman Act, www.ftc.gov/bc/compguide/illegal
Food and Drug Administration, www.fda.gov/ora/fed_state/Small_Business/
    sb_guide
General Services Administration, www.gsa.gov/Portal/home.jsp
Housing and Urban Development Department, www.hud.gov/news/releasedocs/
    HUD Empowerment Zones, www.hud.gov/ezec/locator/
Internal Revenue Service, www.irs.ustreas.gov
    Tax Advantages, www.irs.gov/businesses/small/article/o,,id=100688,00
Justice Department, www.doj.gov.
    Antitrust Enforcement, www.doj.gov/atr/enforcement
    Antitrust Statutes, www.usdoj.gov/atr/foia/divisionmanual/ch2
    Sherman Act, www.usdoj.gov/atr/index
Labor Department, www.dol.gov
    Age Discrimination Act, www.dol.gov/dol/oasam/public/regs/statutes/
        age_act.htm
    Agencies, www.dol.gov/dol/organization.htm
    Bureau of Labor Statistics, www.stats.bis.gov
    Employment Standards Administration, www.dol.gov/esa
    Fair Labor Standards Act, www.dol.gov/esa/regs/statutes/whd/affair.htm
    Family and Medical Leave, www.dol.gov/asp/public/programs/handbook/
        fmla.htm
    Federal Contract Compliance, www.dol.gov/dol/ofccp
    OSHA Standards, www.osha.gov
    Office of Small Business Programs, www.dol.gov/osbp
    Small Business & Minority Affairs, www.dol.gov/dol/osbma
Long Beach, City of, www.longbeach.gov/citygov/budget
Los Angeles, City of, www.cityofla.org
    Enterprise Zones, www.cityofla.org/cdd/icd
    Loans, www.lacity.org/cdd/lending
Los Angeles, County of, www.lacounty.gov.
    Community Development Commission, www.lacdc.org/economic/business/
        index
    Incubators, www.lacdc.org/economic/incubators/innet
    Workforce Investment Board, www.wib.co.la.ca.us/about
New York, City of, www.nyc.gov
    Economic Development Corporation, www.nycedc.com
    Incentives, www.newyorkbiz.com/Business_Incentives
Office of Management and Budget, www.whitehouse.gov/omb/grants/spoc
Overseas Private Investment Corporation, www.opic.gov
Patent and Trademark Office, www.uspto.gov

Securities and Exchange Commission, www.sec.gov/info/smallbus/reachsec.
   Laws Governing the Securities Industry, www.sec.gov/about/law.shtml
   SEC Procedures, www.sec/gov/about/whatwedo.
   SEC Small Business Forums, www.sec.gov/info/smallbus/sbforum
Small Business Administration, www.sba.gov
   Business Development, www.sbaonline.sba.gov/SBDC
   Business Law, www.SBA.BusinessLaw.gov
   Business Opportunities, www.sba.gov/expanding
   Business Plan Outline, www.sbaonline.sba.gov/starting/businessplan.html
   CDC Loans, www.sba.gov/financing/sbaloan/cdc504.html
   E-loans, www.sba.eloans.com
   Eligibility Criteria, www.sba.gov/financing/preparation/eligibility
   Equity Financing, www.sba.gov/financing/basics/equity
   Financing, www.newhorizons.org/NHBS/sba.htm
   Forms, www.sba.gov/library/forms
   Government Contracting, www.sbaonline.sba.gov/GC
   Grants, www.sba.gov/financing/basics/grants
   Loan Application Coaching, www.sba.gov/financing/basics/applyloan
   Loans, www.sba.gov/financing/fr7aloan
   Marketing Program, www.sba.gov/8abd
   Micro Loans, www.sba.gov/financing/frmicro
   Non-profit Organizations, www.sbaonline.sba.gov/nonprofit
   Procurement Opportunities, www.pro-net.sba.gov
   SBIR and STTR Programs, www.sba.gov/sbir/indexsbir
   Small Disadvantaged Business Program, www.sba.gov/sdb
   Starting, www.sba.gov/starting_business/startup/guide4.html
   State/Regional Resources, www.geocities.com/WallStreet/2172
   Venture Capital, www.sba.gov/INV/NMVC/index
   Women's Business Ownership, www.sbaonline.sba.gov/womeninbusiness
Technology Transfer Information Center, www.nal.usda.gov/ttic

# Index